BOB FLOWERDEW'S COMPLETE BOOK OF FRUIT IN AUSTRALIA

BOB FLOWERDEW'S COMPLETE BOOK OF FRUIT IN AUSTRALIA

The definitive sourcebook for growing, harvesting and cooking

REVISED EDITION

London · New York · Sydney · Toronto · New Delhi
A CBS COMPANY

I dedicate this book to my best friend Christine Topping, without whose patience and care I would never have had time to write this book

First published in Australia in 2018 by
Simon & Schuster (Australia) Pty Limited
Suite 19A, Level 1, Building C, 450 Miller Street,
Cammeray, NSW 2062

ISBN 978-1-92575-025-6

10 9 8 7 6 5 4 3 2 1

A CBS Company
Sydney New York London Toronto New Delhi
Visit our website at www.simonandschuster.com.au

Revised and enlarged edition first published in Great Britain in 2009 by Kyle Cathie Limited

Original edition first published in1995

A catalogue record for this book is available from the National Library of Australia

Project Editor Suzanna de Jong
Designer Geoff Hayes
Australian consulting editors Janet Austin, Keran Barrett, Helen Moody, Jan Purser and Paul Urquhart
Picture Researcher Julia Gelpke
Proofreader Simon Canney
Editorial Assistant Catharine Robertson
Production Gemma John

Colour reproduction by Sang Choy
Printed and bound in Singapore by C&C Offset

The paper used to produce this book is a natural, recyclable product made from wood grown in sustainable plantation forests. The manufacturing processes conform to the environmental regulations in the country of origin.

Acknowledgements

With thanks to Kyle Cathie for taking a chance, and to Candida Hall and Penny David for their expertise, patience and encouragement. To Suzanna de Jong for her skill, enthusiasm and constant cheerfulness, Jean-Christophe Novelli for allowing us to use his recipes and Tina Carter for her persistence. Also to Marilyn Ward and Jill Cowley at the Royal Botanic Gardens, Kew; Charles Grace for information on tamarillo; Karen Box and Peter Lipsham in New Zealand; Mike Darcy and the late Robert Fleming in the USA; Simon Hickmott for his willingness to experiment; and Anita Bean, Consultant Nutritionist to the Fresh Fruit and Vegetable Information Bureau. Finally, thanks to Ray Desmond and my wife Gill for her support and administrative skills.

Publisher's note

An asterisk (*) beside a variety name indicates a vegetable which has received an award from the Royal Horticultural Society (see page 268).

Author's note on organic vs. chemical

Since writing the original edition, organic gardening has become mainstream and the choice of available chemicals is being reduced. I am delighted to say that this book is based on organic techniques for pest control. However, if you would prefer to use synthetic chemicals, it is your right to continue to do so – but I won't be coming round for dinner!

CONTENTS

INTRODUCTION

Since the first edition of this book the world has moved on. We are all now aware of the dangers of climate change, the precariousness of our economic position and the continuing threat of wars, famines and fuel shortages. The allotments are full for the first time since the Second World War. Humble dwellings with a large garden are once again desirable, and all the world and their dog want to grow their own organic food.

Yet the talk is always of worthy vegetables; fruit is wrongly considered a luxury, when it is greener, more tasty and less work. We need to get away from the annual, dig, sow, thin, water, feed and weed work ethic and move to a plant, prune and sit-back culture.

Fruit is perennial: you plant it well and it can outlive you. Fruit is less effort. Fruit also locks carbon dioxide into wood, something you try not to achieve with vegetables! And fruit is just so beneficial to wildlife in blossom and habitat, and especially if we fail to protect it.

Indeed, we need to move farming as well as gardening to a more perennial philosophy. Fruit trees should be growing overhead, providing fodder as well as food or even fuel, with other fodder crops growing underneath, getting more from the same land, with fewer energy inputs and with a greater diversity of crops. The world relies on the grasses to provide almost all of our food energy (rice, wheat, maize, barley, oats, sorghum, sugar cane, as well as grazing grass). If, the gods forbid, a disease were to wipe out the grasses we would surely starve. Most of our agriculture is concentrated on these few crops. And almost all meat is grassfed, yet we could feed our animals with fruits and nuts instead. For example, few annual crops rival hazelnuts in fat and protein production.

In our gardens we can start this truly green revolution. If humanity is to survive we need greater, not less, biological diversity. The gardener grows many more crops than the farmer, but still only a few dozen. We need to diversify further, to bring into our gardens different fruits and nuts to spread the risks – and to widen our diets with more nutrients, flavours and textures. And we need to develop better varieties. The apple of today comes from the miserable crab, the strawberry we enjoy did not exist two hundred years ago in either size or flavour. Look to the fruits of the future, those edible berries that have not yet been selected and bred. You could be the breeder to introduce the new huge super-sweet elderberry, the most luscious fuchsia fruit or the biggest, tastiest rose hip ever.

No greater good can one achieve than to feed others, not only with their need but for their delight.

FRUITS AND GARDENS: THEIR HISTORY IS AS ONE

Our earliest diet as hunter-gatherers, millions of years ago, must have included a wide range of seeds, fruits, nuts, roots, leaves and any moving things we could catch. As we lived for the great bulk of the time, according to theory, in warm areas, we would almost certainly have eaten much fruit in our diet. A warmer climate means more fruit in variety all year round.

Nomadic peoples learned to follow circuits to coincide with flushes of food. And of course, seemingly by magic, when they returned to a previous campsite they would find their favourite fruit trees and bushes waiting for them. Moreover, these trees and bushes would be more prolific than 'wild' ones, as the 'magic' trees would be growing on the immensely fertile site of the tribe's midden or waste heap.

Thus, as early populations perambulated, they spread the very plants that sustained them. In those early days the pickings must have been glorious, with vast areas swathed in ripening fruits. But as populations grew, the consequent demand for land caused them to spread to colder and drier regions.

The hunter-gatherer lifestyle became difficult in temperate zones as there is little plant food naturally available for half the year. We developed livestock as a means of storing the food, the summer's harvest becoming winter meat and cheese. Animal culture had other advantages; it was a more readily exchangeable form of wealth, mobile and 'in season' all year round. If enemies threatened, you could head for the safety of the hills with your flocks.

It is no good planting an orchard if you are unsure of next month, let alone next year. As annual crops were more sure than perennial, farming for cereals and quick-return crops predominated and gardens were rare except where civilisation was long established, such as the Hanging Gardens of Babylon. Thus the development of gardening and fruit culture serves to characterise times and places of peace and stability.

The Classical Greek period was a time of wars and there was little chance of gardening. The Roman Empire was the longest time of (relative) peace known. The Romans enjoyed most of our everyday fruits in abundance. They had the apple, pear and quince, the peach, plum, cherry and almond, the mulberry and the grape on sale in their streets and markets along with figs, dates, olives and exotic fruits from around the Mediterranean and North Africa.

One of the earliest places in which gardens developed was the Arab courtyard. Centred on water, representing an oasis, and protected by shading walls, their gardens were planted with the fruit trees, flowers and plants they adored. Their influence extended throughout the Middle East and into the Mediterranean region and trade with Rome. Their fruit gardens were emulated by the Romans, but in more extravagant style. Roman gardens were built around water, fruit trees, bushes and especially vines, and they introduced the idea of organising a garden into areas, 'inventing' the herb garden and the orchard. After the Roman civilisation crumbled, northern Europe entered the Dark Ages. The violence of the period worked against the cultivation of fruit, and almost all the knowledge of the Romans was lost, along with most of their varieties. The little that was preserved was due to the monasteries and royal gardens.

Rich and powerful individuals have always had their own, usually well protected, private gardens. These were often viewed very pragmatically, being usefully filled with fruiting plants and herbs. Many a tyrant prefered to eat fruits he could watch daily, and thus ensure their freedom from poison, and if the oppressed did revolt there was a ready food supply till help arrived.

The monasteries similarly guarded fruits and herbs for their own use and also for their medicinal value. In a time of frequent famine and annual winter dearth, the commonplace scurvy and vitamin deficiencies would have seemed to many people almost miraculously cured by monks' potions containing little more than preserved fruits full of nutrients and vitamin C.

By the time of the Norman invasion, England had become a farming and herding society. The civilising influence returned

and brought back gardens and orchards, mostly to provide the cider which necessarily replaced wine. Most great houses and manors had gardens for fruit, herbs and vegetables.

The Crusades reintroduced Mediterranean fruits which had been forgotten since the Romans and interest in gardening was rekindled. The Low Countries specialised in fruit and market gardening and developed many new varieties during the next centuries. Henry VIII actively encouraged the planting of orchards and fruit gardens to try to break the Dutch monopoly, but they have reigned on and still are the centre of world horticultural trade.

The 'discovery' of the New World by Europeans in the fifteenth century was an enormous upheaval. It brought in so many new and exotic plants that gardening became a respectable hobby for the rich. It could even be a profitable business as people clamoured for these exciting new tastes. The development of the orangery was a breakthrough, as it allowed the over-wintering of tender plants. In response to this, market gardeners started growing many of these new exotic fruits for the home market. Private gardeners with rich patrons wanted such choice fruits for their masters. Early doctors followed on in the traditions of the monasteries and had physic gardens of medicinal herbs and, of course, wanted to include all these new fruits with so much potential value. Thus was born the botanic garden with its hothouses and stovehouses.

As industrialisation proceeded, glass and materials became widely and cheaply available and glasshouses or greenhouses became common. Although many ornamental plants were grown, most effort went into securing crops of very different fruits, both exotic varieties and also common ones grown out of season. It is said that Queen Victoria's gardens had to be able to provide her with four pounds of strawberries any day of the year!

By the end of the Victorian period the humble villager still had a small cottage garden, with fruit trees and bushes underplanted with herbs and simples, and maybe a share in an orchard if he was lucky. Almost every house, from the nobleman's down to the vicarage, had its walled gardens lined with fruit trees and a hothouse producing out-of-season and tropical fruits. Of course, labour and coal were cheap and families and staff were huge. The First World War saw the end of the large garden, as labour and fuel became expensive.

Between the world wars was a time of depression. Prices were cheap, so there was less incentive to grow your own fruit. Moreover, most people had no garden and what gardening was done was by a leisured class who dabbled in rock gardens and alpines – while a man 'did' for them in the fruit garden and vegetable bed.

The Second World War caused tremendous changes in gardening and horticulture, especially in Great Britain, which was threatened with starvation by blockade. The enforced uprooting of vast acreages of commercial fruit trees and bushes to grow more cereals and vegetables meant little fruit was available in the shops. Much was grown at home

Arabic and Mediterranean influences created much of our modern garden

and in the public parks and gardens, which were dug up for allotments. Fruit was discouraged in favour of supposedly more worthy vegetables, but a considerable amount was nevertheless planted – mostly soft fruit such as blackcurrants.

The necessity for home food production, both during the war years and throughout a decade of rationing afterwards, meant an inevitable reaction later. People enjoying improving wealth chose once more not to grow and preserve themselves, but to buy ready made. 'Home made' even became snobbishly regarded as poor or shoddy in comparison with the 'luxury' of imported and commercial products. Clever and expensive advertising ensured we bought our fruits, nor for flavour but on appearance and other features easier to manipulate. One apple variety dominated the market, marketed on its supposed texture, despite it tasting only marginally better than a turnip! Amazingly, even canned fruits were sometimes seen as more acceptable than the fresh, home-grown item.

Then there was a sea change in the public's perception of food in general. Some had already rebelled against the blandness and cost of mass-produced foods. However, the realisation that we had polluted our environment and destroyed much of the ecology of our farms, countryside and gardens was to bring about a real revolution. A mass revulsion against chemical-based methods was mirrored in the rise of organic production and the slowly improving availability of better foods. Vegetarianism also increased as many people turned away from meat, in part because of the barbaric treatment of animals in factory farms. As we became more aware of the true costs of meat production, the health implications of modern farming methods and the need for a balanced diet, many people started eating much less meat. More and more consumers are choosing to buy it from better sources, such as direct-sale organic producers.

These trends mean that there is now a much increased demand for fruits and vegetables as their wider use replaces meat. The simultaneous demands for organic production, fuller flavour and a wider range have led the supermarkets to reassess their position and mean that many of us can now enjoy a very wide choice of fruits on sale throughout most of the year. But there is also a move by people towards growing their own.

Farmers' markets are back in fashion!

The hippie movement back to the land in the 1960s and '70s had shown the way, but few fancied the rigours of life actually tilling the soil. Now, however, there is a new movement back to gardening and home production. The health benefits, ecology and economy of gardening, especially the permaculture aspect of growing fruit, appeal to a greener generation. And, of course, it is all so much easier to use and store for ourselves nowadays, with food processors, juicers and deep freezers.

With dwarfing rootstocks, earlier and later season and better storing varieties, and automatic irrigation, glass or plastic cover, micro-processor controlled heating, shading, cooling and artificial sunlight, it is now possible to grow almost any fruit at home. However, in our rush to make full use of the excitingly exotic, the everyday fruits should not be overlooked just because of their availability. A well stocked garden, brimming full of strawberries, raspberries, currants, apples, pears and plums, is still a most satisfying feast for the eye, the soul and the stomach.

FRUITS

In this section, fruit is defined as plant flesh that we are induced by the plant to eat, in order to distribute its seeds. Included is the closely allied group of nuts, which are in fact the seeds themselves. Presumably the plants are satisfied if a small percentage of the nut seeds are distributed to grow elsewhere.

The fruits covered in the three chapters Orchard Fruits, Soft, Bush and Cane Fruits and Annual Tender Fruits are determined by the manner in which we most usually grow them in temperate gardens. Those that require some protection or cover, such as the annual, perennial and tender fruits, are mostly fruits that are not hardy enough outdoors for the UK and northern European gardener, but are achievable in southern Europe, Australia and much of the USA. Of course, we commonly grow many of these, such as melons, grapes and even lemons, quite easily with the aid of a greenhouse, in cooler regions. I've also included many exotic tropical and sub-tropical fruits on sale in supermarkets and abroad which may be grown (or eaten!) out of curiosity and interest. Most of these were once grown and fruited in Victorian stovehouses, and can often be fruited at home with a modest heated glasshouse or conservatory. Failing that, most of these make spectacular, educational and decorative houseplants. (Please bear in mind, however, the potential final height and size of your humble date palm seedling before you start dreaming of ever ripening a crop!)

The chapter on Shrub and Flower Garden Fruits includes those forgotten and unsung heroes that are called upon only in times of shortage and famine, and by those country folk who appreciate the sharp, strong flavours these piquant fruits offer. The potential of these fruits has often been overlooked; many of them are worthy of deliberate cultivation, and with only a little breeding and selection they could become sweet and tender attractions for our delectation. The strawberry today is gigantic and succulent compared to those of two centuries ago; we can only imagine what new fruits we may conjure from nature's raw materials in the future.

ORCHARD FRUITS

When fruits are mentioned, these are probably the first that come to mind: apples, pears, plums and cherries – the tree-hard or top fruits, as they are known. They consist of two main groups: the pome fruits, which are the apple- and pear-like members, and the stone fruits, which are the plums, cherries, peaches and apricots. The pomes have small seeds in a core around which the 'stalk' from immediately behind swells, enclosing them with flesh. The stone fruits have a single seed in a hard shell around which the flesh forms. Both of these groups are related, as they are both members of the *Rosaceae* family. Mulberries and figs come from different families. Nonetheless, all are similar in hardiness, size and manner of cultivation to orchard trees.

Most of these fruits have been cultivated since ancient times. They were nearly all known to the Romans, who spread them throughout their empire. However, much knowledge of their cultivation was then lost during the Dark Ages. The monasteries, and a few noblemen, maintained fruit gardens and orchards, but the common people reverted to farming and cropping from the wild, with little interest in fruit cultivation. Indeed, fruits were often seen as poor fare compared to meat, and more suited for animal feed. If it was not for the ease with which many of these fruits could be fermented to make intoxicating beverages, they would probably have been even more neglected. After the Norman Conquest of England the new lords proved to be more interested in fruit than the Saxons they had defeated, bringing many of their own improved varieties with them from France. Orchards became more widely planted, and the wealthy vied with one another in collecting the greatest number and variety and in having the earliest and longest-lasting fruits.

In the sixteenth century, Henry VIII brought many new fruit varieties from the Netherlands and France, and the streets of London became full of home-grown and imported favourites. The arrival of completely different and new fruits from the New World aroused more enthusiasm for horticulture, reviving interest in the old fruits as well as the new discoveries. As old trusted varieties were exported to the colonies, new species and varieties were imported. These produced new varieties, which followed the old abroad at the same time as descendants of the first wave were already returning.

By the Victorian era the number of varieties in cultivation had escalated from a few hundreds to many tens of thousands, if you counted local varieties worldwide. The great cities were served by the immense orchards and market gardens that surrounded them.

Every gentleman aspired to a house with grounds that would include an orchard, at least, if not a grouse moor.

In the 20th century, after two World Wars, the labour to maintain great gardens and orchards was not available and the land was needed for more basic crops. Orchards were grubbed up for cereals and more exciting fruits became available from abroad. The British orchard all but disappeared from many counties. Houses with grounds and orchards were demolished to make way for executive hutches at a dozen an acre.

However, the green movement, combined with people's increasing awareness of the utility of trees, the value of fruit, and the ecological advantages of permanent culture as opposed to annual crops, have all caused a reawakening of interest in orchard fruits. More are now being planted than for nearly a century.

Malus domestica from the family *Rosaceae*

CULINARY AND DESSERT APPLES

Tree up to 10m. Life span: medium to long. Deciduous, hardy, sometimes self-fertile. Fruits: up to 15cm, spherical, green to yellow or red. Vitamin value: vitamin C.

Malus domestica apples are complex selections and hybrids of *M. pumila* with *M. sylvestris* and *M. mitis*. Thus the shape of the fruit varies from the spheres of **Gladstone** and **Granny Smith** to the flattened buns of **Bramley** and **Mère de Ménage**, or the almost conical **Spartan**, **Golden Delicious** and **Worcester Pearmain**. The colour can be green, yellow, scarlet orange or dark red to almost purple. The texture can vary from crisp to pappy and they may be juicy or dry, acid or insipid, bitter, bland or aromatic. All apples have a dent in the stalk end, the remains of the flower at the other and a central tough core with several brown seeds. These are edible in small amounts, though there is a recorded death from eating a quantity, as they contain small amounts of cyanide.

The trees will often become picturesque landscape features, particularly when seen in an orchard. They frequently become twisted or distorted when left to themselves. They have soft downy or smooth leaves, never as glossy as pear leaves. The flowers are often pink- or red-tinged as well as snow white.

Apples are native to temperate Europe and Asia. They have been harvested from the wild since prehistory and were well known to the ancient Phoenicians. When Varro led his army as far as the Rhine in the first century BC, every region had its apples. The Romans encouraged their cultivation, so although Cato had only noted a half dozen varieties in the second century BC, Pliny knew of three dozen by the first century AD. The Dark Ages caused a decline in apple growing in Britain and only one pomerium (orchard), at Nottingham, is mentioned in the Domesday Book. However, interest increased after the Norman invasion.

Costard and **Pearmain** varieties are first noted in the twelfth and thirteenth centuries, and by the year 1640 there are nearly five dozen varieties recorded by Parkinson. By 1669, Worlidge has the number up to 92, mostly cider apples. *Downing's Fruits*, printed in 1866, has 643 varieties listed. Now we have more than 5,000 named apple varieties, representing about 2,000 actually distinguishable clones. Several hundred are easily obtainable from specialist nurserymen, though only a half dozen are grown on a commercial scale.

This sudden explosion in numbers was most probably due to the expansion of the colonies. The best varieties of apple trees from Europe mutated and crossed as they were propagated across North America, and then later Australia.

Apples are now grown extensively in every temperate region around the world. The first apples in North America, supposedly, were planted on the Governor's Island in Boston Harbour, but the Massachusetts Company had requested seeds in 1629, and in 1635 a Mr Wolcott of Connecticut wrote he had made 500 hogsheads of cider from his new apple orchard.

CULINARY AND DESSERT APPLES

varieties

The oldest variety known and easily available is **Court Pendu Plat** (mid-winter, dessert), which may go back to Roman times and is recorded from the sixteenth century. It is still grown because it flowers late, missing frosts. The large green **Flower of Kent** (1660) has nearly disappeared in England. This was the apple that prompted Sir Isaac Newton in his discoveries of the laws of motion and gravity. **Ribston Pippin** (mid-winter, dessert) has one of the highest vitamin C contents and superb flavour. It was bred in 1707 and is not happy on wet heavy soils. These and other heritage varieties are still grown in Australia and New Zealand by keen apple fans. Several specialist nurseries propagate and sell old varieties to the public. **Orleans Reinette** (mid-winter, dessert) is known from 1776. It is juicy, very tasty with a rough skin and is not very good on wet cold sites. The year 1785 saw the birth of the rare but choice **Pitmaston Pine Apple** (mid-winter, dessert). This has small fruits with a rich, honey-like flavour.

Bramley's Seedling (mid-winter, culinary), raised in 1809, has one of the highest vitamin C contents of cooking varieties. It grows large, so have it on a more dwarfing stock than others. The **Cornish Gillyflower** is a very tasty, late-keeping dessert raised in 1813. Unlike many other apples, it will flourish in a mild wet climate. It is unsuited to training or cordon culture. One of the best dual-purpose apples is **Blenheim Orange** (mid-winter), a wide, flat, golden-russeted fruit and a large tree. Raised in 1850, **Cox's Orange Pippin** (late autumn) is reckoned the best dessert apple. However, it is not easy to grow as it is disease-prone, hates wet clays and does best on a warm wall. **Sunset**, raised in 1918, and **Suntan**, in 1955, are more reliable offspring. **Beauty of Bath** is one of the best-known earlies, fruiting in early to mid-summer with small, sharp, sweet and juicy, yellow fruits stained scarlet and orange. It was introduced in 1864. It is a tip bearer and not suitable for training.

Egremont Russet (late autumn), bred in 1872, is one of the best russets, a group of apples with scentless, roughened skin and crisp, firm flesh, which is sweet and tasty but never over-juicy or acid. Just a century old is **James Grieve** (mid-autumn, dessert). It is prone to canker, but makes a good pollinator for Cox and is a good cropper of refreshingly acid, perfumed fruits. The ubiquitous **Golden Delicious**, so much grown commercially in Europe, is a conical yellow. It actually tastes pretty good when grown at home, but must be waxed for keeping as otherwise it wilts. It was found in West Virginia in 1916.

Apples exposed to full sun are highly coloured, most aromatic and sweetest

These were fairly well thinned – but they would have been bigger and better if I'd been even more ruthless

Apples in Australia have been bred for warm climat cropping. Red **Lady Williams**, a late apple, originated in Western Australia as a cross between **Granny Smith** and an unknown red apple. **Pink Lady** has a soft pink on yellow skin. It was a cross between **Lady Williams** and **Golden Delicious** in 1973, as was **Sundowner**, a red-fruited apple. Both have a low-chilling factor. Japanese-bred **Fuji**, introduced in 1962,and the New Zealand-raised **Gala** (1934) both have low-chill requirement. **Braeburn**, with its bright red fruit and green stripes, is another popular New Zealand apple. **Delicious** is Australia's most commonly grown commercial variety. **Jonagold** (a cross of Jonathan and Golden Delicious) produces huge red cartoon apples that keep till August.It is interesting to note some varieties have much more vitamin C than others that grow in the same conditions. **Ribston Pippin** typically has 31mg/100g, **Orlean's**

Reinette 22.4mg, **Bramley's Seedling** 16mg, **Cox's Orange Pippin** 10.5mg, **Golden Delicious** 8mg and **Rome Beauty** 3.6mg. Maybe the famous saying should go 'A Ribston Pippin a day keeps the doctor away'.

cultivation

Apples are much abused trees. They prefer a rich, moist, well-drained loam, but are planted almost anywhere and yet often still do fairly well. What they will not stand is being water-logged, or growing on the site of an old apple tree or near to others that have been long established, and they do not thrive in dank frost pockets. Pollination is best served by planting more than three varieties, as many apples are mutually incompatible, having diploid or triploid varieties with irreconcilable differences in their chromosomes. A **Cox** and a **Bramley** will not fruit on their own, but if you add a **James Grieve** all three bear fruit. Crab apples usually prove good pollinators for unnamed trees.

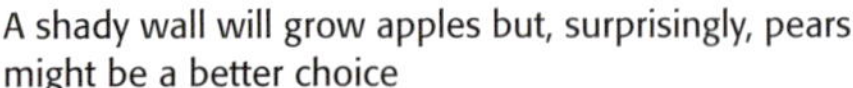

A shady wall will grow apples but, surprisingly, pears might be a better choice

James Grieve

Jonathan is a popular apple for garden orchards as it pollinates most other varieties. **Sundowner** and **Pink Lady** are often planted with **Gala**, **Delicious** and **Fuji** for pollination. Some varieties, especially **Gravenstein** have infertile pollen and cannot be used for pollinating other varieties.

Growing in Containers

On very dwarfi ng stocks apples are easily grown in large pots. They need hard pruning in winter and in summer the lengthening shoots should be nipped out, thus tip-bearing varieties are not really suitable. **Ballerina** apples, which supposedly require little pruning, have been developed for containers. There are six eating varieties: **Waltz**, **Bolero**, **Polka**, **Flamenco**, **Maypole** and **Charlotte**.

Ornamental and Wildlife Value

The pink and white blossom is wonderful in late spring. The flowers are valuable to insects and the fruits are important to birds.

Propagation

Apple pips rarely make fruiting trees of value; however, many of our best varieties were chance seedlings. Apples are grafted or budded onto different rootstocks depending on site and size of tree required. Few grow them from cuttings on their own roots or as standards on seedling stocks as these make very large trees only suitable for planting in grazed meadows. Half-standards

CULINARY AND DESSERT APPLES

are more convenient for the home orchard and these get big enough on M25 stock at about 5.2m high and 6m apart. At the other extreme, the most dwarfing stock is M27, useful for pot culture, but these midgets need staking all their lives and the branches start so low you cannot mow or grow underneath them. M9 produces a 2m tree, still needing staking but good for cordons. On such very dwarfing stocks the trees do badly in poor soil and during droughts. M26 is bigger, growing to 2.8m and still needs a stake but is probably the best for small gardens. It needs 3m on each side. MM106 is better on poor soils, and on good soils is still compact at about 4m, needing 4.5m between trees.

Pruning and Training

Apple trees are often left to grow and produce for years with no pruning other than remedial work once the head has formed. They may be trained and hard pruned summer and winter, back to spur systems, on almost any shaped framework, though rarely as fans. For beauty and productivity, apples are best as espaliers; to achieve the maximum number of varieties, as cordons; for ease and quality, as open goblet-pruned small trees. Stepovers are low single-tier espaliers designed for edging beds or paths; these require pruning hard to spurs, like cordons. Some varieties, especially many of the earliest fruiters, are tip bearers. These are best pruned only remedially as hard pruning will remove the fruiting wood. Minarettes are slender columnar relatively dwarfed varieties; these require minimal pruning and are most suited to tub and patio culture. As important as the pruning is the thinning. Removing crowded and congested, damaged and diseased apples improves the size and quality of those remaining and prevents biennial bearing. Thin after the June drop occurs and again twice after, disposing of the rejects to destroy any pests.

Pests and Diseases

Apples are the most commonly grown fruit tree in much of the temperate zone. They have thus built up a whole ecosystem of pests and diseases around themselves. Although they have many problems they still manage to produce enormous quantities of fruit for many years, in often quite poor conditions. Vigorous growth is essential as this reduces many problems, especially canker. The commonplace pests require the usual remedies, but apples suffer from some annoying specialities. Holes in the fruits are usually caused by

Once the first is damaged the rest will soon follow – don't delay; gather them NOW

one of two pests. Codling moth generally makes holes in the core of the fruit, pushing frass out at the flower end. They are controlled by corrugated cardboard band traps, pheromone traps, permitted sprays as the blossom sets, and hygiene. The other hole-maker is apple sawfly, which bores narrow tunnels, emerging anywhere. They may then eat into another or even a third. They are best controlled by hygiene, removing and destroying affected apples during thinning. Permitted sprays may be used after flower set, and running poultry underneath an orchard is effective. Many varieties are scab-resistant. If it occurs, it affects first the leaves then the fruits and, like brown rot and canker, is spread by mummified apples and dead wood. It is worst in wet areas. All of these problems, and mildews, are best controlled by hygiene, keeping the trees vigorous, well watered and mulched, and open pruned. Woolly aphis can be sprayed or dabbed with soft soap. Sticky non-setting tree bands control many pests all year round, especially in late summer and autumn. Apples also get damaged by birds, wasps and occasionally earwigs, so for perfect fruits, protect them with paper bags. Fruit fly is a serious pest in warmer areas and if not sprayed, results in destruction of the fruit. Fruit can be bagged before they sting fruit, usually starting around November.

An early then a second thinning means these **Discovery** are near perfect

An old fridge makes a good mouse-proof insulated store

Harvesting and Storing

Early apples are best eaten off the tree. They rarely keep for long, going pappy in days. Most mid-season apples are also best eaten off the tree as they ripen, but many will keep for weeks if picked just under-ripe and stored in the cool. Late keepers must hang on the trees till hard frosts are imminent, or bird damage is getting too severe, then if they are delicately picked and kept cool in the dark they may keep for six months or longer. Thus apples can be had most months of the year, provided early- and late-keeping varieties and a rodent-proof store are available. They are best picked with a cupped hand and gently laid in a tray, traditionally padded with dry straw. (This may taint if damp so better to use shredded newspaper.) Do not store early varieties with lates nor near pears, onions, garlic or potatoes. The fruits must be free of bruises, rot and holes and the stalk must remain attached for them to store well. If apples are individually wrapped in paper they keep longer. Apples can be puréed and frozen, juiced and frozen, dried in thin rings or made into cider.

Apple surpluses can easily be dried as rings or pieces

CULINARY AND DESSERT APPLES

culinary

Apples are excellent raw, stewed and made into tarts, pies and jellies, especially with other fruits which they help set. The juice is delicious fresh and can be frozen for out-of-season use, and made into cider or vinegar. Cooking apples are different from desserts, much larger, more acid and less sweet raw. Most break down to a frothy purée when heated and few retain their texture, unlike most of the desserts. **Bramley's**, **Norfolk Beauty** and **Revd Wilke's** are typical, turning to sweet froths when cooked. **Lane's Prince Albert**, **Lord Derby** and **Encore** stay firm and are the sorts to use for pies rather than sauces.

Flying Saucers
Per person

1 large cooking apple
Approx. 3 dessertspoons mincemeat
Knob of butter
7g sesame seeds
Cream or custard, to serve

Wash, dry and cut each apple in half horizontally. Remove the tough part of the core but leave the outside intact. Stuff the hollow with mincemeat, then pin the two halves back together with wooden cocktail sticks. Rub the outside with butter and roll in sesame seeds, then bake in a baking tray in a preheated oven at 190°C/375°F/gas mark 5 for half an hour or until they 'lift off' nicely. Serve the saucers immediately with cream or custard.

companion planting

Apples are bad for potatoes, making them blight-prone. They are benefited by Alliums, especially chives, and penstemons and nasturtiums nearby are thought to prevent sawfly and woolly aphids. Stinging nettles nearby benefit the trees and, dried, they help stored fruits keep.

Malus pumila **from the family** ***Rosaceae***

CRAB AND CIDER APPLES

Kingston Black

Trees up to 10m. Life span: long. Deciduous, often self-fertile. Fruits: 1–7cm, spherical, yellow, green or red. Value: make tonic alcoholic beverages.

Crab apples grow wild in hedgerows and have smaller, more brightly coloured fruits than cultivated varieties. The fruits vary from being unpalatable to completely inedible raw, though they make delicious jellies. Cider apples are more like eating and cooking apples, with fruits in-between in size but similarly bitter and astringent. Selected crab apples are grown ornamentally and are useful pollinators for other apples, so they may be found on semi-dwarfing stocks as small trees. Cider apples were always grown on strong or seedling stock, gaining immense vigour, which they needed to tower above animals grazing underneath.

Crabs have been used since prehistory and doubtless cider has been made for as long. It was probably brought to Cornwall initially by Phoenician tin traders.

varieties

Most crab apples, such as **Golden Hornet** with bright yellow fruit, and **John Downie**, with long golden orange fruits, are grown as ornamentals. Most are mixed hybrids of *Malus pumila* with *M. sylvestris*, which has sour, hard, green fruits and can be thorny, and *M. mitis*, from the Mediterranean region, which has softer leaves and sweeter, more coloured fruits. *M. baccata*, the Siberian crab, and *M. manchurica*, from China, are widely planted for their bright red fruits. Cider apples are more improved and closer to *M. domestica* hybrids. In trials, **Yarlington Mill**, **Tremlett's Bitter**, **Dabinett** and **Breakwell's Seedling** produced ciders that range from light to medium in flavour and sharpness. **Sweet Coppin** and **Reine des Hâtives** produce sweet ciders. In the UK, **Dabinett** is still widely grown in the West Country; ripening in November, it makes a bitter-sweet cider. **Michelin**, raised 1872, is self-fertile, popular in the Midlands and makes a medium sweet cider.

cultivation

Tougher than the finer apples, these may be grown almost anywhere not waterlogged or parched. **Kingston Black** and **Stoke Red** are only suitable for the coldest apple growing areas. They have trouble breaking dormancy in Australia due to their high-chilling requirement.

Growing in Containers

Ballerina crab apples can be fruited in pots; even in the small pots in which garden centres sell them. **Maypole**, used in jellies, grows particularly well. Cider apples are shy and less likely to produce heavy crops.

John Downie

CRAB AND CIDER APPLES

Ornamental and Wildlife Value
The crabs are very attractive in flower and many also in fruit. Cider apples are bigger and less pretty. Both are valuable to insects when in flower and to birds, rodents and insects with their fruit.

Propagation
Although some crabs can be grown from seed they are not reliable. Named varieties are grafted on to rootstocks suitable for the size and site intended. Neither crab nor cider apple varieties are usually available on the most dwarfing rootstocks, but on more vigorous stock they make large trees.

Pruning and Training
Crab apples are usually worked as half-standards on semi-dwarfing stock and are only pruned remedially in winter. Cider apples are worked as standards on strong growing stocks and make big trees. They should only be pruned remedially after forming a head.

Pests and Diseases
Although these can suffer from the same problems as dessert and culinary apples, the crops are rarely badly affected. Crab apples are usually remarkably productive whatever care they get. For cider apples many problems such as scab are also mostly irrelevant.

Harvesting and Storing
Crabs can be picked under-ripe for jellying, but you can hang on, as the birds do not go for them as fast as softer fruits. Cider apples are left as long as possible to get maximum sugar and to soften. If they are shaken down they bruise, so the apples are then best pressed immediately, not stored in heaps to soften further before pressing.

companion planting

The plants that benefit dessert and culinary apples (see page 451) also associate well with these varieties. Both crab and cider apples are often grown in hedgerows and grazed meadow orchards. They seem content with grass underneath and old trees often have mistletoe growing in their boughs, to no obvious detriment.

Malus baccata

A grape press for extracting juice from apples works better if they're pulped first

other uses

Pressed apple pulp can be dried and stored till late winter for wild bird and livestock food.

culinary

Crab apples make delicious tart jellies by themselves, or mixed with other fruits which have less pectin and so do not set so easily. Cider apples are used solely to make cider. They are cleaned, crushed and pressed and the juice is fermented, often with the addition of wine yeast and sugar. After fermentation, cider may be flat, cloudy, sweet or sparkling, green or yellow, depending on local taste. Ciders are made from several varieties of apple, to give a blend of acidity, sweetness and tannin. (Palatable cider can be made from a mixture of dessert and cooking apples.) Some cider is made into vinegar, deliberately.

Crab Apple Jelly
Makes approx 3.5kg

2kg crab apples
Approx.1.5kg sugar

Chop the apples, then simmer them in water to cover until soft. Sieve or strain through a jelly bag and weigh the juice. Add three-quarters of its weight in sugar. Return to the heat and bring to boil, stirring to dissolve the sugar. Boil until setting point is reached, then skim and pour into warm, sterilised jars. Cover while still hot.

Pyrus communis from the family *Rosaceae*

CULINARY AND DESSERT PEARS

Tree up to 20m. Life span: very long. Deciduous, hardy, rarely self-fertile. Fruits: up to 8x18cm. Value: potassium and riboflavin.

Pears very closely resemble, and are related to, apples, but there are no known natural hybrids between them. Pears have a fruit that elongates at the stalk end, which stands proud, whereas an apple's stalk is inset in a dent in the top of the fruit. Some pears such as Conference and Bartlett will set fruit parthenocarpically (i.e., they fruit freely without pollination). However, these fruits are usually not as good as fertilised ones, being misshapen and, of course, lacking seeds. Pear trees resemble apples but have shiny leaves, more upright growth and the fat stems usually have a glossier brown hue and more angled buds than apple. Pears on their own roots make very big trees, too big to prune, spray or pick, and the fruit is damaged when it drops. Pears are thus usually worked on quince roots, which makes them smaller, more compact trees.

Pears are native to Europe and Asia. The first cultivated varieties were selected from the wild in prehistory. The ancient Phoenicians, Jews and pre-Christian Romans grew several improved sorts; by the time of Cato there were at least a half dozen distinct fruits, Pliny records 41 and Palladius 56. A list of fruits for the Grand Duke Cosimo III, in late medieval Italy, raises the number to 209, and another manuscript lists 232. In Britain in 1640 only five dozen were known. This had risen to more than 700 by 1842. In 1866 the American author T. W. Field catalogued 850 varieties. The rapid increase in numbers and quality, from poor culinary pears to fine desserts, was mainly the work of a few dedicated breeders in France and Belgium at the end of the eighteenth century, who selected and bred most modern varieties.

varieties

As pears are used more for eating raw than in cooking, and dessert pears can be cooked, but not vice versa, it is not worthwhile growing purely culinary pears. **Doyenne du Comice** (late season) is by far the best dessert pear. None other approaches it for sweet, aromatic succulence, and the fruits can reach a magnificent weight. These are very choice and deserve to be espaliered on the best warm wall. **Bartlett/Williams' Bon Chretien** (early/mid-season) is widely grown for canning, but is an excellent table fruit – if a bit prone to scab. It is, parthenocarpic as is **Conference** (early/mid-season). The latter is a reliable cropper on its own and is scab-resistant. Raised in 1770 in Berkshire, it is now very widely grown.

Home-grown varieties include the commercially popular **Packham's Triumph** raised in New South Wales in 1896, **Buerre Bosc**, a fi ne textured, flavoursome pear, the late fruiting **Winter Nelis**, a French dessert variety good for baking, and late-ripening **Winter Cole**, raised in Victoria in 1882. **Corella** from South Australia, is a dainty, coloured eating pear with good keeping qualities and excellent taste.

Other classic European pears suited to home orchards are **Buerre Hardy**, **Dr Jules Guyot**, **Durondeau**, **Doyenne du Comice** and **Conference**. Two low-chill varieties, **Hood** and **Flordahome**, are best in warm zones. **Clapp's Favourite** ripens early but has poor keeping qualities. The recently introduced **Beth** is a very tasty early, while **Concorde** is a heavy late cropper. These last two are improved offspring from **Conference**, and **Concorde** is similarly fairly self-fertile.

There are hundreds of other pear varieties, many of which are cooking not dessert, and several species which have more ornamental than edible value.

cultivation

Dessert pears need a rich, well-drained, moist soil, preferably light and loamy. They can be cropped in the open in southern England, but need a wall further north. The blossom and fruitlets need protection from frosts as they flower early in spring. Pollination is best ensured by planting a mixture of varieties. Do not plant deep as pears are prone to scion rooting, which allows them to make big, less fruitful trees.

Nashi or Asian pears

The crisp apple-textured pears of Japan and China (*P. pyrifolia*) are new arrivals to orchardists. They need similar cultivation to European pears but are picked full ripe. Varieties available include **Shinsui**, which ripens around February and March; **Chojuro**, a bland fruit but good for pollinating; **Kosui**, a sweet mid-season fruit; **Tsu Li** a later pear with good flavour; and the popular greeny-yellow **Nijisseiki**, maturing from March.

Growing in Containers

Pears are fruited in tubs. They are amenable to hard pruning, and so respond better than most other fruits to this and to the cramped conditions of a pot.

Pears should not be left till they drop; pick before that point to colour and ripen indoors

Kumoi

Ornamental and Wildlife Value

Why plant an ornamental flowering tree when you can plant a pear? They are smothered with blossom and buzzing bees in early spring. The fruits are splendid, but soon eaten in autumn by insects and birds.

Propagation

Pears do not come true from seed, reverting to their unproductive forms. They may root from cuttings and can occasionally be layered, but get too big on their own roots. Normally they are grafted on to quince rootstocks, which are generally best. For heavy, damp soils and for big trees, pear seedling stock was always used, but there is little demand for this nowadays. Pears have been grafted on to apple stocks and even on to hawthorn. As some varieties do not bond readily with quince stock they are 'double-worked', or grafted on to a mutually compatible inter-graft on the quince. This takes more work and an extra year in the nursery.

Pruning and Training

Grown as trees or bushes, pears can be left to themselves except for remedial pruning. They tend to throw twin leaders which need rationalising. Alternatively, they respond better than most fruits to hard winter pruning and are almost as amenable to summer pruning; thus they can be trained to an endless variety of forms. As they benefit from the shelter of a wall, they are commonly espaliered, and are more rewarding for less work than a peach in the same position. There are many specialised training forms for pears in addition to the cordon, espalier and fan, and equally intricate and specialised pruning methods. These include Pitchforks and Toasting Forks, with two or three vertical stems on short arms, the Palmette Verriers, with long horizontals that turn vertical at the ends, and the multi-curved L'Arcure. Pears will take almost any shape you choose, and you will not go far wrong if you then shear almost all long growths off by three-quarters in summer and then again by a bit more in winter. Take care not to let them root from or above the graft, which destroys the benefit of the rootstock!

Espaliered **Beurre Hardy** is happy on this sunny wall where it pollinates a **Doyenne du Comice** close by

Pests and Diseases

Pears suffer fewer problems than apples. Providing the flowers miss the frosts and have a warm summer they usually produce a good crop of fruits despite any attacks. However, ripening is poor in very cool or hot weather and results in hard or mealy fruits. Leaving the fruit too long on the tree or in storage causes them to rot from the inside out. Pear and cherry slugs appear on leaves in mid-summer. New bio sprays should control it. Codling moth is less voracious in pears than apples, but possums will eat the ripening fruit. Fireblight in New Zealand causes damage resembling scorching. It usually starts from the blossoms. Prune and burn damaged parts immediately, cutting back to clean wood. Scab is a problem in stagnant sites. It affects the fruits before the leaves, which is the opposite from apples.
Sprays are usually unnecessary with the more resistant varieties such as Conference. Good open pruning and healthy growth, not overfed with nitrogen, reduce attacks. Always remove all mummified fruits and dead wood immediately. Leaf blistering is usually caused by minute mites. These used to be controlled with lime and sulphur sprays before bud burst. Modern soft soap sprays have also proved to be effective.

Harvesting and Storing

Early pears are best picked almost, but never fully, ripe. They should come off when lifted to the horizontal. Left on the tree they go woolly. Watch them carefully while they finish ripening. They will slowly ripen if kept cool, faster if warm. Late pears should be left until bird damage is too great, and picked with a stalk. Kept in a cool, dark place, late varieties last for months, ripening up rapidly if brought into the warm. Do not wrap them with paper as one does with apples, and take care not to store the two fruits near each other as they will cross-taint.

other uses

The bark contains a yellow dye and arbutin, an antibiotic. The leaves have been used medicinally for renal and urinary infections. The wood is hard and uniform, so loved by carvers. It is beautifully scented and good for smoking foods.

companion planting

Pears are hindered by grass, so this should not be allowed near them in their early years. However, the pears may be grassed down later, especially if they are situated in rather too heavy and/or damp conditions.

Pear gluts are easily turned into sweet syrup!

CULINARY AND DESSERT PEARS

culinary

Pears are exquisite as dessert fruits and may be used in much the same way as apples, sliced and used in tarts, baked, stewed or puréed. They are delicious pickled with onions and spices in vinegar.

Windfall and over-ripe pears can be chopped and simmered, then sieved and boiled down to a maple like syrup. Nashi Pears such as the **Kumoi** dry to delectable rings, chewier and sweeter than dried European pears and far better than apple rings.

Pear Islands
Serves 4

4 large pears
90g caster sugar
Half bottle sweet Muscat wine
2 level tablespoons cornflour
Splash of milk
Dark chocolate, to taste

Peel, core and halve the pears. Dissolve two-thirds of the sugar in the wine over a gentle heat and poach the pears in this syrup. Place the pear halves on an oiled baking tray, dredge with the rest of sugar and pop under a hot grill for a minute or two until the tops caramelise. In the meantime, blend the cornflour with a little milk and stir it into the syrup. Return to the heat and cook gently, stirring, until thick. Pour the sauce into a serving bowl, grate on some dark chocolate and set the pear halves into this. Serve piping hot or chilled.

Pyrus from the family *Rosaceae*

PERRY PEARS

Blakeney red

Tree up to 20m. Life span: very long. Deciduous, rarely self-fertile. Fruits: up to 10 x 7cm, variable, pear-shaped, yellow, brown or red. Value: make a healthy tonic beverage.

Perry pear fruits are smaller and hardier than their culinary and dessert cousins, while the trees are generally enormous. As these fruits were wanted in quantity for pressing, they were selected for large trees that would stand well above grass and the depredations of stock. The fruits are bitter and astringent, containing a lot of tannin, even though they may often look very appealing. They are pressed for the juice, which ferments to an alcoholic beverage.

Perry pears may have been brought to Britain by the Romans, but they were introduced in force by the Normans. Normandy was by then well established as a perry-growing region and the Normans found parts of the West and Midlands of England equally suitable. Many of the original pear orchards would probably still have been planted for perry without the Norman influence, as early pears tended to be unpalatable raw anyway. The colonists of North America certainly did not start off without perry pears. By 1648 a booklet entitled *A Perfect Description of Virginia* describes a Mr Kinsman regularly making forty or fifty butts of perry from his orchard. Whereas cider has remained a popular drink, perry waned in the nineteenth century. It is now made rarely, except for one or two specialist brands and for local consumption.

varieties

There are some 200–300 perry pear varieties known, though these are called by twice as many names, each district having its own local variation. The **Thorn Pear** is recorded from 1676 and grows on a very upright tree. In the nineteenth century, breeders thought dual-purpose pears would be useful and produced **Blakeney Red** and **Cannock**. The **Huffcap** group all make very big trees with fruits of a high specific gravity. Perry pears were only imported to Australia in 1994. Four varieties, **Gin**, **Green Horse**, **Moorcroft** and **Yellow Huffcap**, are being assessed with Green Horse the fi rst to bear in 1999. Perries are slow to mature, occasioning an old Hereford saying, 'Grow perry pears for your heirs'.

cultivation

Perry pears are less demanding than culinary or dessert pears and will do quite well in fairly poor soils. They do not like shallow or badly drained sites. Information about the development of perry pears may be obtained from the Orange Agricultural Institute (www.dpi.nsw.gov.au/research/centres/orange).

Perry pears are not good eating

PERRY PEARS

Perry pears are smaller, more acidic and often more brightly coloured than dessert pears

Growing in Containers
Although they would resent it by being short-lived and light-cropping, it should be possible to grow these in large tubs.

Ornamental and Wildlife Value
Perry pears make a mass of flowers and are tall attractive trees that live for several hundred years, making them very suitable as estate and orchard trees, but too big for most gardens except on modern dwarfing stock. The flowers are good for insects and the fruits are eaten by birds in winter.

Propagation
British growers use dwarfing quince rootstock but agricultural researchers in Australia have opted to use the D6 rootstock for compatibility reasons.

Pruning and Training
Once the initial shape is formed these are only pruned remedially, though care should always be taken to ensure that such large trees are sound.

Pests and Diseases
These suffer the same few problems as dessert and culinary pears which make little impression on the immense crops. Fireblight is a risk in New Zealand, but not seen in Australia.

Harvesting and Storing
Immense crops are produced; a ton or even two per tree is possible, after a wait of several decades. One tree in 1790 covered three-quarters of an acre and produced six tons per year. Perry pears do not keep and rot very quickly. Perry is usually pressed from one variety only, with sugar and yeast added. Dessert and culinary pears do not make a perry of any value, but can be made into a pear wine.

companion planting

Young trees were usually cropped between cereals or hops and then grassed down as they matured, often grazed by geese.

other uses

The wood is useful for carving and, as firewood, scents the room.

culinary

Perry pears are not normally very good for eating even when they are cooked, though **Blakeney Red** was once considered a good baker.

Pressless Perry Wine

3kg pears
1.5kg sugar
4.5 litres boiling water
Approx. 1 teaspoon wine yeast

Chop the pears, peel and all, into the boiling water. Stir in half the sugar, and bring back to the boil, then allow to cool to 22°C (70°F) before adding the yeast. Seal with a fermentation lock and keep warm for one week, then strain and add the remaining sugar to the liquor. Reseal with the lock and ferment in a warm place until all action has stopped. Siphon off the lees and store in a cool place for 3 months, then bottle and store for a year before drinking.

Cydonia vulgaris/C. oblonga from the family *Rosaceae*

QUINCES

Tree up to 6m. Self-fertile, deciduous, hardy, long-lived. Fruits: 7 x 12cm, yellow and fragrant.

These are small, bushy trees, often twisted and contorted. There are two forms: a lower mounded one with lax branches, more suited to ornamental and wildlife use, and a stiffer, erect type, which bears larger fruits and is better for orchards. The leaves are downy underneath, resembling apple leaves more than pear. They turn a gorgeous yellow in autumn. The decorative pink and white flowers resemble apple blossom, but appear singly on short shoots, up to 12cm long, that grow before the flower opens, so they are rarely bothered by late frost. In some varieties the unfurled flower bud looks like an ice cream cone with strawberry stripes, or a traditional barber's pole. The quinces are hard fruits somewhat resembling pears in shape and colour, often covered with a soft down when young, inedible when raw, but delicious and aromatic when cooked. Because they have long been used as rootstocks for pears and other fruits, they are sometimes found as suckers, surviving long after the scion has passed away.

Quinces are old fruits, still much grown in many parts of Europe though originally from Persia and Turkestan. Dedicated by the ancients to the Goddess of Love, they were promulgated by the Roman Empire as one of their favoured crops and were well known to Pliny and Columella. In 812 AD Charlemagne encouraged the French to grow more and Chaucer refers to them by the French name *coines*. Their pulp makes *Dulce de Membrillo* or *Marmelo*, still popular in Portugal and Spain, and the origin of the marmalade we now make from citrus fruit.

varieties

Portugal is pear-shaped, vigorous and productive with quality fruit. **De Vranja (Berezki)** from Serbia grows strongly but yield is low. The Turkish **Smyrna** matures early and has fragrant, lemon yellow fruit. **Champion**, roundish and mild-flavoured, bears heavily but the fruit is quite small.

The **Chinese Quince**, *Pseudocydonia sinensis*, has a similar large yellow edible fruit but is usually planted for its gorgeous mottled bark and autumn leaf colour.

Cydonia quinces may be confused with Chaenomeles

cultivation

Quinces are popular in country districts with cold winters and warm autumns. They prefer protection from wind and a regular supply of water. Quinces are survivors and tolerate dry summers and neglect but fruit is woody in drought conditions. They do best in heavy soils and can fall victim to iron deficiency.

Plant trees 4–5m apart and stake only for the first year after planting and train to an open-shaped vase. They are self-fertile and rarely need thinning. Trees are prone to many pests and diseases in humid coastal districts.

QUINCES

culinary

Quinces can be made into aromatic clear jelly, jam or a pulpy cheese that goes well with both sweet and savoury dishes. Pieces of quince (if you can hack them off) keep their shape when cooked, adding both texture and aroma to apple and pear dishes.

Quince Cheese
Makes approx 2kg

1kg ripe quinces
1 unwaxed small orange
A little water
Approx.1kg sugar
1 or 2 drops orange flower or rose petal water (optional)

Roughly hack the quinces into pieces. Finely chop the orange and simmer both, with just enough water to cover them, until they are a pulp. Strain the pulp and add its own weight in sugar. Bring to boil and cook gently for approximately 1 1/2 hours. Add the orange flower or rose petal water, if liked. Then pot into oiled, warmed bowls, seal, and store for three months or more before using.

Turn the cheese out of the bowl and slice for serving with cooked meats or savoury dishes.

Ornamental and Wildlife Value
Quinces make excellent small specimen trees as the flowers, fruits, autumn colours and the knotted branches give year-round interest. The flowers feed beneficial insects while the fruits are relished by birds and other wildlife after the apples and pears have long gone.

Propagation
Quinces can be had from seed or by suckers removed from pear trees as these are usually grafted on to quince stocks. Better fruits will always result from buying a ready-formed tree of an already named variety.

Pruning and Training
Quinces can be trained but the twisted contorted growth makes this difficult. They are best grown as bushes or standards, with pruning restricted to removing dead, diseased and crossing wood.

Pests and Diseases
Quince fleck is widespread but spraying with Bordeaux at bud burst controls it. In mid-summer, pear and cherry slug can defoliate trees. Fruit fly is common on the coast but less so beyond the Great Dividing Range. Legally fruit has to be removed by late April in New South Wales to prevent spread. Oriental peach moth and codling moth also cause damage to quinces. Carbaryl cannot be used on them.

Cydonia quinces are very pear-like, but much firmer

Harvesting and Storing
Pick the fruits in autumn before they drop and keep them in a cool airy place. Do not store with apples or pears or vegetables as they may taint.

companion planting

Like pears and apples, quinces may be expected to benefit from underplantings of chives, garlic and the pungent herbs.

other uses

The wood is hard and prunings make good kindling. The fruits are excellent room perfumers and can be used as bases for pomanders.

Prunus domestica from the family *Rosaceae*

PLUMS

Tree 6m. Long-lived, deciduous, hardy, slender, thorny, not usually self-fertile. Fruits: ovoid, usually 3–6cm in any colour. Value: rich in magnesium, iron and vitamin A.

Plums come in more variation than most other fruits. They differ in season, size, shape, colour and taste. We have mixed hybrids, descendants of plums originally selected from fifteen or more different wild species. The European plum, *Prunus domestica*, is thought to be predominantly a hybrid between *P. cerasifera*, the cherry plum or Myrobalan, and *P. spinosa*, the sloe. It is a small to medium, slender, deciduous tree with small white blossoms.

The European plum came from Western Asia and the Caucasus. It naturalised in Greece first and then throughout most of the temperate zone. Pliny describes cultivated varieties from Syria coming to Italy via Greece, and it is likely they were spread by the Roman Empire to Britain and Northern Europe. They were reintroduced in the Crusades. Henry VII is recorded as importing a Perdrigon plum and Brogdale Fruit Research Station have a plum grown from a stone salvaged from the wreck of the *Mary Rose*, Henry VIII's splendid warship. Plum stones were ordered in 1629 for planting in Massachusetts, and plums became widely cultivated in the temperate parts of North America. In 1864 more than 150 varieties were offered in nurserymen's catalogues. Some American plums returned to Europe; California, for example, became famous for exporting prunes – late, dark-skinned plums, which are dried on the tree. Although unsuccessful in cool, damp climates, they can be dried with machinery. Fellemberg and Prune d'Agen are from Europe, but are more widely grown in California.

Czar

varieties

There are hundreds of good varieties, which ripen through the season, although in Australia European plums are less commonly grown than Japanese plums (see pages 466–467). Found in Sussex around 1840, **Victoria** is fully self-fertile, pollinates many others and is always worth having. It has golden-yellow-fleshed, large, yellow, ovoid fruits, flushed with scarlet. **Opal** is like a smaller, sweeter, earlier, better-flavoured Victoria and is even partially self-fertile, and a good pollinator for Victoria. **Coe's Golden Drop** is a shy cropper, but superb. **Czar** has frost-resistant flowers and is self-fertile; it is grown in New Zealand for culinary rather than dessert use. **Angelina Burdett**, an early to mid-season fruit, is one of the commoner plums. It is dark purple with firm flesh. **D'Agen** is a late plum used for drying and pollinating. **President** tends to mature late but stores well. **Fellenberg** is a prune variety, also known as **Italian**.

cultivation

Plums like a heavier, moister soil than many other fruits; however, they do not like cold, damp sites and

PLUMS

Victoria

heavy soils. Rather, plant in fertile loam with some lime and potash. Avoid windy positions and frost pockets.

Most plums have a high-chilling requirement, often over 700 hours. This restricts localities where they can be be successfully grown. In summer, they need watering to ensure the fruit fills up. European plums require additions of potassium to the soil. Feed with complete fertiliser to correct this.

Ornamental and Wildlife Value
Plums are wonderful during their short blossoming. The flowers are loved by early insects and the fruits by birds, insects and rodents, who also chew the bark.

Propagation
Graft on **Pixy** and other new dwarfing stocks, unless you have a big orchard and want immense quantities. Plums can be grown from stones, but take years to fruit and do not come true.

Pruning and Training
Plums make good high standards because, eventually, heavy fruiting branches weep, bringing the fruit down to a skirt. Overladen branches will need propping. Plums are usually grown as a short standard or bush. Leave them alone once a head is formed, except to cut out dead and diseased wood. Any work is best done in the growing season. They can be usefully trained on walls if on dwarfing stock, for example **Pixy**. Plums prefer herringbone, not fan shapes.

Pests and Diseases
Plums get a host of the usual pests, but when they avoid the frost and crop at all they are so prolific there is usually a surplus for private gardeners. They are runed in autumn, winter or early spring – only in late spring and summer and during dry weather. Exotic birds can decimate yields.

Harvesting and Storing
Plums picked under-ripe for cooking will keep for days, but often have poor flavour. Many varieties can be quite easily peeled, and this avoids some of the unfortunate side effects of too many plums.

companion planting

Avoid anemones, which harbour plum rust. In the USA curculios are reportedly kept off by surrounding plum trees with garlic.

other uses

Potent brandy is made from plums in Hungary and in central Europe.

culinary

Plums can be turned into jam, juice or cheese, or frozen if stoned first, and are epicurean preserved in plum brandy syrup.

Prunes in Semolina
Serves 4

250g dried prunes
100ml plum brandy
100ml water
900ml milk
Twist of lemon rind
½ teaspoon salt
7 dessertspoons semolina
2 dessertspoons honey
2 small eggs, separated
Grated nutmeg, to taste

Soak the prunes in the brandy and water overnight. Strain off the juice and simmer it down to syrup. Put the fruits and syrup into the base of a pudding basin. Boil the milk, lemon rind, salt and semolina for 10 minutes, stirring continuously.

Cool a little, remove the lemon rind and stir in the honey and egg yolks. Whisk the egg whites and fork them in. Immediately pour the mixture over the back of a spoon on to the fruit and syrup. Grate nutmeg over the surface and bake in a preheated oven at 200°C/400°F/gas mark 6 for 20 minutes, or until the top is browning.

As delicious cold for breakfast as it is hot for dinner.

Double Victoria
Serves 6–8

500g Victoria plums, halved and stoned
50g honey
25g flaked blanched almonds

For the sponge:
100g sifted self-raising flour
100g vanilla flavoured castor sugar
100g softened butter
2 eggs
pinch of salt

Place the plums in a buttered pudding dish and dribble the honey over them. Beat together the sponge ingredients in a mixer until creamy and light in colour. Dollop the sponge mixture over the fruit, smooth and garnish with almonds. Bake in a preheated oven at 190°C/ 375°F/gas mark 5 for 35 minutes or until golden brown and firm to the touch.

Prunus italica from the family *Rosaceae*

GREENGAGES

Tree/bush 4–5m. Hardy, long-lived. Fruits: 2–4cm, green to red.

Greengages are like plums, fruiting in mid-season with sweet, greeny-yellow or golden, lightly scented flesh. The fruits are smaller, firmer, more rounded and less bloomed than plums. They have a deep crease down one side and frequently russet spotting. The trees are sturdy, not often thorny, and bushier than most plums, though not quite as hardy.

Wild greengages are found in Asia Minor. Possibly introduced to Britain and Northern Europe by the Romans, they disappeared from cultivation during the Saxon period or Middle Ages and were not reintroduced until 1725. Originally known in France as the Reine Claude, the first greengage was brought to Britain by, and named after, Sir Thomas Gage, who lived in Bury St Edmunds, Suffolk – less than 20 miles from where I now write. He was fortunate to live in East Anglia as the conditions suit greengages, which need a drier, warmer summer than plums. The original greengage almost always came true from seed, but there are some larger-fruited selections, and also some good crosses between gages and plums.

Mirabelle

varieties

The **Old Greengage** is original, but can be unreliable; an improved seedling is **Cambridge Gage**. **Jefferson** is similar, later, but not self-fertile.

Greengages are uncommon in Australia, and rarely found in nursery catalogues although recent imports may see them more commonly grown. Among these are the **Transparent Gage**, an old variety from France, honeyed in its sweetness. It has almost transparent golden yellow flesh and is heavily spotted with red. It fruits in late summer. **Mirabelle** is very similar, smaller fruited and of dwarf growth. **Denniston's Superb** comes from the USA and is close to the original in flavour, but is larger fruited, hardier, regular cropping and, most valuable of all, self-fertile. **Reine Claude de Bavay** possibly has a plum as one parent. It fruits a fortnight or so after the previous varieties, in early autumn, but is hard to find. It makes a most delicious jam, a touch more acid and tasty if the fruit is picked a week or so early.

cultivation

Greengages need heavy winter chill and only grow in the colder parts of Australia and New Zealand. They need a rich, moist, well-aerated soil in a cool, sunny location with good air circulation around the branches. They resent hot drying winds in summer and winter front pockets. They are easiest to tend as standards at least 6m apart. Some, such as **Denniston's Superb**,

GREENGAGES

Prunelle liqueur is a warming drink akin to brandy

Early Transparent Gage and **Jefferson's Gage**, will fruit on a shady wall. Gages generally require another tree as pollinator. Even the self-fertile **Reine Claude de Bavay** will yield better if pollinated by another European plum such as **D'Agen**. It is also possible to graft a branch from another variety.

Ornamental and Wildlife Value

As for plums (see page 33).

Harvesting and Storing

Greengages are loved by the supermarkets green and hard, as in that condition they keep for weeks. Picked fully ripe off the tree they are delectable, but do not last, especially if wet. They can be jammed, turned into cheeses, juiced or frozen if stoned first.

Pruning and Training

They are usually grown as low standards or bushes with remedial pruning in late spring once the shape has formed. Overladen branches need propping, but not as much as for plums. As they also tend to irregular bearing, thinning of heavy crops is sensible, but not as effective as for most fruits. Gages are best worked in a herringbone pattern on a wall, and summer pruned.

Pests and Diseases

As greengages are so sweet they suffer particularly from bird damage, and the buds are attacked as well as the fruits! The damage caused also allows dieback to get a foothold. All plums are affected by brown rot. Control by keeping trees airy and open in the centre. Remove any mummified fruit and avoid overhead watering.

Propagation

Gages are usually grafted on to Myrobalan stocks, but newer dwarfing stocks mean that it is easier to fit them on to walls. Cuttings can be taken in late autumn with some success and the oldest varieties come nearly true from stones.

companion planting

Greengages benefit from being positioned on the sheltered, sunny side of the larger plums.

other uses

Prunelle (left) is a liqueur from Alsace and Angers, made from **Mirabelles**. Slivovitsa, an eau-de-vie, comes from the Balkans.

culinary

Mirabelle make the best plum jams. True Mirabelle jam is almost apricot flavoured, but even better.

Greengage jam

Makes 2kg

1kg greengages
1kg sugar
A little water

Wash, halve and stone the gages. Crack a few stones, extract the kernels and add these to the fruit. Pour in enough water to cover the bottom of the pan and simmer until the fruit has softened. Add the sugar and bring rapidly to the boil, then carefully skim, jar and seal.

Prunus species from the family *Rosaceae*

DAMSONS

BULLACES AND JAPANESE PLUMS

Zwetsche

Tree/bush up to 5m. Long-lived, some self-fertile. Fruits: 2cm+, some vitamin value.

Bullaces (*P. insititia*) have globular, bluey-black or greeny-yellow fruits, which ripen in late autumn, at least a month later than most other plums. The fruits are small and generally too acid to eat raw, but make good preserves. The trees are sometimes thorny.

Damsons (*P. damascena*) are closely related to bullaces, with larger, blue-black fruit which more closely resemble plums. However, they are more oval, with less bloom, and have a sweet, spicy flavour once cooked. Damson trees are compact and are reasonably self-fertile.

The **Cherry Plum** or **Myrobalan** (*P. cerasifera*) can be woven into hedges; it is often used as a windbreak. The self-fertile white flowers open at the same time as the leaves, which are glossier than those of other plums. The fruits are yellow, red or purple, spherical and a little pointed at the bottom. They have a sweet, juicy, if somewhat insipid flesh and make good jam.

Japanese plums (*P. salicina* and *P. triflora*) are large, conical, orangey-red or golden fruits without much flavour. They blossom early and are vulnerable to cold, but they are also more productive and tolerant of a wider range of warm conditions than ordinary plums, so are extensively grown in Australia, South Africa and the USA. They have shiny, dark twigs, white flowers on bold spurs and leaves that turn a glorious red in autumn.

Bullaces are native to Europe and Asia Minor, but the current apparently wild stock has probably been inadvertently selected over the centuries. Damsons come from Damascus, or certainly that region, and were brought to Europe during the Crusades in the twelfth century, supposedly by the Duke of Anjou, after a pilgrimage to Jerusalem. Cherry plums come from the Balkans, Caucasus and Western Asia and were introduced to Britain in the sixteenth century. Some of these went to the New World and were interbred with American native species to cope with the harsher climatic conditions. Japanese plums, originally natives of China, were introduced to Japan about 1500 and only to the USA in 1870. Being rather tender, they have never really expanded into Europe.

varieties

Japanese plums, such as **Burbank**, may be available. Similar is **Beauty**, which is red with sweet, juicy, yellow flesh that clings to the stone. The hybrid plum **Wilson's Early** matures before Christmas and is the earliest to ripen. **Mariposa** has a ruby red skin and blood red flesh of good flavour. **Satsuma**, another blood plum, has firmer flesh. **Narrabeen** is a mid-season plum suited to warm zones. **Santa Rosa** needs to fully ripen or the fruit can be tart. It crops well when planted with **Queen Rosa**. **Damsons** are available from heritage fruit groups. **Shropshire** is good for jam. **Merryweather** and some other varieties are retained at research stations and horticultural institutes. The choice of bullaces is down to the purpley-blue **Black Bullace** or the greeny-yellow **Shepherd's Bullace**. Cherry plums are most often called **Red** or **Yellow Myrobalans**. There are several ornamental forms that may fruit.

DAMSONS

Farleigh

cultivation

The chilling requirement for Japanese plums is shorter than for European varieties.

Ornamental and Wildlife Value
The trees are not imposing until they flower, then they froth and foam. Later their displays of fruiting profligacy are quite stupendous. Great masses of fruits continue to feed the wildlife through many months.

Propagation
Japanese plums can bear in three years or so, the others maybe in fi ve. Those on their own roots can be grown from suckers, and seedlings of most will come nearly true. Most types do well on Myrobalan stocks and many on their own roots.

Pruning and Training
As for plums, these are best left alone except for remedial work.

Pests and Diseases
These varieties of plums are generally not as susceptible to brown rot as true plums.

Harvesting and Storing
Bullaces and damsons are supposedly mellowed and taste better raw after frosts, but the birds will have eaten them by then.

companion planting

Avoid anemones, which harbour plum rust.

other uses

As hedges and windbreaks the bullaces and cherry plums are excellent. Damsons can be planted in sheltered sections.

Myrobalans

culinary

Almost all of these fruits are now used culinarily only for jamming, jellying, fruit cheeses, winemaking and liqueurs.

Damson Cheese
Makes 2.5kg

1.5kg damsons
About 1kg light brown sugar

Wash the fruit and then simmer till soft with just enough water to prevent burning. Sieve and boil the pulp with three-quarters its own weight of sugar. Skim off any scum. Cook until the scum has finished rising and the jam is clear. Pot the pulp in warmed oiled bowls and seal.

Prunus armeniaca from the family *Rosaceae*

APRICOTS

Tree up to 6m. Hardy, deciduous, self-fertile. Fruits: 3 x 5cm, yellow/orange. Value: rich in vitamin A and potassium.

This small tree has white flowers (occasionally tinged with pink) very early in spring, well before the leaves emerge. These are spade-shaped and often glossy. The young shoots can also appear glossy, as if varnished in red or brown. The leaves are more similar to those of a plum than those of a cherry or peach, and apricot fruits closely resemble some plums, but the stone is more spherical and the flavour distinct. Some think that Moorpark, one of the commonest varieties, is a plumcot (a plum-apricot hybrid).

The first apricots came from China or Siberia, not Armenia, where Alexander the Great found them. The fruits became loved by the Romans, but they never succeeded in transplanting any to northern Europe. Apricots reached Britain in the thirteenth century and were introduced again, more successfully, in the sixteenth. Bredase may be the oldest variety in cultivation; it closely resembles descriptions of Roman apricots.

varieties

Moorpark is exquisite; the traditional variety, it ripens a little later. **Trevatt** has firm flesh but tends to bear biennially. **Glengarry** needs frost-free positions as it is early to ripen. It has a low-chill factor, the best apricot for warm coastal areas. Its seedling, **Caselin**, bears shortly afterwards, but is less likely than its parent to split after rain. **Divinity** (**Improved Newcastle**) is a good early apricot for most areas but the fruit needs thinning. **Tilton** is best in cool districts and bears late in the season. Other late-maturing apricots include **Autumn Glo** and the mid to late **Helena**. The **Japanese Apricot**, *Prunus mume*, has scented flowers and sour fruit usually eaten salted or pickled.

cultivation

Like most stone fruits, apricots need a cold winter period to rest and warm summers to ripen the fruit. The plants themselves are tough, but the flowers are early so that they are often in danger from late spring frost. The soil should not be heavy nor the site wet. In cool areas, they will only crop reliably against a wall. A warm Mediterranean climate with cool to cold winters to break dormancy and warm to hot dry summers to mature fruit is ideal. Fruit may crack in humid conditions and trees grown where ponding occurs after rain should be grown on plum rootstocks. When grafted onto apricot stocks, trees are fairly drought tolerant. In dry conditions, trees need irrigation for a high yield. Trees tolerate alkaline soil but not high salt levels.

In the southern hemisphere the fruit ripens between November and January. The flavour is enhanced when the fruit is left to fully ripen on the tree. Apricots are self-fertile and do not need another tree for pollination.

Pruning and Training

The least work is to grow apricots as trees, only removing dead and diseased wood as necessary. Cut out all the dieback until no discoloration is seen. The wood is brittle, so watch for overladen branches and prop or prune early. On walls, build a fan of old wood with fruiting spurs. Prune the frame and any dieback in late winter, then prune again in summer to restrict the growth.

Pests and Diseases

Ants may be a problem, and farm scale insects and occasionally caterpillars and aphids may be seen. Apricots do suffer from dieback and gummosis, however, the twigs dying back and resiny gum oozing out of the branches or, worse, the trunk. Both these conditions are symptomatic of poor growth and every

Apricots grown in cool climates are still delicious

APRICOTS

New Large Early

effort should be made to improve the conditions; fewer weeds, more compost, more mulches, more water or better aerated roots, seaweed sprays and hard pruning should do it. Fruit fly is rife in some areas and silver leaf also affects apricots.

Propagation
Apricot trees are obtained budded onto suitable rootstocks, such as **St Julien A** in the UK. This is better for wetter, heavier soils; seedling peach or apricot rootstocks suit lighter, drier ones. Successful trees have been raised from stones.

Harvesting and Storing
Apricots ripened on the tree are heavenly, but soon go over. Picked young enough to travel, they never develop full flavour. Thus they are best eaten straight away, or jammed or frozen.

culinary

Apricots make scrumptious jam and can be preserved in brandy and syrup. Unlike the majority of *Prunus* fruits, most apricots have kernels that are sweet and edible and can be used to make ratafia biscuits.

Apricot Sponge
Serves 6–8

500g apricots
Knob of butter
Coarse, light brown sugar

For the sponge:
55g each of butter; fine, light brown sugar; white self-raising flour
1 large egg
A splash of milk
1 teaspoon real vanilla extract

Halve and stone the apricots (score or remove the skin if you prefer) and place in a buttered flan dish, cut side up. Sprinkle with coarse sugar. Cream together the butter and sugar, stir in the egg, then fold in the flour, together with the milk, if the mixture is stiff, and the vanilla extract. Spoon the sponge mixture over the apricots and cook in a preheated oven at 190°C/375°F/gas mark 5 for about half an hour. When cold, turn out and serve with whipped cream.

companion planting

Do not grow tomatoes, potatoes or oats near apricots, but they benefit from Alliums nearby, especially garlic and chives.

other uses

The wood is brittle, but of use as kindling.

Apricot halves freeze easily

Prunus persica from the family *Rosaceae*

PEACHES

Tree/bush up to 5 x 5m. Generally short-lived. Self-fertile, deciduous. Fruits: 6–8cm, yellow, orange, red. Value: rich in vitamin A, potassium and niacin.

Peach trees are small and the long, lightly serrated leaves resemble willows. They bloom before the leaves appear. The smaller the flowers, the darker rose coloured they are, with the largest being lightest pink. Flowering a fortnight later than almonds, they are closely related – the almond has a tough, inedible, leathery skin over a smooth stone. The skin has a partition line along which it easily splits. Most peach stones are ribbed or perforated with small holes in the shell. In varieties known as clingstones the flesh clings to this shell; in others, the freestones, the fruit is free and easier to enjoy without having to tease it off the stone.

The flesh may vary from white to yellow; there are even blood peaches with red staining. The texture varies with cultivar, soil and climate. The skin colour can be from dull green through yellows and orange to dark red. The most distinctive feature of peaches is the soft downy fluff on the skin.

The peach was known 300 BC to the Greek philosopher Theophrastus, who thought it came from Persia, and so it became named. Early Hebrew writings make no reference to it, neither is there a Sanskrit name, so it seems likely peaches did not reach Europe to any extent until shortly before the Christian period. Dioscorides mentions the peach during the first century, as does Pliny, who states that the Romans had only recently imported it from Persia.

Peaches are, in fact, of Chinese origin. They are mentioned in the books of Confucius from the first century BC, and can be traced back to the tenth century BC in artistic representations. The Chinese still have an immense number of varieties and these were initially spread by seed. The stones produce trees with ease, but of course do not come true. The variability may have accounted for the slow spread to Europe. However, this was more likely to have been because peaches were initially tried in hot countries at too low altitudes. Thus the trees did not get their winter dormancy and would have fruited badly, effectively discouraging further experiments. Pliny indeed mentions that peach trees were taken from Egypt to the island of Rhodes, but this transplantation did not succeed; they were then brought onto Italy.

It took till the middle of the sixteenth century for peaches to reach England and in 1629 a quantity of peach stones was ordered by the Governor of the Massachusetts Bay Colony of New England. The peach found the North American climate highly suitable and spread abundantly. In Australia, peaches were among the first fruit trees brought to the new colony at Port Jackson in 1788. They proved amenable to the climate and are still grown commercially.

PEACHES

varieties

A number of antique peaches can still be found among collections but are not commonly sold. **J.H. Hale**, a freestone, is a fine-coloured early peach, of excellent quality. The late-ripening **Fragar**, originating in Bathurst, ripens in mid-February and still has the best flavour of local peaches. High chill **Cardinal**, a clingstone, is suitable for cold districts. **Flavorcrest** has superior flavour and cropping habits. It carries well too. Two good early low-chill peaches are **Flordagold** (300 hours) and **Floraprince** (150 hours), bred for tropical conditions. Early **Anzac** bears heavily with succulent white fruit of excellent flavour. The freestone **Tasty Zee** was bred by Zaiger's Genetics in California and has sweet fruit late in the season. **Golden Queen** is a late New Zealand peach excellent for bottling. **Pixzee** is a dwarf peach with full-size fruits, well suited to patio and container culture. A very new introduction is **Avalon Pride**, a seedling found near Seattle in the USA, the first leaf curl-resistant variety.

cultivation

Peaches ideally need a well-enriched, well-aerated but moist piece of soil. They prefer open gravelly soils to heavy, and need to be planted at least 6m apart. Peaches need full sun with good air circulation. Rows should be aligned north–south in the orchard. The ideal position allows cold air to drain away but cool air to flow in summer.

Regular and consistent irrigation is needed for good fruit set and yield. Peaches establish quickly if planted early in winter to give roots a chance to spread before bud burst. They need copious amounts of compost and mulches are obligatory to ensure soil retains moisture and prevent evaporation. They respond well to drip irrigation in summer and are heavy feeders. Use a high-nitrogen NPK fertiliser in spring and supplement with poultry manure or blood and bone after harvest. Peaches are most intolerant of any waterlogging. Peaches should not be planted near to almonds, as the two fruits may hybridise, resulting in bitter nuts.

One – or better two – of these must go, or all will be small

It's worth thinning even Peento or flat peaches to get bigger fruits

Growing in Containers

Peaches are good subjects for large pots as they can take heavy pruning if well fed and watered. Pots enable them to be kept under cover during the winter and through flowering and then brought out all summer, thus avoiding peach leaf curl and frost damage. The flowers must be protected from frosts and so must the young fruitlets. The flowers are more susceptible to frost damage after pollination and the fruitlets likewise for a further fortnight.

Ornamental and Wildlife Value

The peach is a pleasure to have. The willowy leaves are held well into autumn and the sight of a good crop of fruits is magnificent. The blossom is wonderful too; peaches in bloom are a joy. The wildlife value of the tree is rather low in wet areas as the trees succumb to leaf curl, but in some drier areas peaches become weeds and are appreciated by birds, insects and rodents.

Thinning to wide spacing gives bigger, more luscious fruits

Pruning and Training

Peaches fruit on young shoots, thus it is essential to have plenty of these growths. They are best obtained by a partial pollarding operation late each winter. This makes the pruning more akin to that of blackcurrants than to that of most other tree fruits. Basically the top ends of the higher branches are removed to encourage prolific growth from the lower branches and stubs. This also serves to keep the peach bushes lower and more manageable.

On walls and under cover, peaches are usually fan-trained. Selected young shoots are allowed to spring from a main frame and then tied in to replace the previous growths, once those have fruited.

Fortunately, if the pruning of peaches is temporarily neglected, healthy bushes respond to being cut back hard by throwing plentiful young growths. More important than pruning is thinning. Peaches are prone to overcropping, breaking branches and exhausting themselves. Thin the fruits hard, removing those touching or anywhere near each other. Do this very early and then again later.

Propagation

Peaches can be raised from stones, but the results are haphazard and take years to fruit. Budded on to suitable stocks, **St Julien A** in the UK, for example, peaches will normally fruit in their third year. Plum stocks are more resistant to wet, but for warmer, drier conditions seedling apricot or peach rootstocks are better.

Pests and Diseases

Peaches suffer most losses from birds and fruit fly. Small paper bags will protect the crop. Earwigs can get inside the fruits and eat the kernel out, but are readily trapped in rolls of corrugated paper around each branch. Protect the bark from animals such as possums. Peaches get minor diseases such as peach scab, but their main problem is peach leaf curl. This puckers and turns the leaves red and yellow and they cease to function properly. Severe attacks cripple the tree and can even kill it. Spraying with Bordeaux mixture prevents the disease if done several times before the buds open in late winter. Dieback and gummosis are symptomatic of poor growth and are best treated by heavy mulching and hard pruning in very late winter. Peach rust and bacterial spot cause markings on fruit and are controlled by fungicides for brown rot.

Harvesting and Storing

A truly ripe peach is a bag of syrup waiting to burst. If picked under-ripe the flesh never develops the full gamut of flavour, or the liquidity. A good peach is a feast, drink and all. As with so many fruits, they are best eaten straight off the tree. They can be picked a few days early if handled with absolute care. Kept cool, they may last. The slightest bruising, however, and they decompose.

companion planting

Peaches are benefited by Alliums, especially garlic and chives. Clover or alfalfa leguminous green manures give the richness they need. Nettles nearby are reputedly helpful at preventing the fruit from moulding.

other uses

Peach stones are used for making activated charcoal for filters. The wood is brittle, but the prunings make good kindling. In some countries, gluts of peaches are used for feeding the local livestock.

Pick just before they drop, peel and eat sun warm

PEACHES

Home-grown peach preserves are exotic fare for the table

culinary

Peach jam, which is potentially more aromatic than plum, is easily over-cooked and the perfume lost. Make it set more easily and sooner by adding apple purée. Fruits that are ripening but starting to rot are best prepared then cooked in syrup. This, if not consumed immediately, can be frozen for winter use. Over-ripe fruits can be juiced, which is the nectar of the gods, and unripe peaches that never look like ripening make excellent chutney.

Peach Macaroon Cheesecake

Serves 4–6

125g macaroons
125g digestive biscuits
100g butter, melted
1kg peaches
15g gelatine
250g cream cheese
125g natural yogurt
100g honey or peach jam
Few drops vanilla essence
125g alpine strawberries

Crush the macaroons and biscuits and mix with the butter. Press into a flan dish. Peel, slice and chill the peaches. Simmer the skins and stones in minimal hot water, sieve and dissolve the gelatine in the warm liquid. Beat the cream cheese, yogurt, honey or jam and vanilla, then stir in the gelatine. Immediately pour over the biscuit base, chill and leave to set. Top with peach slices and alpine strawberries.

Prunus persica from the family *Rosaceae*

NECTARINES

Tree up to 5m. Generally short-lived, self-fertile, deciduous. Fruits: up to 8cm, greenish yellow/orange and red. Value: rich in vitamin A, potassium and niacin, as well as riboflavin and vitamin C.

In almost every way nectarines are just varieties of peach. However, there are several subtle and fascinating differences. Nectarines are more difficult to grow and are less hardy. The fruits are smaller, on average, than peaches. The flesh is firmer and less melting than a peach and more plum-like, less prone to falling apart while you eat it. Nectarines have a definite, almost peculiar, rich, vinous flavour quite distinct to that of a well-ripened peach. The colour of some nectarines also makes them distinguishable from peaches, as many of the older varieties have a greenish or sometimes even a purplish hue over a quite yellowish or greenish ground. Most noticeably, nectarines do not have that downy fuzz on the skin so typical of peaches, but instead are smooth and shiny; indeed they closely resemble a very large, plump plum.

Darwin noted how peach trees occasionally spontaneously produced nectarines, and also the converse; he even noted the case of a nectarine tree that produced a fruit that was half peach, half nectarine and then reverted to peaches. Despite the peach's long history of cultivation, however, rather strangely, no mention is made of nectarines by pre-Christian authors. Pliny mentions an unknown fruit, a duracina, but the first, if indirect, reference is by Cieza de Leon, who lived in the early sixteenth century and described a Caymito of Peru as being 'large as a nectarine'. They were seen growing amongst peaches in Virginia in 1720 and A. J. Downing listed 19 varieties in the USA by 1857. Many dozens of nectarine varieties are now in cultivation, and travellers also report local varieties of nectarine in most of the world's peach-growing areas, so their spontaneous emergence is not really a rare phenomenon.

Early Rivers

varieties

Early and low-chill **FLA 6-3 i**s best for warm areas. Flavoursome **May Grand** ripens early. **Early Rivers** is a white-fleshed mid-season fruit. **Independence** (low chill) is a highly rated fruit mid-season. For mid to late cropping, **Flavortop** has excellent flavour, and late-picked **Fairlane** has yellow flesh. **Nectazee** is a dwarf variety that's ideal for growing in containers on warm patios.

cultivation

Most nectarines are self-fertile and not as hardy as peaches. Good water control is critical to prevent fruit splitting, and so apply thick mulches. Needing more careful siting than peaches, give them protection from a wall or shelter in cool zones.

Growing under Glass and in Containers

Nectarines are more suited than many plants to culture under glass, preferring warmer conditions than peaches. However, they need a cool period of rest each winter or they become unfruitful, so they are best grown in large pots moved outside after cropping and brought back into a cool greenhouse in mid-to-late winter. Being dry under cover prevents peach leaf curl, keeps the frost off the flowers and fruitlets and gets them an early start. But they will only fruit successfully if religious attention is given to watering and ventilation. Hand pollination is desirable.

NECTARINES

Pruning and Training
Exactly as for the peach (see page 42).

Propagation
Nectarines sometimes come from peach stones and vice versa. More often they occur when a peach bud produces a sport. Most varieties are budded on suitable stocks as for peaches.

Pests and Diseases
Nectarines sometimes come from peach stones and vice versa. More often they occur when a peach bud produces a sport. Most varieties are budded on suitable stocks as for peaches.

Ornamental and Wildlife Value
Nectarines are almost exactly the same as peaches and are attractive, with the long, glossy leaves being held late into the season. The pink flowers are beautiful and appreciated by early insects; the lack of fruits reduces their wildlife interest. Nectarines need spraying to prevent peach leaf curl in many areas, so cannot be left to themselves.

Harvesting and Storing
Also as for the peach (see page 42).

Lord Napier

culinary

Nectarines can be used in similar ways to peaches, but as their skin is not fuzzy it is less of a barrier and makes them more toothsome to eat fresh. The firm flesh is also less melting and reduces one's need for a bib to catch half the juice as with a ripe peach. This makes the nectarine a civilised fruit for eating at the dinner table, and this is only enhanced by the succulent vinous flavour.

Nectarine Melba
(all quantities according to taste)

Nectarines, honey, vanilla pod
Vanilla ice cream (the real sort!)
Frozen raspberries
Bitter chocolate, nutmeg

Halve, peel and stone, say, one ripe nectarine per person. Poach half of them, those that are the least decomposingly ripe, in a syrup made by gently warming the vanilla pod in the honey. Poach the nectarines very gently until they are tender but not breaking down, then drain and chill well. Create a bed of vanilla ice cream, interspersed with the chilled ripest halves. Lay the poached halves on this base. Crush the frozen raspberries in the drained honey syrup. Chill, then pour over the nectarines, followed by a generous grating of bitter chocolate and a hint of nutmeg.

companion planting

Again as for the peach.

other uses

As for peaches.

Prunus avium* from the family *Rosaceae

SWEET CHERRIES

Tree up to 10m. Long-lived, deciduous, not self-fertile. Fruits: 2cm, yellow, red, black, rich in riboflavin

Although described as sweet cherries, some varieties, and particularly wild ones, are not actually sweet. They are tall trees, often reaching over 9m, with white blossoms, occasionally pink, which are a massive display at about the same time as the peach. The leaves are plum-like with a lengthening and thinning at the tip. Dangling in pairs on long pedicels, the near-spherical fruits hang in groups along the fruiting branches. The flesh is cream or yellow, sweet or bitter, but once ripe is rarely acid.

The wild form native to Europe, known as the bird cherry, gean or mazzard, is of little value as fruit except in Central Europe, where it is used for liqueurs. Mazzards, little improved from the wild version, still survive and have richly flavoured black fruits only slightly larger than the wild. They make good seedling stocks for better varieties, though if left to themselves they can grow to 20m or more high. Gean fruits were thought to have softer more melting flesh and varieties called Bigarreau had a crisp texture. Years of continuous selection and cross breeding have given us sweet cherries of mixed parentage. One group, the Duke or Royal cherries, have some sour cherry (Morello) blood, which serves to make them tasty and lightly acid as well as generally more hardy.

varieties

Sweet cherries have dark or white flesh, and scarlet or red-black skins. There are countless varieties new and old but finding combinations compatible for pollination is difficult, so the most useful cherries for small gardens are at least partly self fertile. The self-fertile late-maturing **Lapins** cherry has richly coloured, firm red fruit. Partially self-fertile **Sunburst** has very dark red, almost black sweet cherries, maturing mid to late in the season. The white **Napoleon** is compatible with the vigorous and ruby-hued **Stella**, and produces bountiful crops of crisp sweet fruit. Almost any late-flowering cherry will be pollinated by a **Morello** sour cherry planted with them.

cultivation

Cherries demand a cold climate to satisfy a high-chill requirement. They suit cold winter regions and dry conditions. The fruit is prone to rot at maturity if damp. Give them good air circulation, but keep out of wind to keep fruit dry. Cherries flower after almonds but before peaches and usually miss late frosts. They are fully hardy when dormant. Cherries are particular about their pollination partners but Stella is good for many. Other problems are lack of bees at flowering time and hail at harvest. Cover with bird netting in spring to have any hope of obtaining fruit.

Merton Glory

SWEET CHERRIES

Sweet cherries rarely ripen unless protected from birds

Ornamental and Wildlife Value

Sweet cherries are quite staggering to behold in blossom, as if festooned with snow. The fruits are one of the most addictive to birds, and they will come despite all discouragement.

Propagation

Normally budded on to strong-growing rootstocks, which make for big trees, they are now offered on dwarfing stocks such as **Colt**. Stones grow, but the trees take years to fruit and get tall by then.

Pruning and Training

Prune as little as possible after initial head formation. Train young trees to a vase shape and only prune in late summer when cuts heal quickly to remove any dead and diseased wood. Sterilise tools between cuts.

Pests and Diseases

Cherries suffer from bird damage but escape fruit fly by fruiting in early summer. Bacterial canker can prove fatal but copper sprays offer some protection. Purchase certified virus-free plants and improve conditions to reduce risk. Warm drizzle during flowering causes mould and rain or hail during ripening may split fruit. Root weevils may attack and can be trapped with fly-wire skirts on trunks. Cherry slugs (sawfly larvae) can attack the leaves in late spring. Bordeaux spray before bud-burst and at harvest helps control mould.

Harvesting and Storing

Cherries can be picked and kept for several days if absolutely dry. Leave them on the sprigs and do not pack them deep. They can be frozen, but are fiddly as they are better stoned first.

culinary

Sweet cherries often do not make as good culinary dishes as sour cherries because many lack acidity. Their jams and jellies are better combined with redcurrant or whitecurrant juice for this reason.

Pickled Cherries

Makes about 1.5kg

1kg cherries
500g sugar
300ml vinegar
6 cloves
15g fresh ginger, peeled and chopped
Hint of ground cinnamon

Wash and stone (if desired) the cherries. Dissolve the sugar in the heated vinegar and add the spices. Simmer the cherries in the spiced vinegar for a few minutes, then pack them into warmed jars, and cover with the vinegar. Seal and store.

Eat with pâtés, cold meats and especially quiches.

Cherry Jam

2.25kg cherries
3 lemons, squeezed
1.25kg sugar

Wash the fruit thoroughly; remove stalks and stones. Put the fruit into a pan with the lemon juice and simmer gently for 30–35 minutes. Warm the sugar and add it to the cherries over a gentle heat and allow the sugar to dissolve. Then bring the jam to a rapid boil and continue boiling until setting point is reached; this will take about 15 minutes. Test for setting point, remove from the heat and leave for 5 minutes. Pot and cover. Store in a dry place.

companion planting

They are normally grown in grass sward, include clover and alfalfa, to give more fertility. Cherries supposedly suppress wheat and make potatoes prone to blight.

other uses

Sweet firewood.

Stella

Prunus cerasus from the family *Rosaceae*

MORELLO CHERRIES

Tree up to 8m. Long-lived, deciduous, self-fertile. Fruits: 2cm, crimson to black. Value: rich in vitamin A.

Morello cherries, rare in Australia, are similar to sweet cherries, except they are not sweet, so are only useful for culinary purposes. The trees are smaller than sweet varieties, with slightly lax, more twiggy branches and greener foliage that does not have such a red tinge when young. The fruits have shorter stalks, tend to have darker colours and are more acid.

Sour cherries were selected from *Prunus cerasus* (also known as *P. acida*), which grew wild around the Caspian and Black Seas. In about 300 BC sour cherries were known to the Greek Theophrastus and proved so popular with the Romans, who developed at least half a dozen different varieties, that by the time of Pliny, in the first century AD, sour cherries had already long reached Britain. However, during the Dark Ages, the art of their cultivation was lost and the trees had to be re-introduced to England in the sixteenth century by Henry VIII, who had them brought from Flanders. They were soon adopted by the growers of Kent and by 1640 they had over two dozen varieties. The first cherries to reach the New World, the Kentish Red, were planted by the Massachusetts colonists.

Sour cherries get sweeter – if given time

varieties

Before the Second World War more than 50 varieties of Morello and sour cherry were in cultivation, and almost every country had its own wide choice. Now few are grown commercially and only the generic **Morello** is offered by most suppliers. This last favourite, namesake for all its disappearing brethren, is deep crimson to black in colour with a richly bitter, slightly sweet flavour. Late flowering, it misses more frosts than sweet cherries so is more reliable and ripens in mid- to late summer, towards the end of August in southern England. It is self-fertile, and would pollinate almost any other cherry of any type if the flowering period was not so late in the season.

The only other sour cherry offered for sale in Australia is **Montmorency**. It too is self-fertile and late maturing. The red-blushed fruit is large with white flesh used for bottling and home gardens. Sour cherries are divided into **Amarelles** (or Kentish) type and the **Morellos** (or Griottes). A new larger-fruited variety, **Crown Morello**, is claiming to have the largest fruits at more than a dozen grams apiece.

cultivation

Much the same conditions are needed as for pears, with an increased demand for nitrogen and even more

MORELLO CHERRIES

water than needed by sweet cherries. Though the trees will do badly if they are waterlogged, they are more tolerant of poor drainage than sweet cherries. Sour cherries bloom on last season's wood like peaches. They are suitable for espalier or trellis culture.

Growing in Containers
In containers, morellos are the more shrublike cherry and easier to grow. Choose one grafted onto a dwarfing rootstock if you are attempting container culture.

Ornamental and Wildlife Value
Not as elegant or floriferous a tree as the sweet cherry, so of less ornamental value. However, Morellos are well-loved by birds and the early flowers are good for insects.

Propagation
As for sweet cherries (see page 47).

Pests and Diseases
Morellos are afflicted by the same pests as for sweet cherries, particularly birds and pear and cherry slug.

Pruning and Training
Morellos fruit on younger wood than do sweet cherries and thus they can be pruned harder. However, it is usually more convenient to stick to removing dead, diseased and congested growths in spring or summer. Usually grown as standards, they are ideal as low bushes for picking and bird protection, although they can also be trained as fans. They will even crop well on cold walls.

Harvesting and Storing
Cut the cherries off the tree rather than risk damage by pulling the stalks. Morellos were one of the first fruits to be stored frozen and are one of the best. They can be frozen without sugaring and retain their flavour superbly.

companion planting

As for sweet cherries.

other uses

The prunings make good kindling.

culinary

They are primarily a culinary fruit and make fabulous pies, tarts, jams and cakes.

Black Forest Gâteau
Serves 6–8

500g Morello cherries
125g honey
4 tablespoons kirsch
Little water

For the sponge:
100g butter
100g fine light brown sugar
100g white flour
2 large or 3 small eggs
1 heaped teaspoon baking powder
1 heaped teaspoon cocoa powder

For the filling:
600ml double cream
1 heaped teaspoon sugar
1 heaped teaspoon cocoa powder
1 teaspoon vanilla extract
100g dark chocolate, grated

Wash and stone the cherries. Dissolve the honey and kirsch in sufficient hot water just to cover the stoned fruits. Simmer till they soften, then strain (keeping the syrup) and chill. Mix the sponge ingredients and divide between three oiled or lined sandwich tins. Bake in a preheated oven at 170°C/325°F/gas mark 3 for about half an hour. Turn out and cool, then soak the sponge cakes in the syrup. Whip the cream, then stir in the sugar, cocoa powder and vanilla. Build up alternate layers of sponge, cream filling and fruit. Finish off with a covering of filling and grated chocolate.

Morus nigra and *Morus alba* from the family *Moraceae*

MULBERRIES

Tree up to 9m. Long-lived, hardy, deciduous, usually self-fertile. Fruits: 2–3cm, purple, also red through pink.

Mulberry trees are medium-sized trees with a round domed crown, formed by their habit of having no terminal bud on their overwintering twigs. They can become big, gnarled and picturesque in advanced old age. The leaves are heart-shaped, toothed and occasionally lobed, lightly downy underneath but rough on top. The black mulberry, *Morus nigra*, fruits are like loganberries, of a blackish dark red through purple when ripe and stain all they touch. The white mulberry, *Morus alba*, fruits are red or pinkish white, and slightly inferior to eat. There is a red mulberry (which can be almost black), native to North America, and several similar species in hotter climates.

Black mulberries are thought to be native to western Asia. Known at least since the time of the Greeks, they failed to become popular until the Roman Emperor Justinian encouraged them for the production of silk. The trees appeared all over the empire and *M. nigra* was not superseded by *M. alba*, the more productive variety for feeding silkworms, until the sixteenth century. Exceptionally long-lived, the black mulberry may attain some stature; giants found in many parts of the world were planted during the seventeenth and early eighteenth centuries in vain attempts to foster local silk industries. Some mulberries, such as *M. alba* var. *tatarica*, the Russian mulberry, seed freely and become weeds. The red mulberry was native to the Northern Missouri region and along the Kansas river system, where it was an esteemed fruit.

MULBERRIES

varieties

The **Black Mulberry** is mostly grown for fruit. **Chelsea** may be identical with **King James I** and was once the only variety available, though it is now joined by the remarkably similar **Charlton House** and **Large Black**. **Hick's Fancy** has smaller fruit and leaves and is smaller growing. There is also a weeping variety, **Pendula**. **Downing's Everbearing** is often listed as *M. nigra* but is possibly a cultivar of **Red Mulberry** (*M. rubra*). It has red/black fruits and yellow autumn foliage. Less common is the Indian king white mulberry, **Shahtoot** (*M. macroura*). It has the largest fruit at 10cm long. The **White Mulberry** (*M. alba*) has wider leaves and is grown for silkworm fodder, though the fruit is quite edible

cultivation

Mulberries succeed in any well-drained moist soil and grow in all but tropical zones. Plant bare-rooted in winter or in containers in autumn or spring. They like a warm site and are rarely bothered by late frost, as they are tardy coming into leaf and flower. Trees grow quickly and start bearing early after planting. Pendula can be grown in large containers but it needs heavy feeding and watering to maintain health. Cultivated mulberries are mostly self-fertile with unisexual flowers, though the species tend to be dioecious when growing in the wild.

White mulberries

culinary

The fruits can be made into jams or jellies, though they are usually combined and bulked out with apples, and the wine is an old country favourite.

Mulberry No Fool
Per person

Clotted or thick fresh double cream
Some honey
A pot of tea
Biscuits
A mulberry tree in fruit and a sunny day off

Take a bowl with a large portion of clotted or thick cream, honey and the tea and biscuits. Sit peacefully under the mulberry tree, savouring the tea and biscuits while waiting for enough fruits to fall to fill your bowl. Eat them with the cream and honey. In emergencies, tinned or fresh fruit of any sort and a patio umbrella can be usefully substituted for the mulberries and tree!

Ornamental and Wildlife Value
Mulberries become gnarled and attractively grotesque as they age. The traditional situation is in the middle of a lawn with a circular wooden seat around the trunk. The berries are much appreciated by birds and small children.

Pests and Diseases
No significant pests or diseases bother the trees, other than the usual hazards of birds and small children.

Propagation
25–30cm cuttings of newly ripened growth with a heel taken in December are ideal. Layering is possible as are (supposedly) whole branch cuttings.

Pruning and Training
Mulberries can be pollarded hard to give the maximum foliage needed for feeding silkworms. If left to themselves, they make congested heads, so thin out twiggy, dead and diseased growths. Their narrow forks, big heads and brittle wood mean old trees should be carefully inspected and excess weight removed by a competent tree surgeon.

Harvesting and Storing
Mulberries are aromatic and mouth-watering when fresh and ripe, but decompose rapidly, so are really only of use as they drop, and will not store or travel, though they can be frozen.

companion planting

Catmint (*Nepeta spp.*) may repel insects and horseradish is said to encourage fruit. Mulberries were traditionally planted to support grapes in Classical times.

other uses

Of course you can try silkworm production and the foliage is palatable to other animals. The fruits will certainly make dye!

Ficus carica from the family *Moraceae*

FIGS

Brown Turkey

Tree/bush up to 9 x 7m. Hardy, self-fertile. Fruits: pear-shaped, 6 x 10cm, browny green.

Fig leaves are large and distinctive, but vary in exact shape with each variety. Although figs are deciduous, young plants tend to be almost evergreen and are then more tender. Figs can be grown as trees or bushes, but are most often trained on walls. Almost all fig cultivars set the fruit parthenocarpically, without actual fertilisation. However, some old and mostly inferior varieties in hot climates have female fruiting plants and male caprifigs that are separately and specifically cultivated to produce female fig wasps. These wasps will crawl through the minute end hole into the fruits to pollinate them.

Figs are indigenous to Asia Minor and were one of the first fruits to be brought into cultivation. They thus became an intrinsic part of the diet of the Mediterranean basin long before Classical times, though the Greeks claimed they were given to them by the goddess Demeter. Cato knew of six different figs, and two centuries later, in about 60 AD, Pliny notes no fewer than 29 varieties! Figs were certainly brought to England by the Romans as remains have been found, though the plants were not officially introduced until the early sixteenth century. There are more than 600 fig species. Many of the varieties that we encounter today are ornamentals such as the India Rubber Plant (*Ficus elastica*), the Weeping Fig (*F. Benjamina*) and the Fiddle Leaf Plant (*F. lyrata*).

varieties

Brown Turkey is a vigorous tree ripening late summer and producing for over three months. Commonly grown **Black Genoa** has sweet purplish fruit borne in early summer and again in late autumn. **White Genoa** has green fruit also twice per year. **White Adriatic** is an old green-skinned variety recommended for warm areas. The fruit is said to have hints of strawberry. **Black Ischia** is a hardy variety with purple-black fruit, and can be grown in tubs. The small- to medium-sized **Preston Prolific** produces large yellow-skinned figs with rich amber-hued flesh.

cultivation

Plant figs in winter when the plant is dormant. They need wind protection, full sun and plenty of light. Young plants may need some protection from frost but established trees are hardy to –12°C. Trunks may need white-washing in summer to prevent sunburn. Figs fruit better when the roots are restricted in a narrow bed hemmed in by a wall and path or root barrier. They still need well-drained soil and a pH of 6.5–7. Regular water from summer to late autumn avoids fruit split. They can be fed but avoid high nitrogen fertilisers. If left unfertilised, trees usually still bear well.

You rarely see them this big in the shops....

FIGS

.... Okay, well, sometimes you do

culinary

Figs are delicious fresh and they can be made into jams, jellies, cheeses and chutneys.

Savoury and Sweet Figs
Serves 4 as a snack or canapé

12 dried figs
90g mild hard cheese, broken into chunks
Pinch of celery seeds
1 shallot, thinly sliced
25g dark cooking chocolate
50g marzipan
25g each sultanas and raisins
A little Cointreau or sweet liqueur
Honey

Stuff half the figs with small chunks of cheese, a sprinkling of celery seeds and a thin slice of shallot.

Grate the chocolate and marzipan. Mix in the dried fruit and liqueur, then stuff the remaining figs with this mixture. Smear all the figs with honey and put them in an oiled dish in a preheated oven at 180°C/350°F/gas mark 4 for 10–15 minutes. Serve the figs hot or cold.

Growing in Containers
Figs can be grown confined in large pots and can make excellent foliage plants for house or patio, though they will need careful watering and training.

Ornamental and Wildlife Value
The very attractive foliage adds a luxuriant touch to a garden, especially in warmer regions.

Propagation
Layers can be made during summer. 20cm well-ripened or old-wood cuttings taken during the early winter will root, especially if given bottom heat. Seeds produce plants that are unlikely to fruit well.

Pruning and Training
The most fruitful wood is well-ripened, short-jointed and sturdy; long soft shoots are unproductive and better removed. Figs can be pruned any time during dormancy, but are best left until growth is about to start in spring. More importantly, remove any fruit or fruitlet in autumn to prevent these starting into growth, failing and thereby spoiling the second crop that could otherwise succeed.

Pests and Diseases
Fig plants have few problems except birds. Weed near the trunks to prevent rodents nibbling the bark. They may also suffer from twospotted mites and fruit fly.

Harvesting and Storing
The fruits are soft-skinned and do not travel or store well once ripe. In hotter regions figs can be dried and will then keep well.

companion planting

One of the few plants to get on well with rue.

other uses

Figs are known by many for their syrup, administered as a laxative. Also valuable as a food, they contain nearly half their weight in sugar when dried.

A promising crop of **Rouge de Bordeaux** – needs thinning out with the odd one!

SOFT, BUSH AND CANE FRUITS

I prefer to group these fruits as fruitcage fruits because this accurately describes their most common factor: without a cage most of them cannot effectively produce fruits at all. The reasons for their other names are fairly self-evident: soft, because they are not hard fruits such as apples, bush is self-descriptive and cane refers to the slender branches. (The term vine is applied differently depending on region; in some places it is used solely for grapes, in others to plants with long, flexible branches, even Cucurbits.)

The fruitcage members are grouped together by the gardener because they must be netted or grown in a cage. However, as with orchard fruits, most of them come from the *Rosaceae* family. They are shrubby perennials, not tree-like, and thus fairly compact, or can be kept so, quick to crop, and small-fruited. Most are found growing naturally on the woodland's edge and thrive given moist root runs with plentiful humus-rich mould and thick mulches of leafy material. Most will grow and even crop in light shade, though, of course, they usually produce sweeter, better-tasting fruit given more sun. Grapevines will most obviously require much more sun than do the other plants of this group.

The majority of these fruits have been gathered from the wild native species since prehistory and their cultivation will have occurred inadvertently around sites of human habitation, from waste heaps and primitive latrine arrangements. (Both, of course, afford remarkably well-fertilised ground, and thus select for strains that could use such conditions.) Being fast-growing plants and quick to crop, the proximity and opportunity would have created more, but still inadvertent, selection. Such a process would have produced much improved cultivars, spread by migrating peoples, and these may well have influenced wild populations. Today some wild fruits such as the blackberry are just such hybrids in most areas, and it may well be that some supposed native species are in reality escaped cultivars from our distant past.

Thus the cropping potential of some wild fruits may have been raised over the millennia by our own unintended selection. In any case, the wild forms of most of these fruits were so productive and available in such vast quantities that they were simply not brought into cultivation until the end of the Middle Ages, with the important exception of grapes, which have been tended since prehistory. Some, such as the strawberry, have undergone intense development and hybridisation and so have improved dramatically, while others, such as aronia, have remained almost unaltered. Many closely related edible species are available, which could be crossed with cultivated forms, so improved fruits may be only an experiment or two away. The Tayberry is the result of one such crossing, and is better by far than all its similar predecessors.

Rheum rhaponticum from the family *Polygonaceae*

RHUBARB

Herbaceous: 1x2m. Life span: perpetual. Fruits: the stems, 2x60cm. Value: vitamin C.

Manifestly rhubarb is not a fruit, but after several protests it is now included. This most British of fruits is apparently craved by tourists to Britain seeking traditional cuisine, who flock to motorway service stations for the eponymous crumble and custard. The stems are long, succulent and red with a very acid taste. Rhubarb is absolutely inedible raw but widely popular cooked, probably because it is available so early in the year before true fruits arrive.

The first rhubarb to arrive in Europe were for medical use. *R. rhaponticum* is noted first in Italy during 1608. It had been brought from Siberia for its laxative effect and was never eaten for pleasure initially. However, people are adventurous, and though the leaves are poisonous the stems proved tasty when cooked with sugar, as did the unopened pouches or flower heads, which we no longer consume.

Traditional forcing pots are too small – use a stack of car tyres instead!

varieties

It is worthwhile buying virus-free stock as the growth is much stronger than from old infected stools. There are a surprising number of varieties with some differences in colour and taste. **Glaskin's Perpetual** is green and has low oxalic acid levels, so it can be eaten later into summer. **Victoria** is a late, strong grower and crops till well into summer. **Timperley Early** is one of the earliest and best for forcing, but has thin stems. In their native Himalayas other species are also eaten and/or used medicinally. One, *R. ribes*, was the currant-fruited rhubarb. Sadly this appears now to have been lost.

cultivation

Rhubarb is often a neglected crop, seldom getting any attention other than a cursory strawing up and much pulling. It responds to richer conditions by growing well. For forcing, dig good roots in early winter and leave them exposed to cold for a fortnight. Then pot up and keep them in a warm, dark place. These produce better stalks with pale leaves months earlier than outdoor plants, but they are useless and exhausted afterwards.

RHUBARB

Growing under Glass
Most commercial rhubarb is grown in blacked-out sheds from roots originally grown in the open, and discarded after use. However, rhubarb could also be grown as a conservatory border plant.

Growing in Containers
Rhubarb is not very happy cropping perpetually in containers, but it can be briefly forced once and then planted out to recover.

Ornamental and Wildlife Value
There are some inedible ornamental varieties, but ordinary rhubarb is itself imposing enough to be used in the flower garden. Rhubarb provides useful ground cover and dry shelter for small creatures.

Plastic dustbins force well but can get too hot

Propagation
Glaskin's Perpetual and the species can be grown from seed; otherwise pieces of root with a bud are transplanted or potted in early spring.

Weed, Pest and Disease Control
Remarkably free of problems, though occasionally the crown may rot. Starting a new bed elsewhere is the best solution.

Pruning and Training
Longer, tenderer, sweeter stems are had by forcing them to grow up through straw towards the light in a blanching pot, bottomless bucket or chimney pot. Cut out flowering stems before they blossom. After pulling finishes, remove the pot, straw, any mouldy stems and leaves. Weed carefully and mulch well with compost in the autumn.

Harvesting and Storing
The stems are pulled, not cut. Twist outwards as you pull and the stem will detach cleanly. Remove the leaf and top of stem immediately, or the stem will wilt. Stalks will keep only a few days once detached, but stay good on the plant till mid-summer. They can be kept longer if stood in cool, clean water which is changed daily. Roots can be dug up and forced many months early to spread the season.

Keep the stringey bits on so you can get a good colour

other uses

Rhubarb leaves are poisonous and were once boiled with water and soft soap to make an aphicide. Many of the other species are used medicinally. The leaves make cool packing for other fruit.

companion planting

Rhubarb is reputed to deter clubroot and root flies if pieces are planted in the holes with brassica roots.

culinary uses

Rhubarb is eaten stewed, in pies, tarts or as the famous crumble. It can be jammed successfully or made into chutney and even wine.

Rhubarb Crumble
Serves 4-6

500g rhubarb
75g light brown sugar
splash of elderflower wine or cider

For the crumble topping:
175g flour
75g butter
50g light brown sugar
hint of cinnamon

Chop the washed rhubarb into short chunks and put in a pie dish with the sugar and wine. Mix the crumble ingredients with your fingers until they resemble breadcrumbs; add more butter or a drop of water if they do not bind. Sprinkle on top of the rhubarb and bake in the oven at 190°C/375°F/gas 5 for approximately 30 minutes, until it starts to brown. Rhubarb crumble must be served with custard, and for a traditional feel this ought to be a bright yellow proprietary brand.

Fragaria hybrids from the family *Rosaceae*

SUMMER STRAWBERRIES

Herbaceous. 30cm. Life span: short. Self-fertile. Fruits: up to 5x5cm, red, conical. Value: some vitamin C and half as much iron as spinach.

This most delicious of fruits really needs no introduction! Modern strawberries are hybrids based on *F. chiloensis*, the Chilean Pine, and *F. virginiana*, the Scarlet Virginian. The former contributed larger fruit with a pineapple tang and was brought to Europe in 1712; the latter, first mentioned in Massachusetts in 1621, provides the superior flavour, and is still grown commercially as Little Scarlet for jam-making. These two were first combined in the nineteenth century, with intensive development since. Each region has varieties bred to suit conditions.

varieties

Most garden strawberries are short-day varieties, forming flower buds in autumn and winter for spring and summer cropping. Home gardeners have only a few of the new improved strawberries available to commercial growers. **Cambridge Vigour** ripens in October. **Cambridge Rival**, **Tioga** and **Torrey** yield in spring and summer. Other varieties include **Pajaro**, **Chandler**, **Kendall**, the productive early **Earliblush** and mid-season **Redlands Joy** and **Sugar Baby**.

cultivation

All preparation is well repaid. Strawberries need a very rich soil, full of humus, and benefit from slow-release phosphates, such as bone meal. Well-rotted manure or compost, and/or seaweed meal dressings, will be recouped with better cropping. The more space you give them the better they will do and the less work they will be: 60cm each way is the minimum.

Plant strawberries in raised beds for drainage, depth of soil and earlier fruiting. In warmer areas, plant from March to May; in colder areas, in June or July. Queensland grows winter-cropping fruit with runners set in March. Plants require plenty of water – drip irrigation is successful. Some growers erect plastic cloches set over hoops in August to promote early fruiting. Mites attack plants grown under glass.

Growing in Containers

Many containers, often tower shaped, are sold specifically for strawberries. While a good idea, the small amount of root run, their heat in an above-ground position and their low water-holding capacity provide poor growing conditions for strawberries. The plants respond with low yields, which occur in a short period, which makes them neglected for much of the year. However, strawberries can be grown successfully in pots and containers. They need regular feeding as well as copious automatic watering!

Ornamental and Wildlife Value

Rather too straggly to be considered decorative, they would make effective but short-lived ground cover and would not be very productive. By the losses, one must assume that they are valuable to birds!

Straw is essential to stop such low berries getting muddy

SUMMER STRAWBERRIES

Extra early crops indoors planted in the tubs of other fruits such as citrus and grapevines

Propagation

Fresh crowns certified as virus-free are best. Take strawberry runners in the first year when there is less risk of virus infection. Fix the tip of the runner into a pot while it is still attached to the parent to root the crown. The first plantlet on an early runner is chosen, pinned or held to the ground – or preferably rooted into a pot of compost for an easier transplantation. Start new beds in autumn or winter to allow them to establish; they can then crop well the next summer. For a stronger autumn crop, cut back all leaves above the crown in late January. Then, water with seaweed extract over summer to build up crowns.

Pruning and Training

Strawberries will become relatively unproductive after three or four years, so in practice a continual annual replacement of a quarter or a third of the plants is best. Replacing all every four years or so means years of gluts and years of shortages, as they are all the same age. Strawing up is essential for clean crops. Do not straw too early – only when the first green fruits are seen swelling. Remove surplus runners regularly.

Pests and Diseases

Major losses are from birds and mould. Individual bunches can be protected from both with jam jars. Netting is usually obligatory. Mould can be decreased by strawing up and removing fruits that rot, preferably before the mould goes 'fluffy'. After fruiting has finished, tidy the plants, shearing back surplus runners and dead leaves, and in winter tidy them again, removing old straw as well for composting. Aphids spread the dreaded virus diseases, so you should buy in fresh clean stock every ten years or so.

Harvesting and Storing

Strawberries must be used quickly as they keep only for a day or so – they will last better picked with a stalk. They can be juiced and made into syrup, or jammed and jellied – the addition of apple, red- or whitecurrant juice will help with the setting. If frozen they will lose their delicate texture, but are still delicious.

companion planting

Before establishing a new bed, dig in a green manure crop of soya beans to help prevent root rots. Growing borage, any of the beans or onions nearby reputedly helps strawberry plants.

Late Pine

culinary

Wimbledon Fortune

Fresh strawberries, sprinkled with sugar, cream, a shortbread biscuit or two – and a small mortgage, unless enjoyed at home!

other uses

As for perpetual strawberries (see page 60).

Fragaria hybrids from the family *Rosaceae*

STRAWBERRIES
PERPETUAL AND REMONTANT

Herbaceous. 30cm. Life span: short. Self-fertile. Fruits: up to 5 x 2cm, red, conical. Value: some vitamin C and half as much iron as spinach.

These strawberries fall within two groups, everbearing and day-neutral, to distinguish them from short-day varieties. Some have extremely good flavour, probably due to some *F. vesca* ancestry.

These groups have been improved in continental Europe, particularly the Netherlands and in the United States. Short-day types (see pages 58-9) are spring and summer bearers (from September to February) in Australia. They initiate buds in winter when the days are short, hence the name. Everbearing types initiate flower buds both during summer, when days are longer, and during shorter days. Day-neutral types produce fruit from spring to autumn. Production slows in summer in temperatures over 26°C and again with the onset of winter. These are not yet available to the home gardener.

varieties

The Dutch have produced some runner-forming, day-neutral varieties such as **Rapella**. This originated from a cross between **Tioga** and **Rabunda**. Others are **Fern** and **Aptos** but the home gardener will not generally find them in the nursery. **Aptos** bears three months after planting throughout summer and autumn. Fruit is larger than **Tioga**, which is still one of the most common varieties. Among the everbearings, **Rabunda** crops for 8–9 months a year. **Tribute** is under trial but is said to resist root rot and verticillium wilt.

cultivation

Short-day, everbearing and day-neutral types need the same rich, moist conditions. In Australia, they fruit from spring to autumn.

Growing under Glass
Strawberries grown under glass suffer from attacks by two-spotted mite and are more prone to mould and rot diseases. They are best grown in the open and there are recommended varieties for sub-tropical, warm and temperate climates. Local garden centres generally buy only from local runner growers who specialise in the most suitable varieties.

Growing in Containers
Most strawberries available to home gardeners are the short-day type, which produce up to three crops per year under local conditions. Large containers make good use of available space but need regular attention to watering.

Ornamental and Wildlife Value
Climbing varieties can be trained well over trellis and can also be quite decorative, especially when in fruit. Their long flowering period makes these plants valuable to insects, and the fruits themselves are enjoyed by both birds and rodents!

Propagation
Everbearing types tend to produce few runners and instead form multiple crowns. These can be divided in autumn but to prevent disease, it is often recommended to buy fresh virus-free stock from a certified source. All types are planted and otherwise

STRAWBERRIES

treated the same. Some short-day types, **Tioga**, **Torrey** and **Pajaro**, can also be planted in summer.

Pruning and Training

Cut off the leaves about 2cm above the crown in late January, to encourage autumn fruiting. In winter, cut back all plants so they grow clean and fresh in spring.

Pests and Diseases

Because they have such a long season, early mouldy fruits must be rapidly and hygienically removed, or later fruits will suffer exponentially. They are more prone to moulds because of the humidity in autumn and benefit from cloches. Bird damage is less as there are plenty of other attractive fruits around.

Harvesting and Storing

Late autumn cropping strawberries can be juicier than summer varieties, but not always so sweet, and they often rot before ripening. They can be picked green if there is a hint of colouring, and are then fine for culinary use.

Mara des Bois

companion planting

As with other strawberries, they do well with beans and are benefited by onions and borage. Most of all they love a mulch of pine needles.

other uses

Eating strawberries will supposedly whiten your teeth. Strawberry leaves have been used as a tea substitute.

Pop a fresh strawberry or three in a glass of white wine for pleasure

culinary

They can be used just like summer strawberries, but are conveniently fresh from summer till the frosts.

Baked Strawberry Apples

Serves 4

4 cooking apples
A little sugar and butter
Punnet of strawberries
A few raisins

Wash, dry and core the apples and smear with butter. Cut a thin slice off one end to ensure they sit flat in a greased baking dish. Setting aside the four best strawberries, eat some and pass the rest through a sieve. Fill the holes in the apples with strawberry purée. Push in raisins to bring the level over the top. Finish with the reserved fruits and a sprinkling of sugar. Bake at 190°C/375°F/gas mark 5 till the apples are bursting – for approximately 20 minutes. Serve hot with custard, cream or yogurt.

Looks humble, so the strawberry centre is a surprise!

Fragaria **hybrids from the family** ***Rosaceae***

STRAWBERRIES
ALPINE AND WILD EUROPEAN

Herbaceous. 30cm. Life span: short! Self-fertile. Fruits: up to 1 x 2cm. Value: some vitamin C.

Alpine strawberries differ from the common garden strawberries in two distinct ways. The fruits and plants are smaller and they do not form runners. The alpines form neat clumps about 30cm across, with lighter green leaves, and flower all season almost from last to first frost. The other wild (European) strawberries, *F. vesca*, and Hautbois, *F. elatior/moschata*, are more like miniature versions of garden strawberries. With smaller fruits than even the alpines, they do make runners. Indeed some of the wild woodland forms only produce runners and rarely fruit.

These wild forms were the earliest strawberries cultivated and are native to Europe, but only north of the Alps. They were thus unknown to the Ancient Greeks, and although passing reference is given to them by Roman and early medieval writers, it is as wild, not cultivated fruits. In England the fruits are mentioned during the thirteenth century in the Countess of Leicester's Household Roll. By the reign of Henry VIII the fruit was highly esteemed and cost four pence a bushel. At the same time the Hautbois strawberry, *F. elatior/moschata*, was also popular, especially on the Continent. It was one of the most fragrant of all and made few runners. The species from the Americas arrived during this period, but were considered not as good as these native wild varieties. It was not until the nineteenth century that the natives became superseded by 'modern' hybrids.

varieties

Alpines are grown from seed. They are little improved on the true wild form, though yellow- and white-fruited versions are available. **Baron Solemacher** is a slightly larger-fruited selection; it needs nearly 60cm of space each way. **Alexandria** is tastier, juicier and does better in moist half-shade. Wild, runnering strawberries, known as **Fraises des Bois**, are obtainable on the Continent as seed or plants. The **Green Strawberry**, *F. collina/viridis*, has sadly vanished. Wild American strawberries, *F. virginiana*, which were crossed with *F. chiloensis* to give the first modern strawberry are presumably most happy at home in Virginia. The **Beach Strawberry**, *F. chiloensis*, can be grown for the unique flavour though benefitting from pollination by other species such as *F. moschata*. The **Indian Strawberry**, from another genus entirely, *Duchesnea indica*, is a low runner forming strawberry-like plant with a strawberry-like fruit except it's evergreen and the fruit is bland.

cultivation

Alpines are easier to grow, needing less richness and moisture than other types of strawberry, though they will do much better in improved conditions. They can be spaced at 30cm or so apart. Wild strawberries are better grown as ground cover in moist partial shade and allowed to run.

Strawberry flowers are good for beneficial insects too

STRAWBERRIES

The fruits are small but fragrant

Pests and Diseases

Alpine and wild species are much tougher plants than conventional varieties and rarely suffer from pests or diseases. The fruits are also less appealing to birds, so they can often be cropped without protection.

Pruning and Training

As with other varieties and species, it is best to replace the entire stock in stages, normally running over a three- or four-year period.

Growing under Glass and in Containers

Alpines can be cropped under glass to extend the season, but become more prone to red spider mite. Other wild species resent being under cover more. In pots they are easier than more conventional varieties, however, as they need less water and do not run.

Ornamental and Wildlife Value

Alpines make good ground cover and are more decorative than other strawberries, as they form neat mounds. The long flowering period makes them beneficial to insects and the almost evergreen clumps are good shelter and hibernation sites.

Harvesting and Storing

They can be picked under-ripe for culinary purposes. Pick and freeze them until sufficient quantities are gathered, then shake the frozen fruits in a dry cloth and many seeds can be removed. The fruits can be made into jams, jellies, sauces, syrups and compôtes.

Propagation

As true alpines make no runners, they are grown from seed. Rub the seeds off fruits that have been left in the sun to shrivel. Sow in late winter, early spring for plants to put out in spring. Do not cover. A bottom heat of 15°C is helpful. Later in spring the seeds can be sown without heat.

Sometimes the crowns can be successfully divided. The new plantlets can be replanted where required during the growing season.

companion planting

Sixteenth-century poet Thomas Tusser said:

'Gooseberries, raspberries, roses all three
With strawberries under do trimly agree.'

In the wild strawberries are sometimes found growing with vervaine.

other uses

The leaves and fruit of wild strawberries can be used for medicinal purposes.

culinary

Both alpine and wild strawberries are superlatively fragrant and delicious raw, if fully ripe. Cooking brings out even more flavour, from under-ripe fruits as well. These are less moist than ordinary strawberries, so require some water or redcurrant juice to make jam or jelly. They are also firmer after freezing and go well in compôtes.

Alpine Strawberry Tarts

Make individual sweet shortcrust pastry tart cases. Smear the insides with butter, then fill each tart with a mixture of both alpine strawberries and strawberry jam (alpine or otherwise). Bake in a preheated oven for ten minutes or so at 190°C/375°F/gas mark 5. Cool and top each with clotted cream before serving.

Vaccinium species from the family *Ericaceae*

BLUEBERRIES AND BILBERRIES

Bush. 30cm–4m. Life span: medium to long. Deciduous, self-fertile. Fruits: 1cm, spherical blue-black. Value: some vitamins C and B and full of antioxidants and anthocyanins.

Bilberries, blaeberries or whortleberries, *Vaccinium myrtillus*, are low shrubs native to Europe, found on heaths and moors in acid soils. They have slender, green twigs with myrtle-like leaves and spherical pink flowers followed by blue-black fruits in late summer. They are unavailable in Australia.

Highbush Blueberries, *V. corymbosum*, and many near relations come from North America. The Highbush is a tall shrub up to 4m, so lower-growing cultivars for garden use have been bred, though commercial growers still prefer the tall. Many similar species are used as ornamentals because in autumn the leaves turn amazing reds and pinks. The Rabbiteye Blueberries, *V. virgatum/ashei* are similar. The Lowbush Blueberry, *V. angustifolium*, is different, only about 30cm high, and is much hardier, needing a colder climate than the Highbush. The berries are large, sweet and early so this has been crossed with the Highbush.

Bilberries were once highly popular. They would be picked from the wild and taken to market in the towns where they were esteemed for tarts and jelly. They were a staple food to the Scots Highlanders who ate them in milk and made them into wine. Bilberries went into oblivion when the better fruiting blueberries from America became available. Blueberries are a traditional American fruit, with different regions favouring different species, such as Highbush, Swamp and Rabbiteye Blueberries in the warmer areas and the Lowbush, Early or Low, Sweet Blueberry further north. The last was particularly useful as it was easily dried for preservation for winter. The dried berries were beaten to a powder and made into cakes with maize meal. In the north-west they even smoke-dried them for extra flavour.

Conveniently for the home gardener they do not ripen altogether but over weeks

varieties

Many of our blueberry varieties are of mixed American origin. Early-cropping varieties mature in December. **Denise** is an Australian variety for quick picking. **Joyblue** and **Bluecrop** are good for home gardens, the latter bearing for five weeks and with good drought resistance. **Bluerose**, a mid-season fruit from January, needs to ripen on the bush. **Herbert** and **Stanley** are old American varieties for mid-season; the former is considered one of the best flavoured. For late yields until March, try the taller **Brigitta** or **Caroline**. Rabbiteye types, with a low-chill requirement of 400 hours, suit warmer districts. Look for **Premier**, **Bluebelle** and **Delite**. All varieties need to be planted about 1–1.5m apart, but dwarf varieties can be planted closer at 0.6–1m apart.

The **Huckleberry** (*V. ovatum*), an attractive, evergreen shrub with tasty berries and useful for hedging, is rare but found in some cool-climate nurseries.

BLUEBERRIES AND BILBERRIES

cultivation

An acid soil suitable for heathers or rhododendrons is essential; a substitute of peat and leaf mould will do. The tall species prefer wetter sites, the dwarfer ones suffer drier, but all crop better with moister positions. They prefer sunny sites though they will grow in partial shade. Partly self-fertile, they do better if several varieties are grown together.

All these berries prefer a cool winter climate but rabbiteye blueberries grow in warmer coastal districts below southern Queensland. Lowbush blueberries need a very cold climate and are rarely grown.

Growing in Containers
Blueberries have to be grown in containers in many areas as they die on lime soils. Ericaceous compost or a mixture of peat, sand and leaf mould is essential as is regular, copious watering with rain or acidic water. In limy areas avoid tap water!

Ornamental and Wildlife Value
Stunning colours in autumn. There are countless ornamental species and varieties. All berries are valuable to birds.

Propagation
The species come true from seed but better varieties are layered in summer. Suckers can be detached in winter.

Pruning and Training
Blueberries need little pruning except to remove dead or diseased growth, best done in winter. Older bushes should have congested twiggy branches removed, retaining the younger stronger ones.

Pests and Diseases
Apart from the usual losses to birds, this is a remarkably pest- and disease-free family. Any distress will probably be due to an alkaline soil or lime in the water supply.

Harvesting and Storing
The berries should be picked when fully ripe and easily detached or they are too acid. They may be jammed, juiced, jellied or frozen; commercially they are obtainable dried.

companion planting

As these are ericaceous they grow well near heathers. They can also have cranberries or lingonberries underplanted with them as ground cover. I grow wild (English, not French, American or alpine) strawberries with them.

other uses

The leaves were used medicinally. Chewing dried bilberries was a cure for diarrhoea and mouth and throat infections.

culinary

Blueberries and bilberries can be used in pies, tarts, jams, jellies and syrups. Blueberry cheesecake and blueberry muffins are very popular American dishes.

Blueberry Grunt
Serves 4–6

500g blueberries
50g sugar
1 teaspoon allspice
1 small lemon
Maple syrup, to taste
125g white flour
Pinch of salt
1½ teaspoons baking powder
50g butter
300ml single cream

Simmer the washed blueberries gently with sugar, allspice and the lemon's juice and grated rind. Add maple syrup to taste. Meanwhile rub the flour, salt, baking powder and butter into crumbs and blend in enough cream to make a smooth creamy dough. Carefully spoon the dough on top of the blueberries, cover the pan and simmer till the crust puffs and sets. Serve with the rest of the cream and more maple syrup.

Vaccinium species from the family *Ericaceae*

CRANBERRIES AND COWBERRIES

Bush. Prostrate to 60cm. Life span: medium to long. Evergreen, self-fertile. Fruits: up to 2cm, reddish-orange. Value: some vitamin C.

Cranberries are very similar and closely related to blueberries and bilberries, the most noticeable differences being that cranberries have red berries and are evergreen. American selections of cranberry are the only ones cultivated in Australasia. Cranberries naturally grow in peat bogs and marshes in North America. The growing conditions are hard to replicate in Australia and consequently their cultivation is still very experimental. They are more successful in cold parts of New Zealand.

V. oxycoccus, the cranberry, is a native of most northern temperate countries and is found on bogs and moorlands. The low-growing, evergreen shrub is tough and wiry with long, sparsely leafed stems. The leaves are longer and thinner than those of the blueberried *Vaccinium* species. The flowers are tiny, yellow and pink in early summer and are followed by the round, red fruits, which are pleasantly acid to taste. The American Cranberry, *V. macrocarpon*, is much the same, but larger in size and berry. The Cowberry, Crane or Foxberry, *V. vitis idaea*, is also similar, more densely leafed, with rounded ends and clusters of berries, which are more acid and less agreeable than cranberries. The Lingonberry or Lingenberry, or Mountain Cranberry, *V. vitis-idea*, is very similar but even more drought resistant. Resembling a small box hedge, it can be clipped likewise and the berries can be eaten, though they're pretty sour in summer and are better later after the frosts have touched them.

The native cranberry has been gathered from the wild in most cool regions by native peoples throughout the northern hemisphere. The cowberry has not been enjoyed so widely as it is usually too acid to eat raw, though it is excellent after cooking. *Arctostaphylos* species, Manzanitas and Bearberries, are small trees and shrubs, needing similar conditions and producing similar fruits used in similar ways.

varieties

Franklin, **Early Black** (claimed to be most frost resistant) and **Howes** are some American varieties being trialled in Victoria. Some are available from selected cool-climate nurseries. There are several other *Vacciniums* that fall between cranberries and blueberries and have edible berries; *V. floribundum*, the **Mortinia**, is the least hardy and comes from Ecuador. It is an attractive, evergreen shrub with heavy racemes of rose-pink blooms followed by masses of red berries. From East Asia and Japan comes *V. praestans*, a prostrate, creeping, deciduous shrub with sweet, fragrant, glossy, red berries. Some of the other species may possibly prove useful for hybridising.

cultivation

These really need moist boggy conditions, in lime-free soil and water. The best sites are made on the edge of a river or pond by slowly building up a layer of stones covered with a thick layer of peaty, humus-rich, acid soil. They must be moist but not drowned; they need to stand above the water! Most are small, needing as little as 60–90cm each way and even tolerating some light shade.

CRANBERRIES AND COWBERRIES

The commercial cranberry harvest, honest. It's an amazing corner of horticulture, or is it aquiculture, indeed is it fishing?

Cranberries require cold temperatures and can possibly be grown in moist mountain regions with microspray irrigation to maintain cool humidity. Plant in prepared beds enriched with peat and compost.

Growing in Containers
Cranberries have to be grown in containers in many areas as they will die on lime soils. Ericaceous compost or a mixture of peat, sand and leaf mould is essential, as is regular and copious watering with rain or acidic water. Avoid tap water in limy areas!

Ornamental and Wildlife Value
On acid soils cowberries make excellent ground cover. Cranberries are not as dense, so they suppress weeds less well. The berries are loved by wildlife and, being evergreen, the plants will provide good shelter.

Propagation, Pruning and Training
The species can be grown from seed, or by dividing in autumn, or they can be layered in spring. Only remedial tidying is required.

Pests and Diseases
Cowberries and most of the denser-growing species suppress weeds well. Where they appear, weeds must be removed by hand weeding. They do not appear to have the same natural pests in the southern hemisphere. Birds are probably the main pests so plants need to be covered with bird netting or grown in fruit cages.

culinary

Invariably used for the jelly, but also in tarts and pies and added to many other dishes.

Cranberry Jelly
Makes about 3.75kg

500g cranberries
750g apples
Approx. 2kg sugar

Wash the fruits, chop the apples and simmer both with enough water to prevent burning. Once the apples are soft, strain and add 500g sugar to each 600ml of liquid.

Bring the liquid back to the boil, stirring to dissolve the sugar. Cook briefly, skim and pour into sterile warmed jars. Seal at once. Serve with roast turkey.

Harvesting and Storing
Cowberries are made sour by frosts so must be gathered promptly. In Siberia they were kept under water through the winter, so that they gradually became less acid, and were then eaten in spring.

companion planting

They are ericaceous and enjoy similar conditions, root bacteria and fungi as rhododendrons and azaleas so can be used as ground cover between these.

other uses

The leaves and fruits of most of these berries have been used medicinally, Cowberries have been eaten as a cure for diarrhoea.

Ribes sativum from the family *Grossulariaceae*

REDCURRANTS AND WHITECURRANTS

Shrub 2m. Life span: long. Deciduous, self-fertile. Fruits: 1–2cm, globular, glossy red or white.

Redcurrants are reliable, productive plants we rarely notice except when translucent, glossy red berries festoon the branches. Otherwise they are insignificant, similar to flowering redcurrant, *Ribes sanguineum*, which has such prolific pink tassels in early spring. (This sets inedible fruits occasionally.) Whitecurrants are varieties selected without the colour and with their own flavour. I find that the whites crop slightly less extravagantly than reds and are culinarily useful.

Redcurrants, *R. sativum* and *R. rubrum*, are native European fruits. They were not cultivated by the Romans. They gained garden notice in the sixteenth century, when they rapidly became a stalwart of the cottager's garden. Long-lived, they often survive, neglected and unproductive, whereas, given a good site and bird protection, they produce prodigiously. Surprisingly little known in much of Europe and the USA, they are popular in Scandinavia and Russia.

White Versailles

varieties

Raby Castle has *R. rubrum* heritage so is the most hardy of the group. Most often sold are **Fay's Prolific**, an early variety, which can be frost tender, and **Versailles**, which matures mid-season. Also available are **Selection 74/42** and **Jonkheer van Tets**. Whitecurrants aren't common in Australia.

cultivation

Redcurrants respond best to a cool, well-mulched soil. They do not need as rich conditions as blackcurrants or raspberries and may need some afternoon shade in hotter zones, although the berries are sweeter in the sun. The main requirement is protection from birds. Without thorough netting, all else is useless, as these are the bird food supreme.

Pests and Diseases

The major threat to the crop is birds. Currant-borer moth may kill whole branches. Remove and burn affected branches. Two-spotted mites can damage leaves and only need a miticide if severe. Septoria leaf spot cause leaves to drop, especially in wet areas. Spray with Bordeaux before buds open and later with Thiram according to instructions.

Pruning and Training

These are the most easily trained and forgiving of plants. No matter how you misprune them, they respond with new growth and ample fruit. Redcurrants can be made to take any form – cordon, goblet, fan or espalier – and moreover are quick to regrow. They will fruit best on a permanent framework with spurs and need every shoot, except leaders, cut back in summer and again harder in winter. Growing in good conditions, redcurrants can be trained over large walls, including north-facing ones. Moderately pruned as goblet bushes,

REDCURRANTS AND WHITECURRANTS

they need to be nearly 2m apart. As cordons they can be grown two to the metre.

Propagation
The easiest of all plants to root from autumn cuttings.

Ornamental and Wildlife Value
Redcurrants have little value in the ornamental garden as the berries disappear so rapidly. Redcurrants are the most palatable bird snack and so they will be popular in wildlife areas, briefly.

Harvesting and Storing
Currants can be picked from early summer as they colour, for use as garnishes, adding to compôtes and for the most acid jellies. Ripening continues into late autumn in dry years when the fruits become less acid and tasty raw. Being seedy, the fruit is conveniently stored juiced and frozen. Similarly, currants are better as jelly rather than jam. Dry, cool berries keep very well.

companion planting

Redcurrants may benefit from nettles nearby, but the fruit picker will curse. *Limnanthes douglassii* is the best companion and ground cover once the bushes are well established.

other uses

Once popular with apothecaries, as they could be stored for months packed fresh and dry into sealed glass bottles and were thus available as 'vitamin pills' in bleak late winter and spring when fresh fruit and vegetables become scarce. The juice of redcurrants must be the best edible red dye you could want.

Raby Castle

culinary

Redcurrants are immensely useful because of their colour and acidity. They add deep red to everything and their juice makes other fruit jellies set. Redcurrant juice adds tartness and flavour to other juices and can be used in many sweet and savoury dishes.

Whitecurrant juice is a substitute, if not an improvement, for lemon juice and makes even more delicious jellies.

Mint Sauce Supreme
Makes about 1kg

500g whitecurrants
Approx. 500g sugar
125g fresh mint leaves, finely shredded

Simmer the whitecurrants till soft, then strain, or simply juice. Add the same weight of sugar to the juice and slowly bring to boil. Skim and remove from heat. Stir in the finely shredded mint and bottle in warm sterile jars. Cover immediately. This is the sauce for spring lamb roasts, for yogurt dips and for barbecue glazes.

Ribes uva-crispa (Ribes grossularia) **from the family** *Grossulariaceae*

GOOSEBERRIES

Bush up to 1.5m. Life span: long. Deciduous, self-fertile. Fruits: up to 3cm, oval, green to purple. Value: some vitamin C.

Gooseberries you find in the shops are green bullets, for culinary use, nothing like the meltingly sweet, well-ripened dessert varieties. Compared to other *Ribes*, gooseberries have bigger, hairy berries and sharp thorns. They are easy to grow but often handicapped by being grown as a stool. Given attention and good pruning, large, succulent berries can be had in almost any colour and with a delicious flavour, which can range from a clean, acid-sweet taste to vinous plumness.

A European native, gooseberries, *Ribes grossularia*, are first mentioned in purchases for the Westminster garden of King Edward I in 1276. They became popular almost solely in Britain, and by the nineteenth century there were hundreds of varieties, and countless clubs where members vied to grow larger fruits, achieving berries the size of bantam eggs. One variety, London, an outstandingly large, not so hairy, red was the biggest exhibited every year from 1829 to 1867, 37 years unbeaten champion! The wild relation is found in rocky terrain as a small shrub, variable in berry colour, size and in habit of growth, with some being inconveniently lax. American gooseberries, Worcesterberries, are derived from *R. divaricatum*, more disease resistant than European varieties. Gooseberries have low-chill requirements and are now rarely grown in Australia.

varieties

Grow gooseberries in cooler parts of the country, including Tasmania, Victoria, and Stanthorpe in Queensland. Flowers appear in late winter to spring and fruits around December. Experts consider green and yellow varieties have the best flavour. Early variety **Careless** is a heavy cropper of greeny white, large and smooth skinned culinary fruits. The most commonly found variety is **Roaring Lion**, which produces plentiful fruit of reasonable quality. Later maturing, berries turn red when ripening. **Yorkshire Champion** is a vigorous bush with late yellow fruit. Almost spine-free **Captivator** has red fruit, mid-season. **Invicta** is a heavy-cropping pale green disease-resistant culinary gooseberry. **Pax**, a red dessert gooseberry, is fairly mildew resistant and has few if any thorns. From Finland, the **Hinnonmaki Yellow** and **Hinnomaki Red** have sweet aromatic yellow-green or red berries; the former is claimed to taste like apricot. Both are resistant to American mildew.

Think of dessert gooseberries as hairy grapes and skin them for delight

cultivation

Gooseberries love rich, moist, loamy soil and do not like hot, dry, sandy sites or stagnant air, doing better with a breeze. Gooseberries have a low-chill requirement and can only be grown in cold winter districts. Plants need protection from hot sun and wind, and fruit can be damaged by late frosts. Bushes will fruit in part shade.

GOOSEBERRIES

Ornamental and Wildlife Value

The bushes are drab, the flowers inconspicuous and the berries not brightly coloured – the ideal landscaping plant to go with modern buildings! The flowers benefit early insects and the berries disappear.

Propagation

Gooseberries are propagated by 30cm-long cuttings. Disbud the lower end to prevent suckers.

Pruning and Training

Often misgrown as a stool with many shoots direct from the ground, gooseberries are better hard pruned to spurs on a goblet-shaped frame with a short leg. I leave the pruning till late winter so that the thorns protect the buds from the birds, which perversely delight in disbudding gooseberries. To get larger berries or more varieties in a confined space, gooseberries may easily be grown as vertical cordons, fans or even standards.

Pests and Diseases

American mildew is the worst problem, burning tips and felting fruits with a leathery coat that dries them up. Hygiene, moist roots, hard pruning and good air circulation reduce the damage. Sodium bicarbonate sprays and sulphur-based ones (which burn some varieties) are available to organic growers. Some North American wild species have been harnessed in breeding for disease resistance as they have adapted to American mildew. Prune off affected parts if it appears and exercise hygiene control by sterilising tools.

Although delicious in themselves, the reds, even if picked green, will turn your green gooseberry jam red

My favourites are the small whites, such as **Langley Gage**

Harvesting and Storing

Gooseberries do not have as much bird appeal as many fruits and can even be got unripe without protection. Birds and wasps do steal them once they're ripe, otherwise the fruits mellow and hang on till late summer if protected from such pests and damp.

companion planting

Tomatoes and broad beans nearby are reputed to aid them and I always grow them with *Limnanthes douglasii* as ground cover.

other uses

Gooseberries make a powerful wine much like that of the grape.

culinary

Picked small and green, they make the most delicious acid jams and tarts – which turn red if overcooked. As they ripen they become less acid and fuller flavoured for dessert purposes. Ripe fruits for cooking combine well with redcurrants to keep up the acidity and are often jellied to remove the tough skins and seeds.

Gooseberry Fool

Serves 4

500g ripe green gooseberries
Approx. 75g light honey or sugar
300ml thick cream
Dark chocolate and grated nutmeg, to garnish

If the gooseberries are soft, press them through a sieve. If not, warm very carefully till soft first, or freeze and defrost first. Add sweetening to the purée to taste, and cool. Immediately before serving, whip the cream and fold in the purée. Garnish with grated dark chocolate and nutmeg.

Ribes nigrum from the family *Grossulariaceae*

BLACKCURRANTS

Bush 1.5m. Life span: short. Deciduous, self-fertile. Fruits: 1–2cm, black, spherical. Value: very rich in vitamin C.

Blackcurrants are quite different to the other types of *Ribes*, though they are often bundled in with redcurrants. They fruit on young wood, not old, and have dark purple, almost black, berries with a most distinct and unforgettable aroma, which is similar to that of the aromatic foliage and stems.

These, like other *Ribes*, seem to have been unknown to the Ancient Greeks or Romans and were used only medicinally, as quinsy berries, for curing colds and throat problems until the sixteenth century. Then they became more popular as a garden crop and are now very widely grown commercially in Europe, but not so much in the USA. Their rise in fame was due to their very high vitamin C content, and probably also to the fact that sugar, needed to make this naturally sour fruit palatable, became available more cheaply. The native plants can occasionally be found in wild wet areas of northern Europe and Asia, but are now more likely to be garden escapes. Improvement has been done mostly by selection rather than producing hybrids with other *Ribes*, though the Josta is a good example of what is possible.

Blackcurrants can be huge and sweet enough to eat fresh

varieties

Blackcurrants are a minor crop and most are grown on New Zealand's South Island, and in south-eastern Australia where they satisfy their high-chilling requirement and need for cold winters. The main variety in New Zealand, **Magnus**, is now available in Australia. Others that may be obtainable are **Goliath** and **Kimberley**; the latter matures very early. The season occurs from late December to February. Blackcurrants are used for flavouring, syrup and jam. Some American species have been esteemed, such as the fragrant, bright-yellow-flowered **Buffalo Currant** or **Golden Currant**, *R. aureum/odoratum*. *R. americanum*, **American Blackcurrant**, has yellowish flowers and inferior fruit, but turns glorious colours in autumn. **Ebony**, an introduction from Eastern Europe, has particularly sweet currants (15 per cent plus), making it the first dessert variety.

cultivation

Blackcurrants revel in rich, moist ground, the richer the better, and similarly respond to heavy mulching. They do not mind light shade. Late varieties are usually chosen to avoid frost damage during their flowering period.

They prefer a neutral pH and can be planted individually about 1.5m apart or in rows. Plant blackcurrants deeply to encourage shoots to develop below ground and avoid weeding as the roots can be damaged by tilling.

BLACKCURRANTS

Ornamental and Wildlife Value
Rather dingy plants of little decorative appeal, though the smell of foliage and stems is most pleasing. However, the currants are as valuable to birds as to us and thus good subjects for wild gardens.

Propagation
There are no easier cuttings! As blackcurrants are best grown as a stool, the main requirement is for multiple shoots from ground level. Thus cuttings have all buds left on and new bushes are planted deeper than is the standard practice for almost every other subject.

Pruning and Training
In order to provide as much young fruitful wood as possible the optimum pruning is to remove annually all branches over two or three years old, allowing new ones to come up from near ground level. Or annually remove a one-third segment of the stool – like removing a slice of pie from above. The laziest though less effective way is just to cut back totally, down to near ground level once every three years. (Better done to one in three of your bushes each third year in turn or you will have years with no crop.)

culinary uses

The currants have too little liquid to simmer down on their own, so they need water or other juices. Add redcurrant juice to make blackcurrant jams and dishes more pleasantly acid. Jelly is easier work than jam as de-sprigging the berries is tedious.

Bob's Cunning Blackcurrant Jam
Makes about 3kg

1.5kg blackcurrants
500g redcurrants
A little water
Approx. 2kg sugar

De-sprig best quarter of the blackcurrants and set aside. Simmer the rest with the redcurrants, and enough water to just cover them, till they break up. Strain the juice, and repeat the process (if frugal and caring little for the quality). Weigh the (combined) juice, add the reserved blackcurrants and bring to boil simmering till these just start to break up. Then add half the juice's weight in sugar, bring back to boil, skim and pour into sterilised jars. Put the lids on immediately.

Pests and Diseases
Weeds must be kept from encroaching on the stool, but rarely germinate there because of the intense shade. Birds bother these less than most other fruits but still need to be prevented. Mildew is aggravated by stagnant air and dry roots; hygienic pruning and vigorous growth is usually sufficient redress. Big bud is obvious. It is caused by microscopic pests that also carry virus diseases such as Reversion. The simple solution is to replace old infected stock with new clean material after ten or fifteen years or when yields have dropped too far.

Harvesting and Storing
Blackcurrants will keep for several days once picked as they are so firm and tough-skinned. They can be frozen, jammed, jellied and turned into delicious syrups and juices.

They hang on little wiry stems, sprigs, which need careful detaching

companion planting

Nettles nearby benefit blackcurrants. In some parts of the USA blackcurrants may not be grown as they are host to white pine blister rust.

other uses

The leaves have been used as tea for medicinal and tonic purposes; dried currants likewise, especially for throat infections.

Aronia melanocarpa* from the family *Rosaceae

CHOKEBERRIES

Bush up to 2m. Life span: medium. Deciduous, self-fertile. Fruits: 2cm, spherical, black. Value: very rich in vitamin C.

With a name like chokeberry you can be sure the fruits are astringent and sour raw, though fine cooked and sweetened. They are hard, red, ripening to purple or almost lustrous black. They closely resemble blackcurrants in appearance and even in taste, though are more acid and almost pine-flavoured, making them a useful substitute where blackcurrants may not be grown, such as in some parts of their native USA. The bushes are easy to grow, reliable, highly productive, and compact with a height and spread of about 1.5m. White, hawthorn-like flowers and brilliant autumn leaf colours make this a most decorative fruit bush.

Distantly related to the pear and *Sorbus* genus, these berries came from eastern North America in 1700. They were relished by Native Americans who would mix the dried fruits with others to make 'cakes' for winter storage, but it was the autumn colouring that recommended them to European plantsmen. The Royal Horticultural Society Award of Merit was eventually granted in 1972, but still rather for their ornamental appeal than their taste. They are a fruit with great potential. I'm sure they would do better if called the tastyberry!

varieties

Aronia melanocarpa is grown more as an ornamental and has weed potential in some areas. A cultivar of *A. melanocarpa*, **Brilliant**, is available for ornamental plantings because it has exceptionally good autumn leaf colouring. *A. arbutifolia*, the **Red Chokeberry**, also has good autumn colour and produces red berries that were eaten by Native American children for their aroma rather than for their taste. There is also a more erect form. Although completely unrelated, *Rhus glabra*, **Scarlet Sumach, Vinegar tree**, *Anacardiaceae* is very similar. This small easily grown hardy shrub was introduced from North America in 1622 for its spectacular scarlet autumn foliage. It also produces masses of fruits, if both male and females are grown, and these were likewise eaten by native Americans and small boys. They also have a sour taste and were used as a substitute for vinegar; dried and crushed, they were sprinkled over meat and fatty dishes as a seasoning. Some other members of the *Rhus* family have apparently had their fruits or foliage eaten but as they are closely related to Poison Ivy, *Rhus toxicodendron*, great caution is advisable!

Chokeberries are soon robbed by the birds – ignore the seakale leaves underneath, the Aronia's are those small ones nicely colouring

CHOKEBERRIES

cultivation

Chokeberries are easy and do well on any reasonable soil other than very shallow chalk or in very boggy ground. Naturally they will respond to better conditions by becoming larger and more prolific, and are happier with well-mulched peaty conditions. The bushes need to be 2m apart for effective cropping, but possibly closer for displays of berries and autumn colour.

Propagation

The species come true from seed but named varieties are best reproduced from early autumn cuttings or by division.

Pruning and Training

They can tend to sucker, turning them into a stool, but cultivation is easier if they are kept to a single stem. Pruning is mostly remedial, removing suckering, low-growing, congested and diseased growths. I suspect chokeberries would be good trained on wires or a wall – they would certainly be most decorative.

Pests and Diseases

Other than the usual hazards of choking weeds and losses to the birds, these plants are remarkably free from problems. One reason chokeberries are coming into cultivation is that they are as good a source of vitamin C as blackcurrants, but also more productive, with none of their potential problems of big bud, reversion or mildew.

Growing under Glass and in Containers

There seems no need to grow chokeberries under glass as they thrive outdoors and are of little value fresh, only tasty once preserved. However, it is worth growing them in a container if you need a rich source of vitamin C and have no garden space available.

Ornamental and Wildlife Value

The tough reliability, the profusion of spring flowers, huge quantities of glossy black berries and the colour of the autumn leaves make this an essential plant for any area, ornamental or wild, especially if you like birds.

Harvesting and Storing

Chokeberries ripen in mid-summer but the flavour improves if they are left to hang. They will need good bird protection. The best and only sensible means of storage is turning them into preserves.

companion planting

No good or bad companions are yet recognised as they have been little cultivated. I grow mine in a bed with rhubarb and seakale.

other uses

The berries can be used for an edible dye and I can vouch for their being a high-vitamin self-service food for my poultry, who head for them whenever they get out.

culinary

They can be used in the same way as blackcurrants and indeed taste not dissimilar, if more piney and aromatic. However, their preserve goes better with savoury dishes in the manner of cranberry jelly. Jams, jellies and preserves only set well if apple juice or purée is combined with the berries; without it you get berries in syrup.

Chokeberry preserve

1kg chokeberries
500g whitecurrants, or redcurrants if white unavailable
1 small lemon
A little water
Approx. 1kg sugar

Thoroughly wash the berries and currants, chop the lemon and simmer all three with just sufficient water to cover. Simmer till soft then sieve out the skins and pips, weigh the juice and return it to the pan with three-quarters of its weight in sugar. Bring to the boil. Skim well, then pot in small jars. Store for six months before use. Serve with gammon steak, new potatoes and peas.

Rubus idaeas from the family *Rosaceae*

RASPBERRIES

Bush/vine. Life span: short. Deciduous, self-fertile. Fruits: up to 2.5cm, red, yellow, black, conical. Value: valuable amounts of vitamin C, riboflavin and niacin.

Although many have described the strawberry as the finest fruit, others consider the raspberry to be as good, if not better. However, these exquisite berries are not as common by far, because the fruits perish so rapidly. Strangely they are also little grown as garden fruits, although they are amongst the easiest to care for and cultivate.

Raspberries vary considerably in size and are usually red, with black and yellow sorts sometimes encountered. In good varieties, the conical fruit pulls off the plug easily, leaving a hole. Some are less easy to pick and the berries may be damaged in the extrication as they are very soft and thin skinned.

Their young shoots are usually green but soon go red or brown as they grow. Eventually the canes reach 1–3m high. They are often bristly and occasionally thorny. Individually the canes are short-lived, springing from a suckering root system one year, to die the following year after fruiting. The root systems could spread perpetually, though they most often fade away from virus infections. The flowers are small, usually white, with the fruitlet visible in the middle once the petals fall. While the flowers are usually unscented, the leaves have a slight fragrance. This is more pronounced in the North American wild species *Rubus odorata*, which has a resiny smell to the stems, though the pale reddish-purple flowers remain scentless. (Another, *R. deliciosus*, has large, rose-like flowers which are deliciously perfumed.)

R. idaeus raspberries are native to Europe and Asia in hilly areas, heaths and on the edge of woodlands, especially those with acid soils. They are found growing wild in Scandinavia as far north as 70° and have long been gathered. Seeds and debris from the plants have been found preserved in the remains of the prehistoric lake villages of what is now Switzerland. Strangely, like other northern temperate fruits, raspberries went unregistered by the Classical writers. The Romans were such ravenous gourmands that it seems unlikely they did not eat these delightful fruits when colonising cooler, wetter lands than their own. Perhaps because these were gathered from the wild in such profusion they needed no mention, being taken as commonplace. Raspberries are included in the practical poetry of Thomas Tusser and noted by Gerard in the sixteenth century. It seems that at that time the fruit of the closely related bramble was considered far superior and raspberries were used more for medicinal and tonic purposes. There are many similar and wild species which are enjoyed in other temperate countries.

RASPBERRIES

Galante

varieties

There are many *Rubus* species closely resembling raspberries, and others more like brambles or blackberries. The latter are dealt with as a group with Japanese wineberries. In North America they cultivate red and yellow raspberries descended from *R. strigosa*, similar to European raspberries. They also have Black Raspberries, **Blackcaps**, *R. occidentalis*, which are less hardy and with fewer stouter canes more given to branching. Their **Rocky Mountain** raspberry, *R. deliciosus*, is large fruited, delicious but a shy fruiter especially in the UK.

Raspberries can be summer or autumn cropping, though many cultivars vary as much with the pruning method as inherently. Those that readily crop on old wood, last year's canes, are now called floricane varieties while those that crop on this year's new shoots, effectively in autumn, are primocanes. **Autumn Bliss** was long the best primocane for autumn though **Polka**, a Polish variety, has exceptional cropping and flavour and is set to replace it. Another newcomer, **Galante**, is very well flavoured, reliable with large berries and **Joan J** has similar claims made. These last three fruit on and on from mid-summer till the frosts.

As to choice, new varieties of today are soon replaced by others in profusion and no list is ever complete. I still like the almost obsolete but very tasty **Malling Jewel**, an early that crops lightly but holds on well and is tolerant of virus infection, but may infect others. **Glen Moy** is a heavier cropping early, resistant to greenfly. **Glen Ample** is rapidly replacing the very popular **Glen Prosen** and **Malling Joy** as the most reliable mid-season. **Glen Fyne** has by far the best flavour and is aphid resistant and heavy cropping. Lates ripening in August include the superbly flavoured **Malling Admiral**, **Glen Doll**, **Autumn Treasure**, **Octavia** and the Canadian bred and very tasty **Tulameen**. Closely related to the last is **Cascade Delight**, which has very large fruits, is late cropping but very resistant to root rot so best for wet areas.

I love the yellow raspberries: these originated alongside the reds and are less vigorous, with paler leaves and naturally tend towards autumn fruiting. **Golden Everest** is superb with richly flavoured soft sweet berries lacking the sharpness of many reds. **Allgold** may be identical with **Fall Gold,** primocane autumn fruiters much like **Golden Antwerp**, which had the better flavour; one of the oldest varieties it's now rare. **Red Antwerp** is lost; **Norfolk Giant**, another legendary old variety is also no longer obtainable.

Raspberries grow best in cool-temperate areas of Australia like Tasmania, the south-western tip of Western Australia, the Blue Mountains and the Dandenongs. **Willamette** is a summer-cropping variety with another crop in autumn. **Heritage** is a late-summer to late-autumn fruit-bearing raspberry. **Thornless Willamette** is a new release and more will become available as raspberries increase in popularity in cool districts.

cultivation

Preferring cool, moist conditions, raspberries do wonderfully in Scotland. Although they can be grown elsewhere, in most soils, they do considerably better given plentiful moisture, a rich neutral or acidic soil, or at least copious quantities of compost and very thick mulches. With hot, dry summers and wetter autumns the autumn-fruiting varieties can be much more productive, especially on drier sites, and these also suffer less from maggots. Summer-fruiters need a moist site, and do not mind quite heavy shade. They do not like the dry conditions against walls, but can be grown on cool, shady ones with a moist root run.

Fall Gold

Two to pick now, one when you've finished, one for tomorrow and another for the day after

Growing in Containers

I have fruited raspberries in large pots. They resent it and do not crop well or flourish as they really need a bigger, cooler root run.

Ornamental and Wildlife Value

Cultivated raspberries are not very ornamental themselves and the fruit does not last long enough to be called a display! Some of the species are more decorative, and scented, so are worth considering, but are nowhere near as productive as modern fruiting varieties. The birds adore raspberries and will get to them anywhere, so they are good in wild gardens. However, you have a duty to others to eradicate the berries when they become virus-infected. The flowers are very beneficial to bees and other insects.

Propagation

Varieties are multiplied by transplanting any piece of root with a bud or young cane in the autumn. Pot-grown ones may be planted in spring. Summer fruiters should not be cropped the first year but built up first; autumn fruiters may be cropped if they were well established early in the previous autumn. I have found seed can provide very vigorous and productive, if variable, plants, but it is a better plan to buy new, named cultivars.

Pruning and Training

Too lax to be left free, they are best restrained by growing between pairs of wires or winding the tips around horizontal ones. Alternatively, they can be grown as tripods, with three well-spaced stools being joined to an apex. Pruning for summer raspberries is done in autumn; remove all old canes that have fruited or died and fix the new ones in place, selecting the biggest and strongest at about 12cm apart. (It helps to pre-thin these when the shoots emerge in early summer.) Autumn fruiters are easier still: just cut everything to the ground in late winter. (Pre-thinning the canes in spring is, again, quite advantageous.)

Pests and Diseases

Weeding must be done carefully because of their shallow roots. Thick mulching is almost essential. Birds are the major cause of lost crops – no protection, no fruit! The cockchafer beetle can be controlled with hygiene and mulching (methodically rake thick mulches aside in winter to allow birds to eat the pupae) or the use of permitted sprays if necessary. Aphids attack the tips of plants and can spread viral disease. Virus diseases may appear, mottling the leaves with yellow and making the plants less productive. Replacing the stock and moving the site is the only practical solution, but wait till the yields have dropped. Interveinal yellowing is a reaction to alkaline soils; seaweed solution sprays with added magnesium sulphate are a palliative. Compost and mulching provide the most effective cure.

Harvesting and Storing

Pick gently, leaving the plug; if it won't come easily, do not force it! They do not keep for long if they are wet, and less still if warm. If you want to keep them longest, cut the fruiting stalks with scissors and do not touch the fruits. They must be processed or eaten within a

Rubus ideaus

RASPBERRIES

matter of hours as they are one of the least durable or transportable fruits. Those sold commercially are the toughest – and therefore obviously also the least meltingly sumptuous!

companion planting

They reputedly benefit from tansy, and garlic or marigolds and strawberries may be grown close by but not underneath them. Do not grow potatoes nearby as they will then become more prone to blight.

other uses

Raspberry canes are bristly if not thorny. They have little strength or heat value but can be useful for wildlife shelters. I find short lengths, bundled together, then 'Swiss rolled' in newspaper and jammed into a cut-open plastic bottle, will make superb dry but airy ladybird hibernation quarters which I hide in evergreen shrubs. Raspberry leaves and fruits have been used medicinally, and have often traditionally been used as a tea.

culinary

Raspberries make wonderful juices, jellies, drinks and sorbets. They are often combined with redcurrant juice to add tartness. Their wine is delicate and beautifully coloured. Raspberries can be frozen, but have poor texture afterwards.

Kitty Topping's Raspberry Conserve
Makes about 2kg

1kg freshly picked raspberries
1kg caster sugar

Pick fresh raspberries and hurry straight to the kitchen. Wash them and immediately heat them in a closed pan, rapidly but gently, swirling the pan to prevent sticking and burning. Once most berries have softened, but before they break down totally, add the same weight of pre-warmed caster sugar. Stir while heating. One minute after you are absolutely sure all the sugar has completely dissolved, pour into small, heated jars and seal. Keep in the cool and use quickly once opened as the aim of this recipe is the stunning flavour, not keeping quality. Try to use freshly picked fruit only.

Rubus fruticosus from the family *Rosaceae*

BLACKBERRIES

Bush/vine. Life span: medium to long. Deciduous, self-fertile. Fruits: up to 2cm, black, drupe. Value: rich in vitamin C.

Even without its glistening blackberries, the native bramble is known to everyone for the long, arching and scrambling stems armed with vicious thorns. What may be appreciated more by the picker than the walker is that the fruits vary widely from plant to plant. In fact, there is no one native bramble or blackberry, but hosts of them. These have occasionally been crossed deliberately, and often inadvertently, with one another and then again with other garden escapes. Although in some remote areas the stocks remain as several distinct but variable species, they may nevertheless have been altered in prehistory by unconscious human behaviour, as has also been suggested for raspberries (see p504). Certainly now, any blackberry found near enough to human habitation to be picked, is highly likely to be a hybrid. And those nearby will probably be different. Just by looking at the fruits or the flowers in any area you will usually see great diversity.

The common brambles have fern-like leaves, thin purple or green stems, white or light purple flowers and small hard berries. A better and recognisable type of wild blackberry is *Rubus ulmifolius*, which has strong-growing, plum-coloured branches with five-lobed leaflets, which are very light on the underside. It is not self-fertile.

In Europe, an improved form of this blackberry, *bellidiflorus*, is grown ornamentally for its pink double flowers. *Rubus caesius*, the dewberry, is another distinctive species, with three-lobed leaflets on long, thin, creeping, almost tendril-like stems, which can form large mats. The dewberry is smaller than most blackberries, with fruits containing fewer drupelets, which break up as you pick them. These come earlier in summer than the blackberries and do not have the same shiny glossiness, but are more matt, with a whitish bloom similar to a plum's.

Blackberry remains have been found in many of the earliest European habitations and have been an important autumn crop since before recorded history. They were known to the Ancient Greeks, as much for the herbal properties of their leaves as for the fruits. They have always grown in great profusion in woods and hedges, on heaths and moorlands and indeed on every site as soon as it has been vacated by us. So much fruit has always been available free that brambles have never been cultivated on a large scale and even the markets were satisfied by gleaning the wild crop. More recently there has been some breeding, with improved thornless and large-fruited varieties, in effect neglecting flavour, so many people prefer to pick the wild berries rather than use cultivated sorts. Certainly there has been far more interest in the development of hybrids with other *Rubus*. The North American dewberries, which derived from *R. alleghaniensis*, were introduced to Europe. They are less vigorous and larger-fruited than the natives, but have unfortunately also proved more tender. Other introductions have been more successful. The **Himalayan Giant** is an exceptionally vigorous variety which has encroached on the wild populations all over. Strangely enough, the thornless **Oregon Cutleaf** blackberry is not American, as used to be thought, but an old English variety of *R. laciniatus*, or **Parsley-leaved Blackberry**. It has bigger fruits, is nearly evergreen and comes almost true from seed.

BLACKBERRIES

Blackberries never ripen all at once

Their sheer size and exuberance makes them too much for most small, modern gardens, though they do crop handsomely. Heavy dressings of compost and thick mulches will keep up the yields. They do well grassed up underneath, and left to themselves will exclude weeds and anything smaller than large trees.

Growing under Glass and in Containers

They are so easy outside it would be bizarre to grow them under cover. Blackberries do not like the cramped conditions pots afford, and as most of them are thorny they are seldom grown this way. The thornless ones are still too vigorous to thrive in any reasonable pot.

Ornamental and Wildlife Value

The fruiting species are delightful in flower, with a mass of blossom in early summer, and there are many ornamental varieties and species, though most are too vigorous for modern gardens. Their vast quantity of blossom is valuable for bees and other insects and the fruit is an immense feast for wildlife, fattening up the bird population for the winter. The thicket of the bushes makes a snug, dry home for many small creatures, from ladybirds and beetles to rodents and birds.

varieties

Trial plantings of the thornfree blackberries developed in the USA commenced in southern Australia in 1980. They are now grown commercially with high yields for each plant. The brambles are vigorous and blackberries are considered a weed in Australia. The new varieties include **Black Satin**, **Smooth Stem** and **Dirksen**. **Black Satin** is an early thornless blackberry with strong growth and high fruit yield through mid- to late summer. **Silvan** blackberry is thorny, vigorous and tolerates heavier soils; yield is good from early December to mid-January. See pages 84–85 for details of non-feral blackberry hybrids and cultivars.

cultivation

The whole bramble family are gross feeders and love rich, moist soils. They will crop in a light shade but are sweeter in the sun. Their cultivation and control is more like a pitched battle – if you give way they will take over your garden! Each stem arches over, grows down and roots from the tip to form a new stool of stems.

Oregon Thornless

Pick fruits with shiny skins; matt ones are old

Pests and Diseases

Blackberry rust can affect thornless blackberries as well as other cultivated brambles but agriculturalists consider the damage slight compared to the problems of land degradation caused by blackberries in the wild. The rust is considered species specific to the wild forms of the plant.

Propagation

Seedlings come up everywhere, but are variable. The tips readily root and form new plants in the few weeks at the end of summer and into autumn. At this time, make sure the tips go into pots of compost if you want extra plants, or cut them off if not.

Pruning and Training

Blackberries can fruit on wood older than one year old and the canes do not always die, as with raspberries. However the new wood is better and carries fewer pests and diseases so it is best to cut all the old and dead wood out and tie in the new. The canes are much longer and carry heavier loads than raspberries so strong supports are necessary. The young canes need tying in during summer. If new plants are not needed they are best de-tipped in late summer to stop them from rooting wherever they hit the ground.

Harvesting and Storing

Traditionally blackberries are picked as they ripen, from late summer up until Michaelmas, or the first frost, when the Devil was supposed to have spat on them and made them sour. They are unusable red but turn soft to the touch as they blacken. **Bedford Giant** ripens one berry in each bunch way ahead of the others. The berries are fairly tough-skinned, so can travel and last longer than raspberries if picked dry and not so overloaded that they pack down. They are best used as soon as possible or frozen; the spoilt texture when they defrost is no problem if they are to be used in cooking anyway.

companion planting

Blackberries benefit from tansy or stinging nettles nearby and they are a good companion and sacrificial crop for grapevines.

other uses

Brambles make a secure and quick barrier to many four-legged animals and two-legged rats. There are few in the world who will try to come over or through a fence or hedge clothed in any of this thorny bunch. **Himalayan Giant** is so big and tough it will stop almost anything between the size of a rabbit and that of a tank! The prunings are vicious but do burn well and fiercely.

Waldo

BLACKBERRIES

culinary

Blackberries are often too sour to eat raw but once cooked they are much tastier and do not have such a deleterious effect on one's insides. They make excellent jams, though, as they are rather seedy, the jelly is more often made. Frequently apples are included in blackberry dishes, especially jams and jellies, to aid setting and also because the flavours combine so lusciously. Blackberry wine is made by country folk and the berries used to be added to wines and spirits to give a distinctive colour, such as with the Red Muscat of Toulon.

Bob's Blackberry and Apple Pancake Supreme

Serves 4

Approx. 300ml pancake batter
250g blackberries
Golden syrup, to taste
30g cornflour
A little milk
2 apples
Knob of butter
Sugar, lemon juice, lots of cream or yogurt

Prepare the pancake batter and set aside. Wash the blackberries and simmer with golden syrup till soft. Strain, reserving the juice, and keep the fruit warm. To the juice add enough water to make it up to 200ml, return to the heat and bring to the boil. Cream the cornflour in a little milk, pour it into the boiling blackberry juice, stirring all the time, and cook until the juice thickens. Set aside.

Peel, core and chop the apples into chunks. Heat them rapidly with a little butter till they start to crumble at the edges, then remove from the heat and keep warm. Next preheat a grill and a frying pan. Oil the pan. Once it is smoking, pour in all the pancake batter. As the bottom sets, but while the top is still liquid, take the pan off the heat, rapidly spoon in apple chunks, blackberry blobs and stripes of sauce. Swirl slightly so that the liquid batter blends a little but does not mix or cover completely. Sprinkle sugar generously over the top, then add the lemon juice and put under the red-hot grill. Serve immediately the top has caramelised. This goes well with yogurt or cream.

Rubus **hybrids from the family** ***Rosaceae***

LOGANBERRIES

BOYSENBERRIES AND TAYBERRIES

Bush/vine. Life span: medium. Deciduous, mostly self-fertile. Fruits: 6 x 2cm. Value: some vitamin C.

The loganberry resembles a blackberry in manner of growth, but the fruits are more like raspberries: cylindrical, dull red and firm, with a more acid flavour than either, making them sour raw but exquisite cooked. Boysenberry fruits are sweeter, more blackberry-like, larger and reddish-purple. They can be savoured raw with cream but also make the celebrated jam. The tayberry is bigger and sweeter than either, with an aromatic flavour. When fully ripe, the enormous loganberry-like fruits are dark wine red or purple and nearly three times the size of most other berries.

Loganberries were reputedly a hybrid of American dewberry and raspberry, raised by a Judge Logan of California in 1882. Introduced to Britain in 1897, loganberries have remained the supreme culinary berry for nearly a century. The boysenberry has a similar history. It is believed to be another hybrid dewberry but in fact is probably a youngberry x loganberry. It is not as hardy as other hybrids and does better in a warmer site than the rest. The Medana Tayberry was developed by the Scottish Crop Research Institute, who crossed the Oregon blackberry Aurora with a tetraploid raspberry to produce this excellent fruit. It is popular in New Zealand but rare in Australia.

Tayberry

Thornless loganberries

varieties

There are several varieties and similar hybrids. **Loganberry** is a less vigorous, trailing plant (*R. ursinus x R. idaeus*), either thorny or thornless. The thornless variety does not pull off the plug easily but is a heavy cropper with good flavour, maturing mid-November to mid-January. **Boysenberry** (*R. ursinus*) has a similar habit and is also thorny or thornless. I find the **Thornless Boysenberry** not as good a cropper as the thorned. It matures early, around December to mid-January. The **Marionberry** and the **Youngberry** have the habit and appearance of blackberries but the fruits have more flavour. The **Youngberry** is similar to the **Boysenberry** but matures one week later. There is a thornless version as well. The **Black Loganberry** is a New Zealand variety; it has cylindrical tapering fruits and is slow to establish and crop. **Black Satin** and **Loch Ness** have vigorous, semi-erect, thornless bushes with fruit maturing late December to early February. **Lawtonberry** is very thorny, North American in origin, with smaller fruit from early January to mid-March.

cultivation

The hybrids all need much the same, cool conditions and rich moist soils. The boysenberry will cope with drier sites and indeed prefers some shelter. They are generally quite happy on a cool shady wall if they have a moist root run. Loganberries and the American thornless blackberry cultivars are sensitive to sunscald.

LOGANBERRIES
BOYSENBERRIES AND TAYBERRIES

Protect them with afternoon shade, using shade cloth to cover all plants. They grow well on gently sloping ground for improved drainage.

Ornamental and Wildlife Value
Not very useful ornamentally, and thorny, but their flowers and fruits are valuable in the wild garden, bridging the gap between raspberries and blackberries well.

Propagation
As these are hybrids; they will not come true from seed, though interesting results may be had. Tips can be rooted in late summer and early autumn and occasionally the roots can be successfully divided.

Pruning and Training
They grow much like blackberries but can have more brittle canes, like raspberries, so care must be taken when bending them. They mostly fruit on young wood which dies and is cleared completely after the second year. Canes may produce again a third year, as blackberries might, but are usually unproductive, so annual replacement of all the old by new is generally considered a better policy.

Pests and Diseases
The only common major problem is bird losses, which are high as these plants mostly crop after summer fruits but before wild blackberries. The American blackberry rust, introduced to control feral blackberries, can affect some hybrid varieties.

companion planting

Tansy, marigolds and alliums are all beneficial.

other uses

These canes will make good additional barriers with fences and hedges.

Buckingham Thornless

culinary

Generally best flavoured when fully ripe, these fruits are not very acid and benefit from the addition of redcurrant juice to many recipes. Varieties from which the plug is not easily removed, or which even detach a thorny stalk with the fruit, are best used by straining or juicing them first. These fruits make excellent jams, jellies, tarts and pies. The juices are delicious as drinks and make wonderful sorbets.

Summerberry Squash
Makes about 2.5 litres

1kg mixed berries
500g redcurrants
1 litre water
1kg sugar

Wash the fruits and simmer them down with half the water till soft, then strain. Cover the fruit pulp with the rest of the water, bring almost to boiling point, and strain again. Combine the strained juices and the sugar, heating gently if necessary to make sure the sugar dissolves completely. Cool, then pour into plastic bottles when cold and freeze till required. Defrost and dilute with water to taste.

Rubus species from the family *Rosaceae*

JAPANESE WINEBERRIES AND RUBUS SPECIES

Rubus spectabilis – Salmonberry

Bush/vine. Life span: medium to long. Deciduous, self-fertile. Fruits: variable. Value: some vitamin C.

***Rubus phoenicolasius*, the Japanese wineberry, is the best of the vast raspberry/blackberry clan. This delicious and highly ornamental cane fruit resembles a vigorous raspberry covered with russet bristles and thorns. Unlike those of blackberries, these prick rather than jab so are more pleasant to handle and pick. The fruits are smaller than blackberries, orange to cherry red, and they are generally far more palatable.**

Japanese wineberries are not a hybrid but a true species coming from North China and Japan. They certainly do come true, as you will find as they appear all over the garden once the birds spread the seed. Introduced to Britain around 1876, Japanese wineberries were considered worth cultivating and won a First Class Certificate from the Royal Horticultural Society in 1894. During the century since, however, they have not proved popular except with children of all ages who are lucky enough to find them.

varieties

There are no named varieties of any of these species, though there is some variation in leaf and fruit colour so there is scope for improvement. *R. leucodermis*, **Blackcap**, has thorny, bluish stems with light green leaves, white underneath, on a medium-size bush, small white flowers and purple-black sweet fruits with a plum-like bloom. Yellow- and red-fruited forms occur in its native Northwest America. Another, *R. parviflorus*, the **Thimbleberry**, has large, fragrant, white flowers on strong, thornless stems and large, flattened, insipid red berries. *R. parvifolius*, the **Native Raspberry**, was fruited in England in 1825 and has small, pink, tasty, juicy berries. The **Salmonberry**, *R. spectabilis*, has maroon-red flowers on prickly erect stems and acid orange-yellow fruits. Apparently native Americans ate the cooked young shoots. *R. arcticus*, the **Arctic** or **Crimson Bramble**, has amber-coloured fruits that are said to taste of pineapple. Very unusual is the **Rock** or **Roebuck Bramble**, *R. saxatilis*, which grows just like strawberry plants, and is eaten in much the same way. The Russians used to distill a spirit from the berries.

cultivation

Although they will grow almost anywhere, the biggest berries come from plants growing in rich, moist soil well enriched with compost and leaf mould. They will grow in moderate shade or full sun and are self-fertile. Best grown on a wire fence or wired against a wall, after the manner of blackberries, they need a spacing of at least 3–4m apart and wires to at least 2m in height. Like most fruits, they do best when grown in well-mulched, clean soil, but will still produce when grassed down around.

Growing under Glass

These are mostly so easy to grow outside that there is little advantage to having them under glass except to extend the season.

Growing in Containers

Growing them in pots will shorten their life and give greatly reduced yields, but it may be well worthwhile for both their snack and their garnishing value.

JAPANESE WINEBERRIES

Very ornamental and tasty, too

Ornamental and Wildlife Value
Japanese wineberry leaves are a striking light green, with russet bristled stems, bright orangey-red fruits and a star-shaped calyx left afterwards. They are highly decorative – probably the best fruiting plant to train against a whitewashed wall or up a pole for all-year-round interest and colour. Their value to wildlife is as immense as that of the whole clan.

Propagation
These are species, so they come true from seed and the tips can be layered in late summer and early autumn. Remove the old canes and tie in the new each autumn. Plants have a long life if cared for. Prune out any infections early.

Pests and Diseases
Choking and climbing weeds such as nettles and bindweed must be well controlled. There are no major problems other than the birds.

Harvesting and Storing
Japanese wineberries are one of the most delicious of all fruits eaten fresh, though they will keep for a while in the cool of a refrigerator.

companion planting

Tansy, garlic and French and pot marigolds are all potential good companions.

other uses

Their dense growth and prickly bristles make them attractive but impenetrable informal boundaries.

culinary

Very valuable as garnishing for sweet and savoury dishes and simply eating off the plant. Some berries can be frozen to add to mixed fruit compôtes. Japanese wineberry jelly does not set, but forms a treacly syrup, ideal to accompany ice cream.

Wineberry Ripple
Serves 6

1kg Japanese wineberries
Approx 500g sugar
1kg superb vanilla ice cream

Freeze a few berries for garnishing. Simmer the rest till soft with just enough water to prevent sticking. Strain and weigh the juice. Thoroughly dissolve three-quarters of the juice's weight in sugar in the warm juice. Leave to cool completely. Once cooled, interleave scoops of ice cream with the syrup, pressing it all down into a new container. Freeze the new rippled block and then scoop as required, garnishing with the frozen berries.

Vitis vinifera **from the family** *Vitaceae*

GRAPEVINES

Vine up to any height. Life span: long. Deciduous, self-fertile. Fruits: 2–3cm, oval, white, black, red. Value: generally beneficial.

These scrambling vines have smooth, peeling, brown stems, large lobed leaves and bunches of grapes in autumn. The flowers are so insignificant they are rarely noticed but are white and sweet scented. The leaves colour well in autumn; red-berrying varieties tend to go red and white ones yellow.

Grapes have been with us since biblical times; Noah planted a vineyard. The Egyptians show full details of vineyards and wine-making in their relics from 2440 BC. The Romans spread vines all over Europe until, in the first century AD, Emperor Domitian protected his home market and ordered the extirpation of the grape from Britain, France and Spain. Two centuries later, Emperor Probus restored the vine and long after the Roman Empire collapsed the monasteries kept vineyards going.

By the time of the Domesday Book, in the eleventh century, there were still thirty-eight vineyards in Britain. But the climate was cooling and the last UK vineyards disappeared in the eighteenth century. During the nineteenth century grapes were widely grown in glasshouses and the Victorians raised grape cultivation to perfection, almost year round, in hothouses. Without the cheap labour and even cheaper fuel of Victorian times, these hothouse grapes disappeared – though some survived, unproductive, on the sunny walls left after the glass had long gone. In Europe the grape has remained part of life, and in 1494 was already being grown in the New World. Over the last centuries the vine spread to almost every part of the world. Now most grapes are grown on American roots to prevent *Phylloxera* root aphids. Wine grapes are an important commercial crop and strict regulations govern the growing of vines in viticulture regions.

varieties

Dessert grapes are different from wine grapes, though of the same species, so you should be quite clear whether you seek table or wine grapes. *Vitis lambrusca* hybrids are obtained from specialist growers but are suitable for home growing due to their disease-resistance. **Isabella**, **Concord** and **Carolina Black** are grown. Varieties of *V. vinifera* such as **Sultana**, **Black Muscat**, **Italia**, **Waltham Cross**, **Ruby Seedless** and **Emperor** are popular and reliable. Tolerance of cool or humid conditions varies so check with a local supplier.

cultivation

Grapevines are very easy to grow. They are usually too vigorous and do not need rich conditions to crop well. They need a hot, dry autumn to ripen well and thus are usually best grown on walls in cooler regions.

Strict rules govern grape imports and movement in wine-growing areas so check with local agricultural authorities before planting garden grapes.

GRAPEVINES

Little is more pleasing than ripe grapes hanging aplenty

companion planting

Traditionally grown over elm or mulberry trees, grapevines are benefited by blackberries, sage, mustard and hyssop growing nearby and inhibited by cabbages, radish, Cypress spurge and even by laurels.

Ornamental and Wildlife Value

Grapevines are quick to climb over and hide objects and turn bright colours in autumn, so they are valuable where space allows them to ramble. In the wild garden grapevines are useful in both flower and fruit.

Propagation

Phylloxera is an insect that forms galls on roots, eventually killing the vine. It is restricted to areas in Victoria and New South Wales, and all grapes in these areas must be grafted onto resistant rootstocks.

Pruning and Training

There are many ways to prune grapes and many sub-variations, enough to fill a book on their own. Left to themselves vines often produce rank growth and exhaust themselves with overcropping; see sections on pages 91, 93 and 95.

Pests and Diseases

Grapes are attacked by many pests including fungi, powdery mildew and botrytis, which rots the berries. Plants infected with leaf roll virus should be removed. There are several mites, insects such as vine moth and weevils that damage vines but most are controlled by spraying. Birds are the main cause of losses! Mould can be common in damp ripening seasons and mildews in dry ones.

Harvesting and Storing

Kept cool and dry, the grapes hang on the vines well. Cut bunches with a stalk, place the stalk in water and keep the grapes in a cool, dry cellar for weeks. Handle them as little as possible.

culinary

The best are excellent dessert fruits, are easily juiced and the juice can be frozen for year-round use. They make good jellies and any surplus used for wine.

Love Nests

Per person

Approx. 6 large dessert grapes, preferably Muscat
Marzipan, apricot conserve, clotted cream and dark chocolate, to taste
Individual meringue case

Peel and seed all but one grape per portion and fill each with a pellet of marzipan. Smear the meringue bases with apricot conserve, then a layer of cream. Press in the filled grapes, cover with more cream, top with grated black chocolate and the perfect grape. Serve the nests immediately.

Vitis species from the family *Vitaceae*

GRAPEVINE SPECIES

Vine. Life span: long-lived. Deciduous, sometimes self-fertile. Fruit: up to 2cm, in bunches, red or black.

There are hundreds of true grapes, or *Vitis* species, which are mostly ornamental climbing vines. (Very closely resembling them are the *Ampelopsis* and *Parthenocissus*, of which the most common are known as Virginia creepers. These resemble grapevines and even form bunches, which are not edible.) These *Vitis* species are much grown for their covering capacity as they soon hide eyesores, and for their spectacular autumn colour. The fruits are often considered a bonus, but offer different and exciting flavours.

Although the *Vitis vinifera* varieties are almost exclusively used for commercial purposes and wine-making there are countless other *Vitis* species grapes eaten throughout the world, and have been since time immemorial. Their blood has also influenced the *V. vinifera* varieties on many occasions. These are but a few.

varieties

Vitis aestivalis, the **Summer, Bunch** or **Pigeon Grape** is from North America. It has heart-shaped leaves, downy underneath, scented flowers and early black grapes. It was first seen in Europe in 1656. *V. labrusca*, the **Plum, Skunk** or **Fox Grape** is another first brought to Europe in 1656. Its young shoots are covered in down and the leaves are thick, dark green on top, ageing to pink underneath. The fruits are rounded, blackish purple and have a distinctive musk or fox flavour which some dislike. I enjoy it but not in wine! It has given rise to several good cultivars such as **Concord**. *V. vulpina* is similar, with glossy leaves. Both have sweet-scented flowers. *V. rotundifolia* is the **Muscadine** or **Southern Fox Grape**, widely used for wine in southern USA. It produces only half a dozen large fleshy grapes per cluster, usually black, though there are cultivated local white varieties. The **Winter, Chicken** or **Frost Grape berry**, *V. cordifolia* is very hardy and does well on lime soils. The dark purple fruit has to be frosted before it is edible and is used for wine. Some local cultivated varieties have sweeter, tastier, red or black fruits. *V. riparia* is the high climbing **Riverbank Grape** from North America, with large, glossy, deeply lobed leaves and big panicles of male flowers that smell most distinctly and sweetly of mignonette. The fruits are black or amber and very acid. *V. coignetiae* comes from Japan and Korea. It has enormous leaves up to 30cm across. It is strong-growing and the leaves turn crimson and scarlet in autumn so it is much used ornamentally, but the black grapes with a bloom are not very tasty. *V. davidii*, once called **Spinovitis** because it has spines on the shoots, stems and leaves, was brought from China for its glorious, rich crimson, autumn colouring. It also has edible black fruits. *V. californica* was originally cultivated by the native American Pueblo Indians. It must have been good because, to quote Sturtevant, 'The quantity of the fruit that an Indian will consume at one time is scarcely credible'.

cultivation

Most species require much the same treatment as *V. vinifera* grapes. Over-rich conditions should be avoided. For most, a warm site is better, but they do not like warm winters and do best with some chilling in winter. Many of the species grapes listed here are not

GRAPEVINE SPECIES

Some varieties colour beautifully in autumn

commonly sold by nurseries in Australia but may be used in breeding programs by specialist plant breeders.

Growing in Containers

Like *vinifera* grapevines, the species do not enjoy cramped conditions, but they can be grown in large pots. This shortens their life and gives small crops but conveniently controls their vigour, allowing many to be grown in a small area.

Ornamental and Wildlife Value

These are of the highest value as ornamentals and are useful for quick screens and coverings, though they can be too vigorous for small gardens unless hard pruned. Their bountiful flowers and fruit make them very good for wildlife gardens.

Propagation

As these are species they can be grown from seed. Ripe wood cuttings, taken in late autumn, are best, and budding or grafting is possible.

Pests and Diseases

As these are species, they are generally resilient to most of the common grape pests and diseases. However birds are still as much, if not more, of a problem.

Pruning and Training

See also sections on Grapes for Dessert and for Wine. There are many ways to prune grapes and many sub-variations, enough to fill a book on their own. The species are best treated much as regular vines which, left to themselves, often produce rank growth and nearly exhaust themselves with overcropping. For ornamental purposes that is no problem, but for fruit they are best hard pruned and trained on a wall on wires about 50cm apart, and on walls under cover for the more tender varieties. The main framework is formed the first years, covering the wires with stems furnished with fruiting spurs. Thereafter these shoot each spring and a flower truss appears between the third and fifth leaf. After another three or four leaves, each shoot is tipped, as are any replacements as they come. Thinning the number of bunches is recommended, leave no more than three per metre run of cane. In winter new canes are all cut back hard to two buds on a stub on each spur. Many pruning and training methods are available.

companion planting

Species grapevines are probably benefited by blackberries, sage, mustard and hyssop growing nearby and they are inhibited by cabbages, radishes, Cypress spurge and laurels.

other uses

As with other grapes, the grapevine prunings make great kindling.

culinary

Most of these grapes are too small and pippy or sour to be used raw as dessert. They are best juiced or turned into jellies. The strong flavour of some, such as the Fox Grape, can make them unsuitable for wine.

Grape Jelly

Makes approx. 2kg

1kg grapes
Approx. 1kg sugar

Simmer the grapes with only just enough water to stop them sticking. When they are soft, strain and weigh the liquid. Add the same weight of sugar to the juice and bring to the boil, skim until clear, bottle into hot jars and seal.

Vitis vinifera from the family *Vitaceae*

DESSERT GRAPES
UNDER GLASS

Vine. Life span: exceptionally long-lived. Fruits: up to 3cm, oval or round, any colour.

Dessert or table grapes are grown outdoors in Australia and New Zealand but in cold climates they need the protection of a greenhouse. The information contained here is designed for very cold winter climates. The varieties selected make bigger grapes with thinner skins than outdoor varieties. They are hardy, but depend on protection and warmth to ripen in time, so they will not crop outside except in favourable years.

Growing dessert grapes under glass was raised to an art by the Victorians who could afford the heat and labour to produce perfect bunches of fine grapes almost every day of the year. Now cheaper greenhouses and plastic-covered tunnels are within the reach of most gardeners and many varieties can be grown with little or no extra heat, so these gourmet fruits are once again achievable.

Don't spurn small grapes; they are often sweetest and seedless

varieties

If you need to grow under glass, consult a table grape expert for the most suitable variety for the purpose. The following commonly grown dessert grape varieties are normally grown out in the open in Australia, where they will thrive under a hot sun and dry summer conditions: **Black Prince**, **Carolina Black**, **Calmeria**, **Cardinal**, **Chauch**, **Flame Seedless**, **Golden Muscat**, **Gordo**, **Italia**, **Lady Patricia** and **Maroo Seedless**. How well they will perform under glass is not guaranteed but, generally, there would be no need to resort to such practices in most of the southern hemisphere except perhaps for out-of-season fruiting. The information is designed for growers in climates where cold temperatures prevent outside culture of grapes.

cultivation

Amenable to almost any soil, they do not require rich conditions. The best varieties need a long season with an early start. With Victorian heating they were started into growth in early spring. Heat was used to keep them frost-free through spring, and again in autumn to finish off a late crop. However, in a good season, many varieties can be cropped under glass just with the extra natural warmth afforded, the more so if they are grown in pots and brought in after chilling outside.

DESSERT GRAPES

Growing in Containers
This is the only sensible way with grapes. They resent the confined root system and need careful watering and pruning, but become controllable. Several varieties can go in a greenhouse too small for one planted in the ground. In tubs they are also conveniently moved outside for winter chilling then brought under cover for an early start. This ripens them months sooner, allows several to be cropped in turn AND their sojourn outdoors after harvest until the following spring keeps them clean of pests and diseases.

Ornamental and Wildlife Value
Well-pruned vines in pots or trained on walls are very decorative. The framework is easily manipulable so almost any form can be achieved as long as all fruiting wood is kept at roughly the same level and in the light.

Pruning and Training
In pots and tubs vines are grown vertically or wound as spirals around a central supporting post or cane about 2m tall. Once the canes reach the top all further growth and side shoots are removed. Each autumn the canes are ruthlessly reduced to two buds on a stub of new growth, on three or four spurs on the stump. In spring the best four or five canes are chosen when the flowers have set, and all other canes are broken off and the remainder tied to the support. I now do not advise planting in the ground for vines under cover but if you must then the vine is best planted outside, trained in through a hole and then treated much as on a wall. This means wires about half a metre apart and nearly the same distance from the roof to allow for the annual growth. The vine framework is formed over the first year or three, covering the wires with main stems soon furnished with fruiting spurs. Thereafter these spurs shoot each spring, a flower truss appears between the third to fifth leaf, the best placed shoots are left and the surplus broken off. After three leaves beyond each flower truss each remaining shoot is tipped, as are any other further growths. Thinning the number of bunches is essential; leave no more than two per metre run of cane. Thinning the grapes in the bunch is tedious and only for show. In autumn the canes are all cut back to two buds out from each spur.

Pests and Diseases
Grapes can suffer many problems but usually still produce. If the air is too humid when grapes are ripening they may mould. If they are kept too dry before then they get mildew and red spider mite. However, the permitted sprays and usual remedies work well with most problems. Vine weevils can be excluded from vines in pots by making a lid that fits snugly around the stem.

Harvesting and Storing
Under cover they ripen early and hang longer as they are less threatened by pests or weather. Late varieties protected with paper bags may keep almost until the New Year.

Chasselas D'Or sets the standard for reliable sweet transparent yellow desserts

culinary

The dessert fruit *par excellence*, their juice is delicious and freezes well. For wine-making, the flavour and high sugar content go well in combination with outdoor grapes, which have lower sugar and higher acidity.

Recipe
Just eat them as they come, sun warmed.

companion planting

Grow French marigolds underneath the vines to help deter whitefly.

other uses

Pieces of old vine, detached when pruning, make good supports for climbers in pots.

Vitis vinifera from the family *Vitaceae*

GRAPES
OUTSIDE AND FOR WINE

Vine. Life span: long-lived. Deciduous, self-fertile. Fruits: up to 2cm. Some vitamin value.

Vine grapes are as sweet, or more so, than dessert varieties. They have been bred to produce many small bunches rather than large berries, and this suits the vine's natural habit. The grapes are every bit as tasty, just smaller, and if you don't want the wine the juice is still valuable. They are hardier than dessert grapes and many are cropped commercially.

Although wine is predominantly produced in areas with a Mediterranean climate, with warm, temperate conditions, vineyards can be successful in many cool regions. The wines are usually light whites, but new hybrids now produce reds as well. Wine-making has become a popular pastime and its growing popularity means hobbyists need to consider the health of vines as a top priority to protect an important commercial industry.

Reds are more disease-free

varieties

Most wine grapes in Australia are *V. vinifera*, the European grape grafted onto an American rootstock resistant to *Phylloxera*. **Chardonnay**, **Riesling** and **Traminer** produce white wines for cool regions. **Pinot Noir**, **Cabernet Sauvignon** and **Meunier** are grown for red wine. **Meunier** and **Pinot Noir** are not vigorous vines compared to **Cabernet Sauvignon** or **Riesling**. Moderately warm regions are ideal for growing **Semillon** (producing a Sauterne-like white wine), **Malbec** and **Merlot**, which are both red wine grapes.

Ripening Boskoop Glory

Sauvignon Blanc similarly does well in these warmer regions. Hotter climates require special varieties such as **Colombard**, **Ruby Cabernet** or **Muscat Gordo**. **Colombard** grapes produce a fruity white wine. Different varieties are suited to different regions so it is worth investigating the best ones for your location. Any of the outdoor dessert grapes may be used to make wine, to add flavour or just to juice. Indeed this is really their better use as a good juice can be enjoyed from grapes not quite ripe enough to eat.

cultivation

Rich soils should be avoided as they will grow excessively. Obviously the warmer and sunnier the better; wires and supports should ideally run north–south, to give sun on both sides of each row.

Ornamental and Wildlife Value

A vineyard is quite an accessory to any estate. Quote in bottles per year – it sounds bigger. The aim is two bottles per square metre/yard. The wildlife are certainly going to like your vineyard unless you invest in netting against rabbits, rodents and birds.

Pests and Diseases

The major losses are due to bird damage. Wet summers cause mouldy crops with little sweetness – little can be done about this. Mildew is best avoided by growing the more resistant varieties. Vine weevils are controlled by having clean cultivation and keeping chickens underneath, except when the fruit is ripening.

Pruning and Training

There are many different ways of treating vines outside. They can be grown with a permanent framework, as with indoor grapes or those on a wall, and this can be high or low, with benefits from air circulation or heat from the ground. Strong posts and wires up to shoulder

Whites are more prone to rots

GRAPES

height are probably best, so the fruit is borne high enough up to avoid soil splash. Thus the bottom wire should not be less than 30cm high. A modified form of Guyot pruning is often used instead of spur pruning. A short leg reaches to the bottom wire and supports a strong shoot, or two, of last year's growth tied down horizontally to fruit from the buds along its length. Two replacements are allowed to grow from the leg and all other new shoots there are removed. Fruiting shoots are nipped out a few leaves after the flower truss, as with other methods.

Harvesting and Storing
When the fruit has finally ripened enough, but before losses to the birds and mould have mounted, pick the bunches. A dry day after a rainy period gives cleaner bunches. Cut out mouldy bits as you go and press as quickly as possible for juice for drinking or for white wine. White wines can be made from black grapes; only certain Teinturier grapes have red juice. With most varieties the colour only comes from fermenting the skin. Red wines are fermented entire, with the grapes merely mashed. The juice is pressed from the pips and skins later. Extra pips and skins of those squeezed for juice can be added with benefit to the red wine mix as they increase the tannins and sweetness.

companion planting

Asparagus is sometimes grown with the vines in France.

other uses

The vine prunings make good kindling. Big stems are often made into corkscrew handles.

culinary

The juice is one of the most satisfying drinks. It can be used from the freezer throughout the year and is useful as a sweetener. The wine may be even better.

Fruit Salad Soup
Serves as many as you like

Chop and slice finely as many fruits as available and serve in copious grape juice with cream or yogurt and macaroon biscuits.

Triomphe d'Alsace

ANNUAL TENDER FRUITS

Annual tender fruits, such as melons, tomatoes and courgettes, are amazing. They are tender plants from tropical regions, yet they are widely eaten and grown, despite their need for frost-free conditions, in almost every country across the world. They are fruits which are used as often, if not more, for savoury dishes as for sweet. Melons can be grown right across Australia, from the Top End to Victoria, but they need warm conditions in which to ripen. In cool, temperate conditions they benefi t from the protection of a greenhouse or fl eece until late spring or early summer.

Annual tender fruits are mostly very short-lived perennials in their native lands and are grown as annuals in cultivation. They are all, except the hibiscus, in two families: the Solanums and the Cucurbits. Perhaps another common point is that, despite any diffi culties in their cultivation, they can all produce prodigiously from a small area in a single growing season.

Another similarity between so many of these fruits is that, although each has some long-known and cultivated relations in each part of the globe, it was the great exploratory voyages of the sixteenth century that brought them to Europe. Hybridisation and development during the next centuries slowly made better, more hardy and productive varieties available. Annual tender fruits thus grew in popularity, both as a food to eat and in the garden. In particular, the colonisation of the Canary Islands allowed the winter cultivation of many of these fruits within shipping distance of the European markets. The development of cheaper glasshouses and steam boilers then allowed the Victorians to produce most of these fruits nearly year round.

In the garden the availability of myriad varieties has made it possible to grow these fruits in cooler regions with only an amateur greenhouse and a sheltered garden or warm wall. Faster fruiting and hardier varieties have been developed for the commercial market, and we now have thousands of different varieties from which to choose.

Almost every Australian home gardener plants a few tomato plants in their garden over summer – strange surroundings indeed for tropical South American plants!

Lycopersicon esculentum from the order *Solanaceae*

TOMATOES

Herbaceous. Life span: annual/short-lived perennial. Self-fertile. Fruits: from 1cm to 10cm weighing from a few grams to over 500g, red or yellow. Value: rich in vitamins A and C.

A sprawling climber normally grown as an annual, the tomato is perennial but short-lived and only survives where the temperature does not fall below about 15°C. The racemes of yellow fl owers are produced between leaf joints on the stems. Each fl ower is self-fertile, but better pollination is obtained by tapping the plant or by bees. The fruits have thick walls, making cells for the seeds in a thin jelly. In varieties such as San Marzano, an excellent culinary plum tomato, this jelly has been reduced; it is less watery and more fl esh-like.

Once known as Gold, Peruvian or Love Apples, the tomato was originally golden, rarely red, but now reds predominate, though yellow and striped varieties are sometimes grown. The early fruits were deeply ribbed and fl attened; the beefsteak variety Marmande still sometimes exhibits such an appearance. Tomatoes are fi rst recorded in 1554 in Italy, called Tomati. They had been found in Mexico, grown amongst maize, but originated from the mountains of Peru and had already long been cultivated in South America. They were only an interesting novelty for more than two centuries until becoming popular in Italy at the beginning of the nineteenth century and later throughout the USA, Europe and Australia.

varieties

There are many different types and varieties. There are those for greenhouse or outdoor culture; round or large ones with thin skins for salads, or thick-skinned ones for travel; plum varieties for juicing and cooking; cherry tomatoes for bite-size snacks. It is well to try several till you find what suits your site, soil and conditions.

cultivation

Tomatoes need warm, sunny sites, support and rich, moist soil. They can be grown outside in cooler areas only if started off early under cover. Although most crops are rotated, many biodynamic gardeners grow tomatoes on the same site every year, and may feed them with compost made from tomato leaves.

Growing under Glass

Tomatoes are most reliably grown this way in colder areas (see pages 102–3).

Growing in Containers

Tomatoes do best and are least work grown in the ground as they suffer many problems with the confined root run and sporadic watering in a pot. In the open garden grow tomatoes in the soil. Under glass, pots are still a poor alternative to the border soil, but see the greenhouse tomatoes on page 102.

Ornamental and Wildlife Value

Several tomatoes are useful decorative plants, for example, those bush varieties designed to trail in hanging baskets, such as **Tumbler**, the patio or dwarf varieties such as the delicious **Minibel**, and those with brightly striped fruits like **Tigerella**.

If you leave the ripe one on, fewer fruits will follow

TOMATOES

Small tomatoes give cleaner fruits as they never touch

Propagation
Tomatoes are easily grown from seed and they usually come true unless they are F1 hybrids. To save tomato seeds, scoop the pulp into a jar of water and allow them to ferment for two days in a warm room, sieve, wash the seeds, sieve again and dry well. Tips, suckers and detached shoots can be rooted and the stems layered.

Pruning and Training
Most tomatoes are grown on a single stem. This may be extended almost indefi nitely, limited only by the growing conditions. A single stem cordon may be vertical or sloping, for convenience, but tomatoes can also be trained with more stems as fans or espaliers. The stems need support, tied to a cane or wound round a string. Each stem needs frequent pruning, nipping out all side shoots from the leaf joints while small to prevent crowding. Some varieties are determinate (i.e. they form bushes and do not grow well as cordons). These kinds are not pruned, and all shoots are left to form a rambling bush, best supported on netting or straw to prevent the fruits touching the soil.

Weed, Pest and Disease Control
Tomato plants may suffer several problems, but are reliably productive, given basically good conditions. Whitefly and aphid attacks are a threat while the plants are small, but are easily remedied. Bird damage occurs to outdoor crops and several diseases may make the plants short-lived, but they should have set a good crop by then anyway.

Harvesting and Storing
Red tomatoes start green, ripening to yellow orange then red. They ripen best if left to hang, but green fruits can be ripened in any warm place. They are sundried in hot regions and can be frozen whole without preparation, but take less space puréed. (Slip the skins off frozen tomatoes by putting them in hot water just for an instant.)

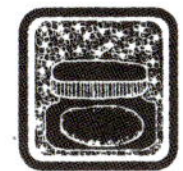

other uses

Surplus fruit feed poultry and many animals.

Classic companion planting with French marigolds

companion planting

Tomatoes should be kept away from brassicas and potatoes as they mutually suffer blight. French marigolds, basil, carrots, onions, garlic and asparagus are beneficial grown nearby.

culinary uses

Although definitely a fruit, tomatoes are now used predominantly in savoury dishes and as salad vegetables. The juice makes good stocks and sauces.

Bob's Economical Marmalade
Makes about 2.5kg

1kg yellow tomatoes
500g whitecurrants
1 lemon
Approx. 1kg sugar

Chop the tomatoes and simmer with the whitecurrants till soft, then strain. Add the squeezed and very finely sliced lemon to the juice and weigh. Bring back to the boil, add the same weight of sugar, boil till the sugar has completely dissolved, then pour into warm, sterilised jars. Cover at once.

Lycopersicon esculentum from the order *Solanaceae*

TOMATOES
GROWN OUTSIDE

Herbaceous. Life span: annual. Fruits: from 1cm to 10cm weighing from a few grams to over 500g, red or yellow. Value: rich in vitamins A and C.

Outdoor varieties are much the same as indoor ones and some are dual purpose, such as the superb Gardener's Delight. Generally, however, outdoor plants are hardier, preferring more airy conditions, and may suffer in the close humidity of a greenhouse. Outdoor varieties from hot countries are often not suitable for the low light and close, damp conditions in an equally hot, but northern greenhouse, and are better off grown in front of a hot wall, having been started off under cover.

I grow two lots: one reliable crop under glass and plastic, but I always prefer the fl avour of the crop grown and ripened outside, even if they are often beaten by the weather.

Much breeding has gone into making tomato plants hardier, so they can be grown further north, and faster, so that they can be cropped in a shorter time. This also helps us to grow them in the short summers at high latitudes, but even so they have to be started off under cover and planted out, so that the fruits can be ripening before the frosts of autumn kill the plants. Another serious problem with outdoor tomatoes is potato blight which is now affecting them most summers, indoor crops rarely suffer this until later if at all.

varieties

For sheer speed coming into production and for the ability to crop even in winter (under glass and kept warm of course) is **Sub Arctic Plenty**. (I grew this on a sunny windowsill some decades ago when it was released – apparently NASA or some agency had bred it to crop reliably in low light – it managed a couple of fruits in mid-winter though the plant was a pretty miserable sight.) Currently my favourite outdoor varieties, for flavour of course, are the small fruited **Gardener's Delight**, **Sweet Million** and the orange **Sungold**. For tasty usual-size fruits the potato-leafed **Stupice** is reliable and well flavoured. For outdoor productivity, the **Grosse Lisse** and **Tommy Toe** are also reliable, and the yellow **Golden Sunrise** sometimes fools the birds, who wait for it to ripen. Big beefsteak Marmande types like **Mortgage Lifter** produce massive, wonderful-tasting fruit early in the season, though you have to restrict each plant to only a couple of fruits at a time. Plum tomatoes such as **San Marzano** and **Super Roma** produce mid- to late season crops of egg-shaped fruit and are so tasty once cooked. They're also much more blight resistant than most other types. Other blight-resistant varieties include **Red Currant** and **Bite Size** cherries.

cultivation

A warm spot with full sun and rich, moist soil is needed, so incorporate copious quantities of compost beforehand. A shovelful of wood ashes per square metre will provide the potash that tomatoes crave. Shelter is very beneficial, so provide a good site in front of a sunny wall or, failing that, in front of other, tougher plants. Strong supports are essential, but in cool regions tomatoes are unlikely to swell, let alone ripen more than half a dozen trusses, so posts need only be shoulder high.

Growing in Containers

Tomatoes do badly in containers compared to growing in the soil, especially if they are unevenly watered. If no soil is available then a large, deep pot is better than a flat plastic bag, as it allows deeper roots with less risk of water saturation in the bottom. Grow plants singly. Do not plant several in a bag, as often suggested, as this produces fewer fruit for the same effort. Water religiously and feed frequently. Feed made from rotted

TOMATOES
GROWN OUTSIDE

down comfrey is perfect once diluted; seaweed and fish emulsion feeds are also benefi cial.

Ornamental and Wildlife Value

As suggested on page 98, tomatoes can also be used decoratively. Their value to wildlife is small, as the fruit often rots before it ripens. Self-sown seed also rarely lives long enough to reproduce itself.

Propagation

Start off outdoor tomatoes six to eight weeks before the last expected frost date. Sow them singly in small pots in a warm, light place. Pot them regularly, make sure they are well hardened off, protect them the first few nights, and again on cold nights. Plant them deep to encourage basal rooting.

Pruning and Training

Pot up often, support with a cane and nip out sideshoots. The first truss should be ready to flower when they go out. You should nip out the tip after six trusses.

Weed, Pest and Disease Control

The worst problems are cold weather and late frosts. In warm, damp seasons potato blight may cause problems, but it can be prevented with Bordeaux mixture. Birds eat the ripe fruits.

Harvesting and Storing

Pick the ripe fruit or protect it from the birds. Once frosts are likely, cut off the stems and hang them upside-down in a dry, airy shed to ripen the green fruit on the vines.

These need picking and using before they shrivel

other uses

The poisonous leaves have been used as a pesticide.

companion planting

Tomatoes should be kept away from brassicas and potatoes, as they mutually suffer blight. French marigolds, basil, carrots, onions, garlic and asparagus are benefi cial grown nearby.

culinary uses

Outdoor tomatoes have better flavour than those grown indoors, so I use them first for salads and then for drinking juice.

Stuffed Tomatoes

Serves 4

1 large onion
1 garlic clove
Knob of butter
1 large carrot
1 large potato
A few French beans, topped and tailed
1 cob sweetcorn
1 bunch of peas
Mayonnaise
Black pepper
4 large tomatoes

Chop and fry the onion and garlic in butter until transparent. Cool. Boil the carrot, potato, French beans, sweetcorn cob and peas till cooked. Drain and cool. Scrape the corn off the cob, cut the carrot and potato into pea-sized cubes and chop the beans into short lengths. Mix all together with enough mayonnaise to bind it, and add plenty of black pepper. Cut a lid off each tomato and hollow out the centre. Fill with the vegetable and mayonnaise mixture.

Lycopersicon esculentum from the order *Solanaceae*

TOMATOES
GROWN UNDER GLASS

Herbaceous. Life span: annual, potentially perennial. Fruits: from 1cm to 10cm weighing from a few grams to over 500g, red or yellow. Value: rich in vitamins A and C.

Greenhouse tomatoes are similar to outdoor varieties, but have been specially bred for rapid cropping in warm, low light conditions and for their disease resistance. Some will not grow outdoors at all, as they need shelter and warmth, but many varieties are dual purpose and grow happily in a favoured outdoor site.

It is quite amazing that a plant native to the mountains of tropical Peru could become a major commercial crop throughout the year in temperate countries of the world. The first winter tomatoes were brought from hotter regions such as the Canaries to the markets of Europe. Development of large greenhouses and heating allowed these tender fruits to be grown in favoured areas of Europe such as the Channel Islands. Eventually better varieties and improved technology made even the cool countryside of Holland one of the largest producers of salad tomatoes.

varieties

The best and quickest varieties change yearly. **Vivian** thrives both indoors and outdoors, while **Tiny Tim** is a good container plant. **Moneymaker** does well under glass, and the bite-sized **Gardener's Delight**, **Sungold** and **Suncherry** are best grown near the door where they get the cooler air and more importantly can be quickly got at for wee snacks. Likewise under cover **Super Roma** and **San Marzano** plum types prefer cool greenhouse conditions to steamy hothouses if you want them to produce loads of firm-fleshed cooking toms with superb flavour. If you want to get crops way out of season see **Sub Arctic Plenty** on page 100.

cultivation

The soil should be well enriched with copious compost, wood ashes and seaweed meal. Calcified seaweed or lime should be applied every other year and forked in. Ideally, automatic watering systems should be arranged, preferably to the roots to keep the foliage dry. Strong supports are also necessary for a good crop. Ensure ventilation and heating are adequate.

Pear-shaped toms are often best cooked

TOMATOES
GROWN UNDER GLASS

San Marzano

Growing in Containers

It is said that tomatoes should be grown in containers as the greenhouse soil becomes unsuitable for them with regular use. For most gardeners, the work of changing the soil every six years or so, if this degradation does occur, would still be less than the six years of carrying in and out all the containers full of potting compost and the extra water and feed they require. Still, if containers you must have, use big ones, one plant to each, and arrange a religious watering and feeding regime.

Ornamental and Wildlife Value

Patio and hanging varieties can both be used most decoratively, without taking up too much space, in either a conservatory or greenhouse. Tomatoes are happy in similar conditions to humans, while both find conditions for cucumbers and melons too humid.

Propagation

Best grown from seed for the cleanest plants, side shoots from existing stock can be layered or taken as cuttings. Plants for heated and lit greenhouses can be started at almost any time, although for heated greenhouses without lights, the earliest sowing time is late winter as otherwise there is not enough light to produce good growth or fruit as the plants mature. If the greenhouse cannot be heated, plants are best sown about six weeks before the last hard frost is expected.

Weed, Pest and Disease Control

Aphids and whitefly can appear and require the usual remedies. The worst problems are usually caused by poor growing conditions. Tomatoes need warmth, light and a buoyant atmosphere to crop well under glass; if it is humid and close they may get moulds. Blossom end rot is a black corkiness of the flower end of the fruit, often caused by poor watering of plants with a confined root system. Green tops to fruits are similarly caused, especially with high temperature conditions.

Pruning and Training

Good ventilation is essential under cover, so regular pruning is needed, usually to a single stem. Lower leaves are also removed, once they start to fade, to allow better air circulation. Obviously mouldy leaves, fruits and fl owers should all be removed just as soon as they are spotted.

Harvesting and Storing

Under cover, fruits can be left to hang but watch out for mould. With dry conditions in a frost-free but otherwise unheated greenhouse, they may still be usable off the vine in the winter. The fruits are said to ripen more quickly with bananas near them.

companion planting

Always have plenty of French marigolds as they keep whitefl y away. Alyssum is a good pollinator attractant and basil grows well with tomatoes, as they enjoy similar conditions.

other uses

Puréed plum tomatoes are an invaluable antidote to a dose of skunk perfume.

culinary uses

Tomatoes grown indoors seem to have less flavour and acidity than the same varieties grown outside. Nonetheless, they are delicious and glass protection lengthens the season for fresh tomatoes to more than half the year. Plum tomatoes are the best both for purées and pasta sauces.

Proper Breakfast

Per person, all quantities to taste

Pork sausages
Bacon
Plum tomatoes
Mushrooms
Eggs
Buttered toast
Mustard

First fry sausages and bacon and set aside to keep warm. Then slice the tomatoes in half and lengthways before frying with the mushrooms in the meat fat. Set these aside and fry the eggs. Serve altogether with some hot buttered toast and mustard.

Capsicum species from the order *Solanaceae*

HOT AND SWEET PEPPERS

Herbaceous to semi-shrubby, up to 1m. Life span: annual or perennial. Tender, self-fertile. Fruits: from 2.5cm to 15x7cm, spherical to box-shaped, often with dented sides. Usually yellow, green or red. Value: very rich in vitamin C.

A true fruit, though mostly used in a savoury manner, the capsicum, or sweet pepper, has large, oblong fruits, which are green, ripening to yellow, purple or usually red. These have thick, crunchy walls enclosing a void and small seeds adhering to white ligaments. The fruits of chillies, or hot peppers, are much smaller and pointed, usually green ripening red, and thin-walled. The fruits are borne singly, following the white flowers which come from leaf axils and where stems divide. Both plants are tender, with a long growing season, so need starting under cover and, in cooler regions, are best staying there.

The hot and sweet peppers come from tropical America, and are not closely related to white or black peppercorns, which are the seeds of a South Asian native climber, *Piper nigrum*. The first fruiting pepper in Europe was recorded in 1493 as having been brought back from the so-called New World with Columbus. It was pungent and all early interest was in the fiercely burning hot or chilli form, now called *Capiscum frutescens*. It probably helped to disguise the putrid food of the times. The subtler flavour of the milder, sweet peppers, *C. annuum*, were ignored until recent times, when they became particularly valued for salads, for flavour and for their high vitamin C content.

HOT AND SWEET PEPPERS

The fantastically hot, but incredibly, tasty Big Sun Habañero

varieties

Very much a matter of taste: **California Wonder** is a sweet and crunchy capsicum. **Big Bertha** has fruits that are bigger and blockier than even supermarket best. Tapering and sweet **Marconi** (**Rosso**) is very good, and **Chocolate** is as sweet and dark as its name. For hot peppers I like **Hungarian Hot Wax**, which is yellow to crimson depending when picked; it's mild and never gets too fierce. **Jalapeno** is long, thin and red hot, and like most chillies it's evil. **Cayenne** is the one for the pepper and **Tabasco** for the sauce. There are a staggering number of carefully selected fiendishly hot varieties from around the world, usually the smaller the fiercer. Take care with **Scotch Bonnet Peppers**, especially the very hot, very flavourful golden **Big Sun**; you have been warned!

cultivation

Easier than tomatoes, peppers will require a moderately rich, moist soil, warmth and light. Some support is needed for the huge crops. Otherwise they rarely have any problems.

Growing under Glass

I have succeeded in occasionally growing good crops outdoors, but unless the site is very warm and sheltered, these plants really require the protection of a greenhouse. Safe inside, they are then both admirable and productive subjects.

Growing in Containers

These are more suited than many plants to growing in pots. They must have careful watering and crops will be smaller, but they are neat and simple to look after. The pot size effectively controls that of the plant. Keep the sunny side of pots shielded with aluminium foil or white card as their roots will not grow into hot soil.

Ornamental and Wildlife Value

The compact habit, glossy foliage and brightly coloured fruits make these very attractive. The long chilli varieties are smaller-leaved and fruit even more prolifically, making them extremely decorative for a long time.

Propagation

Start the seeds off singly in small pots, keeping warm, light and airy as for tomato plants, and pot up regularly. They can also go in their final position once the warmth can be sustained, and outside after hardening off, but only in a very favoured spot. Cuttings can be taken

Peppers need cool roots so light coloured bags are good, if ugly

and the seed will come true of non-F1 varieties grown alone.

Pruning and Training

Nipping out the tips of leggy plants and supporting heavy crops are all that is needed. Take some fruits unripe to relieve any crowding.

Weed, Pest and Disease Control

The worst problem is whitefly and aphid attacks when the plants are seedlings, which may attack growth. Slugs will eat them and damage the fruits. Mould may appear in humid conditions in late autumn.

Harvesting and Storing

They can be eaten green, but are less challenging when ripe, which usually means dark red, when they have a rich, sweet flavour. Hot peppers are invariably cooked or pickled. The fruits can hang on the bushes for a while, especially the hotter varieties, but for long-term storage they are best sliced and dried or frozen. They travel well and should keep for days.

Green peppers, unpierced, cooked in rice will give it a divine flavour

You need a greenhouse or conservatory, or at least a coldframe, to grow these

other uses

The seeds and fruits have been used medicinally.

companion planting

These plants give off exudates that kill Fusarium moulds, so they benefit tomatoes grown nearby and enjoy similar conditions. Both will also get on well with basil.

HOT AND SWEET PEPPERS

Peppers drying

culinary uses

The seeds and white ligaments in hot peppers contain most of the pungent heat; removing them reduces it considerably. Paprika and pimento are made from hotter varieties of sweet peppers. Tabasco is made from fiery, small chilli hot peppers, and cayenne pepper is made from powdered dried fruits. Just because they are grown in a cool country does not make them any less hot.

Sweet Starter

Per person

1 dark red sweet pepper
Equal measures of chopped celery, grated apple, grated carrot, peas and mayonnaise
A half measure of chopped onion
Some paprika and a little parsley

Cut off the top of the pepper, remove the seeds and white ligament and fill with mixture of vegetables and mayonnaise, Garnish with a sprinkle of paprika and a sprig of parsley. (A measure of grated hard cheese can be included in the mix if wished.)

Solanum melongena from the order *Solanaceae*

EGGPLANTS AND HUCKLEBERRIES

Herbaceous, up to 1.5m. Life span: perennial grown as an annual. Fruits: variable size and shape, from 1cm spheres to 6x25cm cylindrical whoppers, purple, ivory or white.

Unlike tomatoes or peppers, eggplant (also known as aubergine) fruits are not sweet or edible raw. The large, purple, glossy, smooth-skinned fruits are carried on waist-high, stiff bushes with large, soft, almost downy leaves. The flowers are purple, resembling the potato more closely than the tomato, and spring from the stems between leaf joints. They frequently have spines on the stems.

Called the eggplant because the early forms, which you may still find, are white or ivory and egg-shaped, it was also known formerly as the mad apple. A native of Asia, it was unknown to the Ancient Greeks or Romans. Its first mention is in fifth-century Chinese writings. It became known in the Mediterranean region in the twelfth and thirteenth centuries from Arab sources, and finally reached northern Europe in the fifteenth and sixteenth centuries. However, it was still not widely grown in Europe until the nineteenth century. Even now, it is still not commonly appreciated.

varieties

The purple varieties dominate, with **Black Beauty** producing enormous fruits. Most varieties are similar in growth, so the larger-fruited ones make the best choice as there is much less waste when they are peeled. Avoid the white egg or funny shaped and most small-fruited varieties, except out of curiosity, as they are relatively poor croppers.

S. muricatum, **Alligator Pear**, **Melon Pear** or **Pepino**, is very similar to an eggplant but the oval purple-striped fruit is sweeter, more melon-like and can be used as a dessert fruit or cooked with sugar. This plant is a tender perennial, however, and can be productive for several years though prone to pests. *Solanum quitoense*, **Naranjilla** or **Quito Orange**, is a larger, decorative-leaved but spiny, half-hardy shoulder-high shrub which has small orange-like fruits which are much esteemed in their native Peruvian Andes for their sweet, fragrant green pulp.

Huckleberries, *S. intrusum*, are surprisingly closely related and similar with small insipid sweet black berries, remarkably like those of the poisonous *S. nigrum*, **Black Nightshade**. They come from Africa and are sometimes eaten in parts of North America though frequently confused in literature with **Viburnum Huckleberries**, and the far more popular **Gaylussacia Huckleberries**, which are *Ericaceae* much resembling *Vacciniums*.

Heavy crops need good supports before the plants topple

EGGPLANTS AND HUCKLEBERRIES

What does she polish them with?

cultivation

Eggplants and similar species all need warmer conditions than tomatoes or peppers and a long growing season. They need a rich, moist soil and some support for the heaviest crops.

Growing under Glass

Unless grown in very warm sheltered sites, eggplants need a greenhouse, though I find they do better in a polythene-covered walk-in tunnel.

Growing in Containers

Can be grown in large pots and are more amenable to this than tomatoes, but not as good as peppers. They need regular watering and feeding.

Ornamental and Wildlife Value

Not very attractive plants, rather dingy in fact, but the fruits can be impressive. They have little value to wildlife.

Propagation

Best grown from seed, which is, however, difficult to save. Cuttings may be possible. Start the seed off early and keep potting up until their final position is warm enough. Eggplants prefer warmer conditions than peppers or tomatoes, but do not like it as humid or shady as cucumbers or melons.

Pruning and Training

No pruning is needed. Removing dead leaves and any mould is good practice. The heaviest crops will benefit from support.

Weed, Pest and Disease Control

Given good conditions and a long growing season they are usually productive regardless of the odd aphid or red spider mite attack. These necessitate only vigilance and the usual remedies.

Harvesting and Storing

If left too long on the vine, the seeds form and make the fruits less desirable. Picked too small and young, they may be woody. They have a tough skin and travel well, keeping for up to a week or more. The fruits can be peeled, chopped, salted and fried in oil with garlic before freezing, when they are then useful for winter recipes.

companion planting

Eggplants need similar conditions to peppers and tomatoes. They are benefited by peas, beans, tarragon and thyme nearby.

The flower is typical *Solanaceae*

culinary uses

The tough peel is probably best removed. The flesh is often salted, and rubbed with lemon juice or garlic before cooking. Eggplants will absorb lots of oil and thus acquire flavour in early cooking, and later will become a thick purée.

Super Rat

Serves 6 (quantities are all approximate, add more or less according to taste and what is available)

1 large eggplant
Salt
1 garlic clove
1 large onion, sliced
Olive oil
2 zucchini
1 red and 1 green pepper
1 ear of sweetcorn
6 plum or cooking tomatoes
Red wine
Bread
Parmesan cheese
Black pepper

Peel and chop the aubergine. Salt and rub with garlic. Leave to stand for 10 minutes, then fry in the oil with the onion. Add the sliced courgettes, chopped red and green peppers, stripped corn and skinned tomatoes. Simmer slowly, adding a slug of red wine. When the vegetables have all softened, serve with bread, more wine and some grated cheese and black pepper.

Physalis **species from the family** ***Solanaceae***

CAPE GOOSEBERRIES
AND GROUND CHERRIES

Herbaceous. Life span: annual or short-lived perennial. Fruits: up to 6cm, yellow to purple in papery husk. Value: rich in vitamin C.

The *Physalis* are distantly related to tomatoes and potatoes. Their best known member is the old garden perennial **Chinese Lanterns**, *P. franchetii*, and the incredibly similar if slightly less vigorous and smaller-lanterned **Bladder Cherry**, *P. alkekengi*. Both have straggling stems, heart-shaped leaves, small pale flowers and bright orangey scarlet papery lantern calyces surrounding a red fruit. Both are often said to be poisonous – even though *P. alkekengi* has been eaten at least since the Greek Dioscorides in the third century AD, and many also think *P. franchetti* is but another variety, not a species! However, the calyce, foliage and even the fruits of some uncommon species are poisonous. ALL are dangerously similar – do not eat unknown unusual varieties!

The **Ground Cherry**, **Strawberry Tomato** or **Cossack Pineapple**, *P. pruinosa*, is low-growing, up to knee level, and has small, green fruits ripening to dirty yellow. Sweet and acid, they are vaguely pineapple-flavoured. *P. peruviana*, the **Cape Gooseberry**, **Ground** or **Winter Cherry**, is taller (about 1m) with yellower fruits. Both fruits are enclosed in similar, though duller, papery husks to those of the **Chinese Lantern**. Another similar fruit is the **Tomatillo** or **Jamberry**, *P. ixocarpa*, which is perennial, with much larger green or purplish berries filling the husk.

The annual *P. pruinosa*, which grows wild in North America, was popular with Native Americans and, apparently, also with Cossacks. It was introduced to England in the eighteenth century, but never caught on. The perennial **Cape Gooseberry**, *P. peruviana*, comes from tropical South America and became an important crop for the settlers on the Cape of Good Hope at the beginning of the nineteenth century. *P. ixocarpa*, the **Tomatillo** or **Jamberry**, comes from Mexico, but has become popular in many warm countries as it fruits easily and reliably and makes good sauces and preserves.

P peruviana

varieties

P. ixocarpa has some improved forms with fruits up to 6cm across, yellow or green instead of the usual purple. Named varieties include **Purple de Milpa** and **Toma Verde**. **Golden Gem**, *P. edulis*, is also available in Australia, producing medium-sized golden fruit.

cultivation

Seeds are best started under cover and planted out. The perennials ripen and crop outdoors until frost overtakes fruit production. They all prefer a rich, light, warm soil and a sunny position. Little support is really necessary, though they do flop.

CAPE GOOSEBERRIES
AND GROUND CHERRIES

P. ixocarpa

Growing under Glass
All the family give better and sweeter fruits grown under glass and present no major problems; indeed they seem to be designed for it.

Growing in Containers
P. pruinosa is easily grown in pots. The larger ground cherry can be grown in pots, but prefer a bigger root run. The decorative *P. alkekengi*, known as **Chinese Lantern**, is an ornamental and worth having in a pot just for the show it provides.

Ornamental and Wildlife Value
Most of the productive species are nowhere near as attractive as their more ornamental cousin, the **Chinese Lantern**. They have small value to wildlife, though the flowers are popular with insects.

Propagation
Normally grown from seed, the perennial varieties can be multiplied by root cuttings or division in the spring. Start them off early and pot up regularly to build up a large root system.

Pruning and Training
They need little attention other than tying in the lax growths and clearing away the withered stems after cropping. The roots of perennial varieties can be got through mild winters under protection for earlier crops the following year.

Pests and Diseases
They are remarkably pest- and disease-free. The **Tomatillo** is especially useful as it can be used much like a tomato, but can ripen as early in cool conditions and does not suffer blight as tomatoes may.

Harvesting and Storing
The fruits must be fully ripe to be edible. They can hang on the plant till required as they are rarely attacked by pest, disease or bird. The husk is inedible and must be removed.

companion planting

There are no known companion effects.

other uses

The ornamental **Chinese Lanterns** can be dried for winter decoration and have been used medicinally.

Pretty in a pot but not good eating

culinary

Most *Physalis* berries are relatively tasteless and insipid raw but make delicious preserves, sauces and tarts. The Cape Gooseberry often tastes best on first acquaintance and may rapidly lose its appeal after the initial elusive strawberry flavour. It was once imported in vast quantities from South Africa, when it was known as Tippari jam or jelly.

Tippari Jelly
Makes approx. 2kg

1kg Cape Gooseberries
A little water
Approx. 1kg sugar

Remove the husks from the fruit and boil them with just enough water to prevent the fruit from sticking. Strain the juice and add its own weight in sugar. Simmer till fully dissolved, skim off scum, then jar and seal.

Hibiscus/Abelmoschas esculentas and *sabdariffa* from the family *Malvaceae*

OKRA

LADIES' FINGERS, GUMBO AND ROZELLE

Herbaceous shrubs, up to 2m. Life span: annual. Selffertile. Fruits: long green seedpod/fl eshy sepal calyx. Minor nutrient value.

Hibiscus, now properly *Abelmoschas*, species are related to cotton and mostly known for the opulent fl owering sorts. However, two others provide fruits loved by culinary enthusiasts. *H. esculentus*, **Okra, Ladies' Fingers** or **Gumbo**, is the more common of the two. These are long, pointed, occasionally spiny, green seedpods that break down when cooked to a mucilaginous texture appreciated for thickening savoury dishes. The **Rozelle** or Roselle, the **Indian sorrel**, is a very similar plant, *H. sabdariffa*, commonly grown in India, Florida and its native West Indies. After the fl ower petals fall, the thick fl eshy sepals remain, forming a swollen calyx around the short fruit. These are made into sweet dishes; rozelle jams and jelly are even sold commercially. Both hibiscus are tender, shrubby annuals with a long growing season. The Rozelle has reddish stems. Okra fl owers are usually yellow and live for only an hour or two; Rozelle fl owers are red or white.

Okra comes from tropical Africa and has long been cultivated in the Middle East and India. In the nineteenth century it was seen growing wild on the banks of the White Nile. Okra was probably fi rst introduced to Europe by the Spanish Moors;

Abdul-Abbas el-Nebati, a native of Seville, described the plant in detail in 1216. As soon as the New World was discovered it travelled there and was known in Brazil in 1658. There are now many local varieties in the southern United States, where it is much appreciated, as well as in Africa and around the Mediterranean. The Rozelle, *H. sabdariffa*, travelled in the opposite direction, from the West Indies to Africa, and then on to India. In Asia they make a pickle from the petals of our familiar *H. rosa-sinensis*, the **Chinese Hibiscus**, and other species are used in much the same ways in many countries of the world.

You need about this many for a good gumbo

varieties

The fruits of **Clemson Spineless** are conveniently so. This is the most popular variety of okra. The fruits are best picked when small and the plant will then crop heavily. **Green Velvet** is also very good, velvet-fruited and heavy-cropping. The **Rozelle** is found in both red- or white-flowered forms and a greenish-fruited form known as **White Sorrel**.

cultivation

They need a warm, open soil and continuous unchecked growth. Stiff plants, usually growing only to waist height, the crops are light, so no support is necessary and they can be planted at 75cm apart.

OKRA

LADIES' FINGERS, GUMBO AND ROZELLE

Growing under Glass
In anything other than in a hot climate they must be grown under glass. Rozelle also needs hothouse conditions. Start them early as they have a long growing season, but only when you can give them enough warmth and light.

Growing in Containers
Okra resents confinement in pots and does best on hotbeds, as is the case with melons and cucumbers.

Ornamental and Wildlife Value
The flowers are brief and not showy and the fruits hard to spot. The okra flowers are valuable to insects in warmer climates.

Propagation
As these are annuals, they are grown from seed. They do best sown in situ.

Pruning and Training
They need no pruning or training, but the fruits must be picked as they swell. If not they prevent others forming and become tough and fibrous.

Weed, Pest and Disease Control
They may suffer from aphids, but red spider mite is not often a problem as long as there are sufficiently humid growing conditions.

Harvesting and Storing
Okra pods must be gathered while they are small or they prevent others forming and they get tougher. If there is a surplus they are best cut in half and dried. They can be stored thus in sealed jars or pulverised to a powder first.

companion planting

Okra gets on well with cucumbers and melons. The rozelle is often grown in hot countries as an intercrop between other slower plants while they are establishing. Both species must be kept away from cotton as they share pests and diseases.

other uses

The seeds apparently make the best substitute for coffee beans.

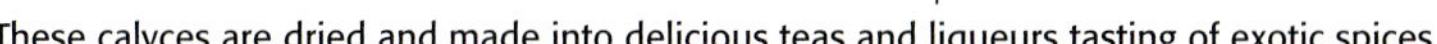

These calyces are dried and made into delicious teas and liqueurs tasting of exotic spices

culinary uses

Fresh or dried okra is added to soups, stews and casseroles especially in Egyptian, Indian and Creole cuisine. The seed pods may be battered and deep fried or, pickled young, they can be pickled like capers. Rozelle fruits are made into delicious tarts, a beverage called sorrel drink, puddings, jam and jelly.

Gumbo
Serves 4

500g thinly-sliced okra
3 small onions, sliced
2 garlic cloves, crushed
25g butter
1 large red pepper, chopped
4 large cooking tomatoes, peeled
½ teaspoon cayenne pepper
Salt, to taste
900ml good meaty stock
75g long-grain rice, pre-soaked in cold water for 1 hour

Fry the okra, onions and garlic for 5 minutes in the butter. Add the chopped pepper, tomatoes, cayenne pepper and salt. Add the stock and simmer for an hour or two. Add the rice and simmer for at least 30 minutes before serving.

Cucumis melo from the family *Cucurbitaceae*

MELONS

Herbaceous vine. Life span: annual. Self-fertile but requires assistance as separate male and female flowers. Fruits: 5–25cm spheres, whiteish cream to green, netted or smooth. Value: rich in vitamins A and C, niacin and potassium.

Melons belong to a very wide family of tender, trailing annual vines, much resembling cucumbers in habit. They have broad leaves, softly prickled stems and small yellow flowers, followed by fruits that can be any size from small to very large, round or oval. Melons are characterised by a thick, inedible rind covering succulent, melting flesh, which encloses a central cavity and a battalion of flat, pointed oval, whitish seeds.

The tasty, sweet, aromatic melons we know were apparently unknown to the Ancients. They certainly grew similar fruits, but these seem to have been more reminiscent of the cucumber. Pliny, in the first century AD, refers to the fruits dropping off the stalk when ripe, which is typical of melons, but they were still not generally considered very palatable. To quote Galen, the philosopher-physician, writing in the second century AD, 'the autumn (ripe) fruits do not excite vomiting as do the unripe'. By the third century they had become sweeter and aromatic enough to be eaten with spices, and by the sixth and seventh centuries they were distinguished separately from cucumbers.

The first reference to really delicious, aromatic melons comes in the fifteenth and sixteenth centuries, probably as the result of hybridisation between many different strains. The seeds were left wherever humans ventured. Christopher Columbus returned to the New World to find melons growing aplenty where his previous expedition had landed and eaten the odd meal of melons, liberally discarding the seeds. Likewise, both deliberately and inadvertently, melons have reached most warm parts of the globe and are immensely popular crops for the home garden in many countries. The Victorians developed reliable varieties that were successfully cropped year-round under glass, but in Australia they are grown outside where summers are not too humid and temperatures not too cool.

MELONS

varieties

There are countless varieties, literally hundreds if not thousands, and many more go unrecorded worldwide. Most of those that are available, either as seed or commercially, fall into three or four main groups. **Rockmelon** or **Cantaloupe** varieties usually have orange flesh. The fruits tend to be broadly ribbed, often with a scaly or warty rind, but not netted. The flesh is sweet and aromatic. For home gardens, grow **Hale's Best**, resistant to powdery mildew, or **Planters Jumbo**, which has excellent colour and flavour. **Early Dawn** is an early-maturing variety. **Honeydew melons** have a white or yellow skin and sweet green flesh. **Honey Melon** has large fruit while **Greenflesh** has cream skin. **Dewcrisp** is a popular commercial variety. **Galia melons** are an Israeli strain. They are round with green to yellow skin turning to gold. The green flesh is very sweet and popular in Europe. **Musk melons** are netted or nutmeg melons and have distinct netting, lighter in colour and raised from the yellow or green rind. The major variety grown in Australia is **Emerald Delight**. **Hami melons** originated in China and several hybrids are available. They are oval with a speckled skin and pale salmon flesh.

cultivation

Melons are not difficult if soil is prepared before planting with well-rotted manure and organic matter. Plants are grown in well-drained positions often on mounds spaced 1m apart. They prefer even temperatures around 21–25°C and fruit takes four to five months to mature. They are not suitable for cool summer areas. Fruit is prone to fungal attack, especially powdery mildew, so avoid overhead watering. Long wet periods and high humidity can damage the crop. Ground irrigation in the morning is preferable. Sow seeds July to October in southern Queensland; September to December in coastal New South Wales and Western Australia; October in northern Victoria. Flowers are only open for a short time, so hand pollination with a small brush may be needed to encourage fruit set.

Growing under Glass

This is only necessary in cool climates or where summer warmth is less than the required time needed for maturing of the fruit. Usually melons are grown in the open with great success. Some may prefer to start seedlings early in a greenhouse or cold frame for a quick start when the weather warms. Cold greenhouses can produce light crops, heated ones far more. A cold frame or curtained area in the greenhouse is better still, and the ease of providing extra warmth and humidity more than makes up for the diminished light. A cold frame set on a hotbed, or with soil-warming cables, in a greenhouse or polytunnel, is the best environment attainable by the average gardener and can produce an impressive crop. Indoors, pollination is advisable as a precaution.

Yellowing is a sign of approaching heaven

Growing in Containers

Melons are one of the easiest plants to crop well in a large pot, provided they are kept warm, well watered and fed regularly with a liquid feed. (I even grow them successfully in bags of fresh grass clippings topped off with a bucketful of sieved garden compost to seal in the heat and smell. The seed is sown direct in a mound of sterile compost set on top of that and covered with a plastic bottle cloche. The bag stands in my polytunnel, a self-contained mini hotbed. When the plant is growing, the bottle is reversed to make a useful watering funnel.)

Ornamental and Wildlife Value

These are not really very decorative plants, but can impress with their luxurious growth. The scent of ripening melons is heavenly. The fruits are well liked by rodents and birds, making these useful for the wild garden in warmer countries.

Cantaloupe

Propagation

Melons are normally started from seed, which does not come true when self-saved unless you are very careful, as Cucurbits are promiscuous cross-pollinators. The seed needs warm, moist conditions to start and the plants need continuous warm, rich, humid conditions. Avoid the roots making a tight ball in the pot, but do not over-pot. The stems can be layered or even taken as soft cuttings to continue the season.

Pests and Diseases

Providing the growing conditions are just right, melons usually suffer no major problems. The slightest drop in humidity and two-spotted mites may need controlling, as this can check the plants. It is worth introducing the commercially available predator *Phytoseuilis persimilis* if mites are spotted. Aphids and whiteflies sometimes appear, requiring the usual remedies. Melons do suffer occasionally from neck rot where the stem enters the soil, usually during cold conditions. Sterile compost, warmth and clean, carefully applied water usually prevent any occurrence. European Victorian gardeners always grew melons on little mounds to keep the neck dry. If neck rot appears, rub with sulphur dust and then earth up with moist, gritty compost to encourage rooting from the base of the stem. Rodents and slugs attack the fruits.

Harvesting and Storing

Their heavily perfumed, aromatic sweetness and luscious, melting texture make them divine when ripened to perfection – though too often they are taken young to travel and are then not sweet, but woody and never well perfumed. For sybarites, they really must be ripened on the vine until they are dropping – the nets are not there to support but to catch the fruits! Once they are ripe enough to scent a room, the fruits should be chilled before eating to firm the flesh and then removed from the refrigerator a short while before serving to allow the perfume to emerge fully.

A tile slipped underneath prevents a yellow bottom

At this stage, beware of slugs creeping in

companion planting

Melons like to ramble under sweetcorn or sunflowers, enjoying their shelter and dappled shade. They also get on with peanuts, but do not thrive near potatoes. **Morning Glory** seed sown with melons is said to improve their germination. Most of all, melons need the same hot, humid conditions as cucumbers and there seems little problem with their pollinating each other. However, there might be if you want to save seed.

other uses

Melons accumulate a great deal of calcium in their leaves, making them especially useful for worm compost. The empty shells make good slug traps. *Cucumis melo dudaim*, **Queen Anne's Pocket** melon, is grown for its strong perfume, but the flesh is insipid.

MELONS

Melon chutney

culinary

Quintessentially a dessert fruit, melons are nevertheless most often served as a starter in the place of savoury dishes. They may be combined with savoury or sweet dishes and are exquisite as chunks combined with Dolcelatte cheese and wrapped in Parma ham. Melons can be made into jam or chutney, added to compôtes, and used as bowls for creative cuisine.

Melon Sundae

Quantities to taste

Ripe melon
Vanilla ice cream
Toasted flaked almonds
Sultanas
Honey
Dark chocolate
Glacé cherries

Remove balls of melon with a spoon. Layer these in sundae glasses with scoops of vanilla ice cream, almonds and sultanas. Then pour over the melon juice thickened with honey. Top with grated dark chocolate and a glacé cherry.

Cucumis sativus from the order *Cucurbitaceae*

CUCUMBERS

Herbaceous vine. Life span: short. Fruits: variable in size and shape, normally 4–5x25–30cm, but some 'mini' ones are 2–4x12cm, green. Vitamin value: poor.

Cucumbers are tender, short-lived, perennial, scrambling vines, very closely related to, and resembling, melon plants but with matt, grapevine-like leaves and long, green fruits. These may be prickly, especially in the hardier outdoor varieties, and the very similar gherkins, *C. anguira*. We prefer these fruits to be green and unripe, not mature and bloated as we do those of most other crops.

Originally from southern Asia, cucumbers were grown by the Ancient Greeks and Romans. Early varieties were incredibly bitter and used more medicinally than culinarily. Breeding parthenocarpic fruits that swell without being pollinated has fruits with no bitterness, and their tendency to cause flatulence has been decreased. Recent all-female versions have been improved to the point of trustworthiness.

varieties

Indoor cucumbers are smooth-skinned, and modern all-female F1 varieties remove the chore of continuously searching for and eliminating male fl owers. Australian F1 varieties like **Carmen**, **Saroya**, **Neptune** and **Biet Alpha** have proved remarkably productive as, like the plethora of other newer varieties, they have excellent disease resistance. The old varieties **Telegraph** and **Telegraph Improved** are still preferred by some for growing in cold greenhouses and frames, as are the **Amazon** and **Jasper** hybrids. Japanese cucumbers such as **Kyoto** are usually longer and not as uniformly shaped as indoor varieties; they can do well indoors though intended for outdoors and are staggeringly productive! Outdoor or ridge cucumbers are shorter fruits, very prickly. They are grown outdoors but started off earlier under cover. **Burpless Tasty Green**, **Masterpiece** and **Marketmore** are popular. Gherkins such as **Cornichon de Paris** are very similar to ridge cucumbers, though with a different genetic ancestor; they have prolifi c small prickly fruits that must be picked while still small. Odd heirloom varieties are interesting such as **Boothby's Blonde**, a creamy yellow pickler. **Crystal Apple** is another old variety; it produces round apple-sized fruits which are thought especially tasty.
Femspot

CUCUMBERS

cultivation

All cucumbers need rich, moist soil, though outdoor varieties and gherkins demand less than indoor sorts. The indoor varieties require similar warm, humid conditions to melons; like the latter they do well on hotbeds and do not share well with Solanums. Despite the name, ridges are not at all necessary for outdoor varieties, but all cucumbers are best started atop small mounds to keep their necks dry and prevent neck rot.

Growing under Glass
Indoor varieties must be grown under glass; they need heat and high humidity. Outdoor varieties, especially Japanese and gherkins, may be grown in coldframes and unheated greenhouses to advantage, with the opportunity of earlier and longer cropping.

Growing in Containers
Cucumbers crop in large pots fairly easily, but need careful watering and feeding. The soil must always be moist but should never be wet, especially around the cucumber neck.

Ornamental and Wildlife Value
Outdoor varieties can be grown over arches or a trellis, but have little wildlife value.

Pruning and Training
No pruning is needed, but tying in must be done regularly as cucumbers scramble, needing support indoors. Outdoors they are best grown over straw or on a trellis. Indoor fruits must be pollinated, so remove all male flowers; with the outdoor varieties, however, this does not matter.

Gherkins and Ridge Cucumbers have small spines

Weed, Pest and Disease Control
Cucumbers are susceptible to neck rot (see page 116 for treatment) and cucumber mosaic virus. They can get red spider mite badly if not kept humid enough and in fact commercial predator introduction is almost a necessity. Mildews and other diseases are rarely a problem with modern varieties. Leaves may scorch in bright sun, necessitating shading.

Harvesting and Storing
The end swelling on indoor fruits means that they are pollinated and will be bitter, so the swellings should be removed before they prevent others setting. For the same reason fruits should be removed before they swell – though they were once preferred in this fully ripe stage. Gherkins are picked sooner and more frequently.

You cannot pick gherkins too small

companion planting

Indoor cucumbers grow well with melons. They will also benefi t from tansy and dill, which goes well with them in pickles. Outdoor cucumbers will enjoy the light shade of sunfl owers or sweetcorn. All prefer to be near peas, beans, carrots or radish, not near potatoes or strong herbs.

other uses

The fruits have long been used as a skin conditioner and medicinally.

culinary uses

Eaten raw with salads and savoury dishes, cucumbers may also be cooked or pickled. Outdoor cucumber and gherkins are most usually pickled.

'More tea, Vicar?' Sandwiches

Cucumber
Malt vinegar
Soft white bread
Butter

Slice the cucumber very thinly and leave it soaking in the vinegar. Thinly slice the bread, thickly butter it and sandwich the drained cucumber between. Remove the crusts and cut into triangles before serving.

Citrullus lanatus/vulgaris from the family *Cucurbitaceae*

WATERMELONS

Herbaceous vine. Life span: annual. Self-fertile. Fruits: variably large, green. Value: rich in vitamins and minerals; a serving contains more iron than spinach.

Watermelons are scrambling, climbing vines. Their leaves are darker, more bluey-green, hairy and fern-like than melon leaves; the flowers are similar, small and yellow. Watermelon fruits vary in size from small to gigantic, from light green to dark green or yellow in colour. The thin, hard rind is packed with red flesh, embedded in which are small, dark seeds. Eating the very juicy flesh is like drinking sweet water.

This productive and nutritious, thirst-quenching fruit comes from Africa and India, but was first mentioned by botanists and travellers in the sixteenth century. The fruit became widely cultivated, but it appears to have been little improved until it reached North America. There it was developed to produce examples weighing over 45kg and many varieties with different coloured flesh, rind or seed. These included a sub-group with ornamental 'painted', 'engraved' or 'sculptured' seeds.

varieties

The flesh is always exceedingly juicy and sweet and red, but once it varied in colour with black, white, cream, brown, purple and yellow-fleshed forms. Now few varieties other than the reds are grown on any scale. The most popular large-fruited type is **Candy Red**, resistant to fusarium wilt and anthracnose. It weighs up to 14kg. **Sugar Baby** is small, only 4kg, and takes up less room in the row. **Country Sweet** is good for fruit salad while **Minilee** is small but very sweet.

cultivation

Warm (21°C plus), well-aerated soil is necessary. If necessary, pre-warm the site with opaque plastic sheet laid flat, with another clear sheet raised above on sticks or whatever. Start in warmth and do not plant out in cold, or the roots will rot. Although copious water is needed at the roots to swell the large fruits, watermelons prefer less humid conditions. They also do not need the same high degree of fertility and thrive in any reasonable sandy soil, as they benefit from watering as much as from feeding. In temperate areas with hot summers, the watermelon can be grown outdoors as it produces more quickly than the melon does.

Growing under Glass

Grow watermelons in mounds or hills spaced 2m apart and set two or three plants in each hill. If sun is particularly hot, the fruit can scald. Protect it with its own leaves or temporary shade protection. Temperatures under 25°C limit flower and fruit set but there are cool tolerant varieties like **Sweet Siberia** available from heirloom seed suppliers.

Growing in Containers

Watermelons can be grown in large pots though they resent the restricted root run and lack of aeration. Use an open, gritty compost and ensure that regular watering and feeding are maintained throughout the season.

WATERMELONS

Ornamental and Wildlife Value
The vines are much more decorative than those of melons. The fruits are appreciated by wildlife in hotter countries.

Propagation
These are readily started from seed, but need regular potting up. Watermelons are not as easy to layer as melons. They prefer clay pots to plastic ones and react very badly to over watering or to compaction of the compost.

Pruning and Training
Watermelons do not need stopping like melons, but it is a good idea to limit each vine to one fruit to ensure a decent size. The plants are best allowed to ramble. If they are trained up anything, provide support for the immensely heavy fruits. On the ground they are best laid on straw or a tile to keep them clean.

Pests and Diseases
Very prone to two-spotted mites. Introduce predatory mites to control them. Although watermelons like it as warm as melons, a similar degree of humidity does not suit them and will aggravate attacks by mites. Fusarium wilt is kept in check by crop rotation. Sunburn can lead to fungal attacks where the fruit is scalded so provide some cover on hot days.

Harvesting and Storing
Watermelons are ripe when they sound taut and 'hollow' to a tap from the knuckle. If they are really ripe and well grown they will split open as soon as the knife bites. However, if left intact, they will keep for a week or more.

companion planting

Watermelons do not object to potatoes, as melons do, and may run amongst the plants to advantage in warm countries.

Although small when grown in the UK, they still get luscious and very sweet

other uses

The closely related *Citrullus colocynthis*, **Colocynth**, **Bitter Gourd**, is like a small, intensely bitter watermelon. It is used medicinally and occasionally pickled or preserved after many boilings.

culinary

Watermelons are best eaten fresh. Their seeds may be eaten – they are oily and nutritious. The pulp can be made into conserves, or reduced to make a sugar syrup.

Watermelon Ices
All quantities to taste

Watermelon
Melted chocolate
Grated desiccated coconut

Freeze bite-size cubes of watermelon on a wire tray. Once they are frozen solid, dip each quickly in cooling melted chocolate, sprinkle with grated coconut and freeze again. Serve them nearly defrosted, but still just frozen, with piped cream and macaroon biscuits, if liked.

Cucurbita pepo and species from the order *Cucurbitaceae*

SQUASHES

PUMPKINS, MARROWS AND GOURDS

Herbaceous vine. Life span: annual. Fruits: variable, from 10cm spheres to 1m flattened spheres, in yellow, orange or green. Value: riboflavin (vitamin B2), niacin, potassium and vitamin A.

These are very vigorous, tender, rambling vines with enormous leaves and big yellow flowers followed by fruits in all sizes, shapes and colours, but usually green or yellow. There is an immense number of closely related and interbred species and varieties. Marrows are large and cylindrical; zucchini (courgettes) are the same but small. Most squashes are round or bottle-shaped; Custard or Scalloped Squashes have a distinctive pie-like appearance. Hubbard and Turban Squashes are keepers for winter use. They are richer in nutrients and vitamin A than the summer sorts. Pumpkins are very large, round and usually orange or yellow.

Various members were grown for millennia in Africa, the Americas and Asia. They only appeared in Europe in the sixteenth century, and over the next centuries developed into the myriad forms we know today. Marrows, courgettes and zucchini are respectively the English, French and Italian developments, while most squashes and pumpkins come from North American strains. All are similar in most ways and promiscuously hybridise all too readily.

You cannot give them too much sun

varieties

In these more than in most, variety is a matter of taste. Try them all for yourself. I believe zucchini such as the ridged **Romanesco**, prolific **Blackjack** and **Greenskin** or mini **Bambino** give the best value. Avoid novelty spherical, coloured or tapered varieties if usable production is your aim. Summer squashes do not store, and come when much else that's tastier is available, though **Patty Pan**, despite its silly shape, is a favourite. Winter squashes are for storing so are far more useful; the **Butternut** series are proving widely popular. **Crown Prince** is tasty, very long keeping and

At this stage rest it on a smooth board or brick to improve the bottom

Courgettes are best taken small then more come

has a blue skin. **Gold Nugget**, and **Queensland Blue** pumpkins keep well with good flavour, but I find many squash, especially **Spaghetti Marrows**, disappointing. If American and European varieties are not enough, many more species are grown around the world. *Momordica charantia*, the **Balsam Apple/Pear** or **Bitter Gourd**, *Trichosanthes cucumerina*, the **Snake**, **Serpent**, **Viper's** or **Club Gourd**, and *Sechium edule*, the **Chayote**, are all very similar tropical Cucurbits used culinarily – the last for sweet as well as savoury dishes. **Chayote** also furnishes an edible farinaceous root rather like a yam to taste.

cultivation

A warm, rich, moist soil is needed for full cropping. They are all happiest growing on a compost or muck heap. Spacing depends on variety; compact bush zucchini need only a metre apart, but pumpkins will need more room.

Growing under Glass
Some of the more tender species such as **Loofahs**, *Luffa cylindrical*, **Lagenaria Gourds** and **Cushaw Pumpkins/Crookneck Squashes**, *C. mixta/ moschata*, can be grown under cover to advantage, if the space is available. Zucchini are often grown under glass for early crops, but produce mostly male fl owers if kept too hot.

Growing in Containers
These can be grown in large pots if given copious water and feed, but they are much smaller than when they are given a piece of ground to romp in. Propagation These are started from seed. The plants hybridise, so it is best not to save seed. Old seed is said to give more female flowers. They are most reliable sown one per pot, potted up often, hardened off and planted out once the last frost is past, but sown in situ they tend to make better plants.

Pruning and Training
These may be trained over a trellis or arches. Remove zucchini as fast as they form. No pruning will be necessary for these plants.

Ornamental and Wildlife Value
Some colourful fruited varieties, especially the inedible gourds, are very attractive. The seeds are loved by rodents.

Weed, Pest and Disease Control
They are so vigorous that they rarely suffer from weeds.

Storing squash must have a decent length of stem attached

Silly shapes waste flesh!

Virus infections may occur occasionally from dirty water, and slugs, snails and late-summer powdery mildew can cause problems. Generally, however, these are considered to be productive and trouble-free crops.

Harvesting and Storing
Zucchini are best picked often and while small. Remove swollen large ones anyway, or they will prevent others forming. Summer squashes and marrows are best before full size is reached. Pumpkins and winter squashes need to ripen on the vine to store well and may keep over several months. To keep well they must have a finger-length stub of stem left attached to shrivel and dry up.

They get bigger given some support underneath

companion planting

Grow these rambling under sweetcorn or near peas and beans, but not near any potatoes. Datura weeds may make the plants healthier.

other uses

Luffa cylindrica is very similar. Usually grown under glass in Britain, **Loofahs** are the prepared dried fruits. *Lagenaria siceraria*, is the **Bottle Gourd**, the dried fruits of which are used as containers.

SQUASHES

PUMPKINS, MARROWS AND GOURDS

Their flavours go well together

culinary uses

These are used in a multitude of ways – baked, boiled, jammed, served in sauces, pickled, chutneyed or fermented. There are hull-less seeded varieties to make eating the nutritious kernels easier: these are good raw or fried and salted. Even the flowers are considered edible, stuffed or fried in batter.

Marrow and Ginger Jam
Makes about 2.5kg

1.5kg marrow
1 large lemon
Approx. 1kg sugar
7g powdered ginger

Peel the marrow, removing the loose flesh with seeds. Cut the firm flesh into bite-sized chunks and mix in the juice of the lemon. Weigh and add half the weight in sugar. Leave in a cool place overnight. Strain off the juice and bring to the boil. Add the strained chunks, ginger and finely sliced lemon rind. Bring back to the boil again and simmer for half an hour. Add the same weight of sugar again, bring to the boil, then skim and pot into sterilised jars.

PERENNIAL TENDER FRUITS

Whereas the annual tender fruits are nearly all members of just two families, these perennial fruits are diverse, each belonging to a different family. Indeed, in some cases they are the only, or the main, constituent members of that family – loquats and pomegranates, for example. Others such as the passion fruits and persimmons have many similar and edible relations worldwide.

With the exception of Actinidia, all these fruits have long been in cultivation and their use from wild stocks pre-dates history, so early on they spread well beyond their native lands. This is probably due to the fact that most of them possess thick, rind-like skins and thus have some ability to travel and store well, when compared with other fruits, anyway. Certainly it is otherwise hard to see why a fruit such as a pomegranate, which is relatively poor value, could be so widely distributed at such an early date.

The human desire for new tastes and flavourings made each of these fruits an important item of commerce, as they are all distinctly different from other fruits. Once sampled, they become desired, and as world trade started to increase in the seventeenth century, most of them became expensive luxuries and thus indispensable for the developing European, and later the American, markets. We are sometimes deluded by our supermarkets piled high with exotic fruits into thinking we have such largesse by virtue of our 'modern' skill and cunning. Far from it. Many such fruits were widely on sale in 'olde' England. After all, Nell Gwynne, the mistress of King Charles II, was a street orange seller by trade.

At first, the difficulties of long-distance transport prevented these fruits from saturating the market, even though they could survive longer journeys than most. However, they had become common by the Victorian era, as increased production in warm temperate regions, such as around the Mediterranean basin and in California and Florida, displaced longer-distance imports. These areas became so competitive that few of these fruits have ever become worth growing commercially under glass in colder regions, despite the relative ease with which they can be cultivated.

The other interesting connection between these fruits is that they are all very nearly hardy, or have nearly hardy members which can survive in quite northerly, cool countries. The gardeners of the time of Henry VIII, and for the next century or two after, believed that if you kept moving plants northwards they would slowly acclimatise. They built the great orangeries of Europe, at tremendous cost, to overwinter the fruit trees while they grew hardier. Of course, these plants still need glass and heat to ripen crops. Nonetheless, all of them can be grown for a while, even if not fruited, outdoors in a cold country such as England, despite their origins in much warmer regions. Perhaps the early gardeners were right after all, but they were mistaken in looking for improvements in a few generations, not over hundreds of years.

Citrus species from the family *Rutaceae*

LEMONS, ORANGES
AND OTHER CITRUS FRUITS

Tree/bush up to 8m. Life span: medium to long. Evergreen, self-fertile. Fruits: variable size, orange, green or yellow. Value: rich in vitamin C.

Citrus fruits of the *Rutaceae* family are small, glossy-leaved evergreens with green stems that are occasionally thorny, especially in the leaf axils. Typical of this family, the leaves have glands which secrete scented oil. The small, white, star-shaped flowers are intensely and similarly perfumed, and are followed by the well-known fruits, which take up to a year to ripen. These swell to a size which ranges from that of a cherry to a human head, depending on the species. They are yellow or orange with light-coloured flesh inside a tough, bitter and scented peel. The flesh is sweet or sour, always juicy, and segmented. Each piece may contain a few small seeds.

Originally from China and Southeast Asia, some species and closely inter-related cultivars have been in cultivation since prehistory. They moved slowly westward to India and then on to Arabia and thence to the Mediterranean countries. The Ancient Greeks seem not to have been aware of any citrus. The Romans knew the citron, which is recorded in Palestine in the first century AD, but probably arrived several centuries before. They were widely planted in Italy in the second and third centuries, becoming especially popular near Naples.

The Romans were such gourmands that they would hardly have failed to notice a delight such as an orange. These did not reach Arabia until the ninth century. It was recorded as growing in Sicily in the year 1002 and was grown in Spain at Seville, still famous for its oranges, while it was occupied by the Moors in the twelfth century. It is said St Domine planted an orange in Rome in the year 1200 and a Spanish ship full of the fruits docked at Portsmouth, England, in 1290; the Queen of Edward I received seven. These were probably bitter oranges, as many believe the sweet orange did not reach Europe till later. First seen in India in 1330, the sweet sort was planted in 1421 at Versailles; another planted in 1548 in Lisbon became the 'mother' of most European sweet orange trees and was still living in 1823.

The lemon reached Egypt and Palestine in the tenth century and was cultivated in Genoa by the mid-fifteenth century. The new fruits were soon spread around the warmer parts of Europe, and then further afield, with the voyagers of the fifteenth and sixteenth centuries. Columbus must have scattered the seeds as he went, for they are recorded as growing in the Azores in 1494 and the Antilles in 1557. They had reached orchard scale in South America in 1587 and by then Cuba was covered in them. They are now mainly grown in Florida, California, Israel, Spain and South Africa, though every warm to tropical area produces its own and more.

LEMONS, ORANGES
AND OTHER CITRUS FRUITS

varieties

The various types are of obscure parentage and were probably derived by selection from a distant common ancestor. *Citrus aurantium* is the **Seville, Bitter** or **Sour Orange**. Too sour to eat raw, this is the best for marmalade and preserves and was the first sort to arrive in Europe. *C. sinensis* is the **Sweet Orange**, often known by the variety such as **Valencia Late, Jaffa**, which is large, thick-skinned and seedless, or the nearly seedless and finest quality **Washington Navel**. Blood Oranges, such as the **Maltese**, are sweet oranges with a red tint to the flesh.

C. limon is the lemon. The fruits are distinctly shaped yellow ovoids with blunt nipples at the flower end and the characteristic acid taste. The commonest are **Lisbon, Eureka** and **Villafranca**; the hardiest and most convenient for a conservatory is the compact **Meyer's Lemon**.

C. aurantifolia is the lime. This makes a smaller tree of up to 3.5m. The small, green fruits are mainly consumed locally or made into a concentrate. The **Tahitian** lime is mostly seen in warm temperate climates but for tropical gardens, the **Mexican** or **Key** lime is more common and said to have the better flavour. The similar *C. limetta*, **Sweet Lime**, is insipidly sweet when ripe. True limes require near tropical conditions.

Citrus under cover usefully crop from mid-winter

The scent of their blooms alone make them worth having

C. paradisi is the grapefruit. Not as acid as a lemon, this is relished for breakfast by many. They may be a hybrid of the **Pomelo** or **Shaddock**, *C. grandis*, which is similar but coarser. **Marsh's Seedless** is the commonest variety of grapefruit, with greenish-white flesh; but some prefer the Texan varieties with pink flesh.

C. reticulata is the Mandarin**,** Satsuma**,** Tangerine or Clementine. These names are confused and interchanged for several small, sweet, easily peeled and segmented sorts of small orange. *C. medica* is like a large, warty lemon and is now mainly produced in a few Mediterranean countries for making candied peel. There are many other citrus species and hybrids, **Uglis, Ortaniques** and **Tangelos**, to name but a few. The **Kumquat** is not a citrus, but belongs to the similar genus *Fortunella*. The fruits are very like small, yellowish, tart oranges, and are especially good for making preserves. *Aegle marmelos*, **Bael fruit**, is another relation with hard-shelled 'oranges' used fresh, for sherberts and marmalade.

cultivation

Citrus need a warm, rich, moist soil, well aerated and never badly drained. They are all tender, though lemons and oranges have, despite the odds, been grown successfully outdoors in favourable positions in warm sheltered positions in cool climates receiving frost and snow. In warm countries they are spaced about 5–6m apart each way and are in their prime at ten years old. Trees with fruits of orange size will give a crop of over 500 each winter; small fruits, such as lemons, will crop more than 500; while big fruits, such as grapefruits, will crop less.

Citrus are gross feeders and should be fed regularly with a complete fertiliser or special citrus food. This is

If the fruits feel soft, the plants need more water

applied around the drip line, or the outer edge of the foliage. Mature trees need 2kg per year spread over three applications in spring, summer and autumn; start younger trees with much less, about 200g per year. Plant young trees on a raised mound to improve drainage and keep lawn grass well away from the trunk and drip line as grass robs trees of nutrients they need.

Growing in Containers
Citrus adapt well to pot culture but must be kept well watered in the growing season and fed with organic fertilisers to prevent build-up of salts in the soil. They must have a well-aerated, well-drained, but rich compost. Avoid plastic pots or give them extra perforation. Old school gardeners always reckoned that diluted, stale urine was the best feed for citrus.

Ornamental and Wildlife Value
Very decorative in leaf, flower and fruit, all of which have a wonderful scent, these are ideal subjects for a conservatory and for a warm patio in the summer. The flowers are loved by insects; the fruits are less use to wildlife – which is fortunate for us.

Propagation
Commonly, commercial plants are grafted or budded, often on *Poncirus* stock to dwarf them and to introduce added drought and frost hardiness. Cuttings can be taken. I find some succeed quite easily in every batch. Seedlings are slow to bear fruit and may not be true; however, citrus seeds occasionally produce two seedlings, one being a clone copy of the original plant and the other normal. Seedlings are often more vigorous and longer lived than worked plants, which may offset their slow development.

Pruning and Training
Citrus rarely need any special shaping and are allowed to develop a natural shape. Light pruning of straggly, unfruitful, diseased and long shoots replenishes bushes. Cut back before growth starts in early spring.

Pests and Diseases
Citrus are subject to scale and sooty mould. Soft soap and oil sprays are useful against them. Bronze orange bugs destroy new shoots and are best controlled by manual means. Fruit fly is a problem in areas where it is prevalent. Baits help control this. Citrus leaf miner and citrus gall wasp can also be a problem.

If the fruits don't yellow well, they're too hot

Harvesting and Storing
Usually picked too young so they can travel, they are of course best plucked fresh off the tree and fully ripe. They do not all ripen at once and picking may continue over many weeks. The rind contains the bitter oil which can be expressed to give a zest to cooking.

Satsumas give very good value for their space

LEMONS, ORANGES
AND OTHER CITRUS FRUITS

These containers make it easy to move the citrus outside to the orchard for summer and autumn

companion planting

In warm countries citrus are benefited by growing aloes, rubber, oak and guava trees nearby. However, they are also said to be inhibited by *Convolvulus* or possibly by the *Ipomoea* species.

other uses

The leaves, flowers and fruits, especially of *C. bergamia*, the **Bergamot** (NOT the herbaceous *Monarda didyma*), are used in perfumery. The empty shells of the fruits make slug traps and firelighters if dried. *Citrus/ Poncirus trifoliata* is hardier than the others and heavily thorned; it is used as a hedge in mild regions.

culinary

The fruits can be juiced – much of the world's crop is consumed this way – or jammed or jellied and made into marmalade. The peel is often candied or glacéed. Small amounts of lemon juice prevent freshly prepared fruits and vegetables oxidising and give a delightful, sharp, clean taste to most things, savoury or sweet. The Victorians grew the seeds for the young tender leaves to add to salads. The peels are much used for liqueurs and flavourings.

Orange Sorbet
Serves 4

4 large unwaxed oranges
Mace
Sugar
Egg white
Parsley sprigs

Cut the tops off the oranges and scoop out the contents. Freeze the lower shells to use as serving bowls. Strain the juice from the pulp and weigh and measure it. Simmer the chopped tops of the oranges with the pulp and a small piece of fresh mace in half as much water as you have juice, then strain out the bits and add half the juice's weight in sugar. Once it has dissolved, mix this sweetened water and the juice and partially freeze. Take it from freezer and beat vigorously, adding one beaten egg white per 450g of mixture, refreeze, then repeat the beating. Serve, partially thawed, in the reserved shells with a garnish of parsley.

Orange marmalade

Olea europaea from the family *Oleaceae*

OLIVES

Tree up to 10m. Life span: long. Evergreen, self-fertile. Fruits: up to 2.5cm, ovoid, green to black. Value: rich in oils.

Cultivated olive trees are gnarled and twisted with long, thin, dark leaves, silvered underneath, though the wild species are bushier with quadrangular stems, rounder leaves and spines. The inconspicuous, sometimes fragrant, white flowers are followed by green fruits that ripen to brown or bluey-purplish-black, and occasionally ivory white, each containing a single large stone.

Found wild in the Middle East, olives have long been cultivated. They were amongst the fruits promised to the Jews in Canaan. According to Homer, green olives were brought to Greece by Cecrops, founder of Athens. They were certainly the source of its wealth. By 571 BC the olive had reached Italy and in the first century AD Pliny records a dozen varieties grown as far as Gaul (France) and Spain. These are still the major producing areas; olives are also grown in California, Australia and China.

varieties

There are several dozen varieties grown commercially in different regions but usually unnamed 'olive' trees are offered. **Manzanillo** is a green pickling olive with medium fruit. **Verdale** has good dual-purpose pickling and oil fruit. **Sevillano** has a low oil content and not the best flavour.

cultivation

Olives grow well in arid sites that will not support much else. They prefer a well-drained, light, lime-based soil. They will grow, but rarely fruit well, outside Mediterranean climatic regions. Small strong trees, they need little support. Plant trees in full sun in well-drained gritty soil and preferably on sloping ground. Olives are drought hardy but benefit from regular water. They suit inland areas with hot, dry summers and cold, wet winters. Summer rainfall areas produce fruit with insipid flavour.

Growing in Containers

Olives make good subjects for containers, though they are unlikely to be very productive. They must have a free-draining compost and then are fairly trouble-free.

Ornamental and Wildlife Value

Very attractive shrubs, these are worth having. The flowers are beneficial to insects, and some are fragrant. They are dense evergreens, making good shelter, and the fruits are rich in oils, so these are useful plants for wild gardens in warmer climes.

Propagation

Seeds may not come true, though they are often used, and the resulting plants can be slow to come into fruit. Cuttings with a heel can be taken in late summer but, like the seed, need bottom heat to ensure success. Grow seedlings on for a year or two in large pots before planting out – they get tougher as they get bigger.

Pruning and Training

Olives bear on the previous year's growth; remove the dead and diseased or crossing branches in late winter or early spring. They can be trained as fans on walls for extra protection. If the tops are frosted, they can still come again from the root and can be cut back very hard or pollarded. Old trees often throw suckers as replacements.

Pests and Diseases

Olives have very few problems in private gardens, though scale insects can bother them occasionally. Protection from frost and good drainage are more important factors.

Not the South Downs yet…

OLIVES

Green olive crops come before the ripe black and are more attainable in the UK

Harvesting and Storing

In the Mediterranean region the trees bear when they are about eight years old. They produce about 25kg of fruit each, which reduces to about a quarter to half that weight in oil. The green fruits are ones picked unripe and pickled; the black fruits are ripe and ready for pressing for oil or preserving. The oil that is squeezed out without heat or excess pressure is called extra virgin (an interesting concept). Cheaper grades are produced by heating or adding hot water to the mass.

companion planting

Oaks are thought to be detrimental to olive trees.

other uses

The oil has many industrial as well as culinary uses. Much is used in cosmetics and perfumery and it was once burned in lamps.

culinary

The oil is used in many ways – in Mediterranean countries it is used in preference to animal fats – and the fruits are added to various dishes. The fruits are also eaten as savoury accompaniments such as pickled in brine, often stuffed with anchovy or pimento, or dried. If beaten to a paste, olives will make a delicious savoury spread.

Olive Bread

Makes 1 loaf

500g strong white flour
1 packet dried yeast
Water
60g black olives, stoned
Olive oil
Poppy seeds

Mix the flour and yeast with enough water to form a dough. Knead and allow to rise until it is half as big again. Knead again and work in the olives. Rub the dough with olive oil; place it in an oiled tin to rise again with a sprinkling of poppy seeds. Once it has risen to half its size again, put it in a preheated oven at 220°C/425°F/gas mark 7 for 20 minutes or till brown on top. Serve as an entrée with a crisp green salad and a sharp dressing.

Actinidia chinensis/deliciosa from the family *Actinidiaceae*

KIWI FRUIT
OR CHINESE GOOSEBERRY

Vine, up to 10m or more. Life span: medium. Deciduous, some not self-fertile. Fruits: up to 5cm, flattened ovoid, brown, hairy. Value: very rich in vitamin C.

The kiwi fruit or Chinese gooseberry is the best-known member of a small number of deciduous clambering and twining shrubs closely related to camellias. The kiwi has large, hand-sized, heart-shaped leaves, downy underneath, on softly bristled stems. The flower is like a small, poorly developed rose, off-whitish and fragrant. The brown, furry fruits are thin-skinned and firm with luscious green pulp containing many tiny black seeds around the centre.

These were not known in the West till the end of the nineteenth century, when they were introduced from Japan and East Asia, more for their use as decorative climbers than for their fruits. Though now commonly known as kiwi fruit, they are not native to New Zealand, but were introduced there in the early years of the last century and became more popular as a fruit when greenhouse growers needed to look for alternative crops to their oversubscribed tomato market. Recent breeding has developed self-fertile varieties. A dwarf, shrubby, form would be handy.

varieties

A. deliciosa **Hayward** is the most widely available and the main commercial variety. It is not self-fertile so needs planting with a male. It is not as vigorous as other varieties and the fruit keeps well. **Tomuri** is similar. **Blake** is very high-yielding (up to 90kg per vine is claimed). It is self-fertile and needs protection for the lower stems in cold regions. *A. arguta*, the **Siberian Kiwi** or **Tara Vine**, is very vigorous with fragrant, triple, white flowers, followed by green, sweet fruits. The copious sap is drinkable. *A. kolomikta* has large, oblong leaves which start green then go cream and pink. The single, white flowers are sweetly perfumed and followed by long, yellowish, sweet berries. *A. polygama* is a native of Japan and has large, heart-shaped leaves that open bronze, maturing to green on red stems, with white, fragrant flowers and yellow fruits. Early **Bruno** has very large brown fruit with less resilient storage. It is a heavy cropper as is **Monty**, which may need hand thinning to ensure a decent yield. **Abbott** is the earliest to flower. For pollination, plant **Tomuri** for **Hayward** and **Matua** with early bearing varieties. There are many more sweet edible species.

cultivation

Kiwis require a warm site, rich, loamy soil and strong supports. They will grow, but not crop, in shade. Some of the early varieties are female only and require one male to be planted to every half dozen females. Modern varieties are self-fertile, though they may perform better if planted with others to cross-pollinate. Some species similarly need pollinators, so it is often best to plant several (more than three) to be sure of getting one male for several female plants.

Leave a space of 7m between each trellis and plant male and female plants close to each other for insects to carry out pollination. Prior to planting, add half a kilo of blood and bone to the planting hole. Fertilise in October/November with a mix of compost and animal manure. Kiwi fruit needs a minimum of 400–700 hours below 7°C to form fruit. If winters are too warm, fruit is unlikely to form. Plants may take four years to bear and need shelter from wind. Plants can be girdled (remove 3–4mm of bark) in February/March to induce flowering to avoid biennial cropping.

KIWI FRUIT

Ornamental and Wildlife Value
Kiwis are very attractive climbers. The young shoots are particularly pretty as they are covered in many fine, red bristles. Kiwis are hardy enough to be used to cover eyesores, but they are not likely to crop unless they are given a warm site. The species are equally useful.

Propagation
The species can be grown from seed, but varieties are grown from half-ripe summer or from hardwood autumn cuttings rooted with bottom heat in a frame.

Pruning and Training
The fruits are borne on sideshoots. Unless these are left there are no fruits, so these must not be hard pruned, but may be shortened. Kiwis must be well trained or they form an unruly thicket; therefore give them plenty of space. Old shoots die, so tie in replacements in spring. Good supports are necessary for these vigorous plants.

Pests and Diseases
There seem to be no major problems with these fruits, save dieback in cold winters. Give them extra protection if you are after fruits.

Harvesting and Storing
The fruits ripen late; hang well with protection against frosts from the elements, ideally under glass.

Their fruits swell early but hang on late

Long after the leaves fall the crop hangs on making picking easier

companion planting

There are no known companion effects.

other uses

These plants are useful for covering old trees and other eyesores.

culinary

Kiwis can be eaten raw or made into juices, jellies and jams and are much liked for decorating other dishes, usually sweet but occasionally savoury. They contain an enzyme that breaks down gelatine, so should not be used to make dessert jellies. This enzyme can also tenderise meat.

Kiwi Meringue Pie
Serves 4

4 individual meringue bases
Green gooseberry jam or preserve
Clotted cream
4 kiwi fruits
Toasted chopped nuts
Glacé cherries

On each meringue base build a thick layer of jam, then a layer of clotted cream covered with very thin, overlapping slices of peeled kiwi. Top with nuts and a cherry or two.

Passiflora from the family *Passifloraceae*

PASSION FRUIT

Herbaceous vine up to 10m. Life span: short. Semi-deciduous, self-fertile. Fruits: from 2.5cm to 10cm, spherical to cylindrical, yellow, orange, red, brown, black or green. Value: rich in vitamin C.

Passion fruit are a family of perennial climbers with tendrils, deeply lobed leaves, amazing flowers and peculiar fruits. These vary in size from that of a cherry to a coconut, and in colour, coming in almost any shade from yellow to black. They are usually thick-skinned with a juicy, acid, fragrant, sweet pulp inside, almost inseparable from smooth, black seeds. The passion fruit, *Passiflora edulis*, is the most widely grown species. It has white or mauve flowers fragrant of heliotrope and purple-black fruits that are best when 'old' and wrinkled. A yellow-skinned form, *P. edulis flavicarpa,* is also popular in Brazil.

Passion fruit are native to America and were first recorded in Europe in 1699. The flowers caused quite a stir in European society, with many contemporary Christians claiming that they were a sign of Christ's Passion (the Crucifixion). The three stigmas represented the nails, the central column the scourging post, the five anthers the wounds, the corona the crown of thorns, the calyx the halo, the ten petals the faithful apostles, and the tendrils the whips and scourges of His oppressors. These delightful climbers, with their stunning flowers and delicious fruits, are popular in most warm countries, even acquiring a sort of cult status in Australia, where it is grown throughout the entire continent.

varieties

Passiflora edulis is the tastiest variety. Improved varieties are preferred nowadays. **Nellie Kelly** has large dark purple fruit and is the benchmark fruit. Also growing in popularity are coloured fruits such as **Panama Red** and **Panama Gold**, which ripen up to three weeks ahead of the regular purple kinds. The fruit is also slightly more acid. Yellow passion fruit (*P. edulis f. flavicarpa*) prefers a more tropical climate, where selections such as **Panama** and **Marsh** perform well. **Lacey**, **Purple Gold** and **Barlow's Special** were popular until more disease resistant forms like **Supersweet 1** and **Tom's Special** replaced them. The banana passion fruit *P. mollissima* has pink flowers and edible fruit. Less common are the **Giant Granadilla** *P. quadrangularis* for tropical regions; *P. incarnata* **Maypops** used in hybridising; and *P. ligularis*. None are as tasty as the common passion fruit.

cultivation

Passion fruit are grown all over Australia, even in cool areas, though pollination is sometimes affected in a cold spring. A humus-rich, moist soil and a sheltered position on a warm wall suit the hardier varieties. Plant in spring and, once established, feed with a high nitrogen fertiliser or citrus food every two months throughout the summer. Mature vines need 2kg spread over three separate applications per year. Train plants

Old and wrinkly is better!

PASSION FRUIT

Big crops of tasty tender *P. edulis* can be had under cover

to a support that faces north to get the most warmth in cool zones. Plants should not be allowed to dry out as it checks fruit growth and the plant's immune system, making it more prone to disease. Rain at flower set may interfere with pollination, which only occurs in the morning. In prolonged bad weather, a light cover may thus be needed to keep flowers dry for pollination. The vine will bear the following season and fruit matures in 12 weeks.

Ornamental and Wildlife Value
The fast growing vines are popular for covering ugly sheds and fences with a dense green canopy.

Propagation
Passion flowers can all be grown from seed, which can give good results for they are still relatively unimproved and most are true species. But plants may not be as disease resistant as grafted stock. In cool areas, *P. caerulea* is used for understock. In warmer zones, forms of *P. edulis f. flavicarpa* resistant to fusarium wilt are preferred.

Pruning and Training
Train plants from an early age by tip pruning and tying down new side shoots horizontally. Prune late winter or early spring as they bear on new season's wood.

Harvesting and Storing
Best ripen the fruit on the vine till they drop, though picked young for transport they keep well. As they ripen they will shrivel, appearing old and wrinkled, and the flavour is then at its best.

Yellow Granadilla

other uses

The empty shells make good slug traps for the garden.

culinary

Thirst-quenching raw passion fruit are made into juice which is a popular drink in many countries, much as orange juice and squash are in others. They can be made into jams, liqueurs and sorbets.

Passion Fruit Sorbet
Serves 4–6

12 ripe passion fruit
Approx. 120g sugar
Mint sprigs

Scoop out the fruit pulp and seeds and sieve. Discard the seeds. To the juice, add half its weight in water and the same of sugar, stir till the sugar has dissolved and freeze. Partially thaw and beat vigorously, then refreeze. Serve partially thawed, scooped into glasses and decorated with mint sprigs.

Punica granatum from the family *Lythraceae*

POMEGRANATES

Bush up to 4m. Life span: medium. Deciduous, self-fertile. Fruits: up to 8cm, spherical, orange. Value: good source of vitamin C.

Pomegranates have coppery young leaves that yellow in autumn, glorious orange or red, camellia-like blooms, and orange fruits with a rough nipple and thin, leathery rind. Inside they have bitter yellow pith and are stuffed with seeds embedded in pink, sweet pulp. They are infuriating to eat. Natives of Persia, the pomegranates were cultivated in Ancient Egypt and other Mediterranean countries. American and Russian cultivars with a lower seed to fruit ratio are slowly entering the market. If planning to grow for fruit rather than for ornamental purposes, use one of these new forms.

varieties

Wonderful has rich red colour and full-flavoured fruits. From Russia come **Gulosha Azerbaijani**, **Veles**, and **Kazake**. Only grow named varieties for fruit.

Pomegranates outdoors will do best not far but sheltered from the sea

cultivation

Pomegranates are best suited to hot, dry summer areas. They are not fussy about soil, though a heavier soil is said to produce better flavour. In dry conditions, plants need irrigating to stop fruit drop and develop juice. With a low-chill requirement, trees grow satisfactorily in mild climates but place in a dry spot in humid summer climates. Plant trees 4–5m apart and remove suckers that appear.

Growing in Containers

Trees grow easily in pots but produce inferior fruit. The dwarf variety, **Nana**, is purely ornamental.

Propagation

By seed, layering or half-ripe summer cuttings using bottom heat.

Pruning and Training

Pomegranates are mostly grown as small trees in the open. They only need light pruning to improve access to picking and remove old wood. The plants fl ower in late spring or early summer at the ends of branches. Prune lightly in late winter or early spring.

Harvesting and Storing

They travel very well, keeping for weeks, so are easy to distribute.

Pests and Diseases and Companion Planting

Pomegranates suffer from few problems and no companion effects have been noted.

other uses

They grow densely enough to be used for hedges in warm countries. A dye is made from the fruit peel. The peel and the bark are used as native cures for diarrhoea and dysentery. In Brazil the rind is boiled and the extract used as a gargle for throat infections.

culinary uses

The juice is used for drinks, syrup, conserves and fermenting.

Pomegranate Pastime

Sit down under a shady tree with your ripe pomegranate. Cut open the rind, pick out the seeds individually with a pin and eat the pink pulp. The seed may be swallowed or rejected.

Diospyros kaki from the family *Ebenaceae*

PERSIMMONS

Tree/bush, up to 6m. Life span: medium. Deciduous. Fruits: 5–8cm, round, orange-red. Value: rich in vitamin A and potassium.

Persimmons have lustrous, dark green leaves. The fruits are large and glossy, like orange tomatoes or Christmas baubles. Japanese persimmons were first seen in 1776. Extremely popular in Japan and China, they are now relished by fruit connoisseurs in Australia and New Zealand as a delectable and valuable winter fruit.

varieties

Fuyu is one of the best non-astringent varieties with fruit in April–May. **Izu** is earlier and **Kuro-Kumo** has small fruit. Astringent types like **Dai Dai Maru**, a common home garden fruit, have flatter fruit. Late maturing **Flat Seedless** is excellent and **Hachiya** bears alternate years. **Mabolo**, *D. blancoi*, or **Butter-fruit** resemble small orangey winter squashes smelling of cheese – but once you get the skin off, their creamy white flesh is surprisingly sweet and tasty. *D. digyna*, the **Black Persimmon** aka **Chocolate Pudding Fruit**, from Mexico has thick, finger-sized dark greeny-black soft fruits that mixed with spices and sugar resemble real chocolate pudding and are thus exceedingly popular.

cultivation

Persimmons have a wide climatic range though, in general, non-astringent types are more suited to subtropical conditions while astringent varieties like cool summer climates and grow better in cooler southern areas. Plants require good drainage but soil needs to be constantly moist, especially inland, for the fruit to develop. They require a long mild summer for good fruiting. Plant bare-rooted trees in winter in a wind-free position. Remove any weeds and water regularly when establishing. Train the tree into a pyramid or vase shape.

Ornamental and Wildlife Value

These are very attractive small trees, grown for their autumn colouring and ornamental fruits. The fruits are of value to birds.

Propagation

By seed or grafting for the better varieties.

Pruning and Training

Only remedial pruning is needed, so plant about 6m apart. Thin the fruits to get bigger ones.

Pests and Diseases

Root rot kills trees in poorly drained soil. Fruit fl y affects early ripening varieties and fruit left on the tree to ripen. When skins are hard, they are less of a problem. Parrots and flying foxes damage crops.

Harvesting and Storing

Cut rather than pick to retain the short pedicel. This way they keep better. Store cool and dry until ripe – up to four months, as they are best when soft. Place in a plastic bag with an apple or banana to hasten ripening. They can also be frozen like tomatoes and similarly de-skinned as they thaw.

other uses

The fruits are successfully used as pig food. Pounded persimmons dropped into a pond stupefy the fish.

culinary

Persimmons are eaten fresh, dried or candied, but rarely cooked. They can also be made into a yummy ice cream.

Percinnammons

Serves 4

4 soft, ripe persimmons
Cinnamon
Apricot conserve
Cream
4 glacé cherries

Peel the fruit and cut in half. Dust each half with cinnamon, cover with conserve and top with cream and a cherry.

Eriobotrya/Photinia japonica from the family *Rosaceae*

LOQUATS
JAPANESE MEDLARS OR PLUMS

Tree/bush, up to 10m. Life span: medium to long. Evergreen. Fruits: up to 5cm, pear-shaped, orange. Value: minor.

Loquats have large, leathery, corrugated leaves, woolly white underneath, and fragrant, furry, yellowish flowers. The fruits are orange and pear-shaped with big, brown-black seeds and sweet, acid, chewy pulp on an attractive small tree. First reported in 1690, these were imported from Canton to Kew Gardens in London in 1787. Widely cultivated in the East, they are popular in Mediterranean and sub-tropical climates, and were a feature of older gardens in Australia's warmer temperate zones.

varieties

Select named varieties like **Mizuho**, **Bessel Brown** or **Nagasaki-wase** for fruit.

cultivation

Any well-drained soil and a warm, well-drained site will suffice. Flowers suffer from frost damage and flowering time is winter so frost-free conditions are desirable. Loquats are heavy feeders. Apply citrus food in spring, summer and autumn. Fruit is prone to fruit fly attack and netting is needed if any fruit is to be gathered. Don't expect decent fruit from common varieties. Insist on a named cultivar. Thin to avoid small, inferior fruit.

Growing in Containers
Loquats make big shrubs, so they are usefully confined in large pots.

Propagation
Loquats can be grown from fresh seed, or layers, or soft wood cuttings taken in spring with bottom heat.

Ornamental and Wildlife Value
Very architectural plants with a lovely scent, they will also make good shelter for birds and insects.

Pests and Diseases
Fruit fly is a major pest!

Pruning and Training
Only remedial pruning is needed. They are best trained on a wall and allowed to grow out from it or grown as bushes in pots. Trim back any dead and diseased growths in spring.

Harvesting and Storing
The fruits need warmth and protection to ripen in late winter/early spring, so they must be grown under glass in cold countries.

companion planting

These are dense evergreens that will kill off any plants grown underneath.

other uses

These shrubs make tall and attractive screens in countries with warmer climes.

culinary

Loquats are eaten raw, stewed, jammed or jellied. They are made into a liqueur in Bermuda.

Loquat Jam
Makes approx. 2.4kg

1.4kg loquats
Approx. 1kg sugar

Wash and stone the loquats, then simmer till soft with just enough water to prevent burning. Weigh and add three-quarters of the weight in sugar. Stir to dissolve the sugar, then bring to the boil. Skim and pot in sterilised jars. Store in a cool place.

Opuntia ficus indica/dillenii **from the family** *Cactaceae*

PRICKLY PEARS

BARBERRY FIGS

Herbaceous up to 2m. Life span: medium to long. Evergreen, self-fertile. Fruits: 5–9cm, ovoid, red, yellow or purple. Value: minor.

These are typical cacti, with round or oval, thick, fleshy pads covered with tufts of long and short spines. The flowers are large, 5–7cm, yellow, with numerous petals, stamens and filaments. These are followed by red, yellow or purple, prickly, oval cylinders which are the fruits. Under the skin the flesh is very acid and sweet.

These are natives of the Americas, where they have long been used. The prickly pear that overran Australia in the nineteenth and twentieth centuries was a different species.

varieties

Burbank, the great American breeder, raised a spineless prickly pear. Many other *Opuntia* species have edible fruits: *O. compressa/fragilis/goldhillea/humifusa/macrorisa/maxima/phaeacantha* and *rutila*. Other cacti with edible fruits are: *Brachycereus* spp. **Rositas**, a trailer with red flowers and small fruits; *Borzicactus aequatorialis*, **Zoroco**, a fragrant white-flowered cacti with white-fleshed fruits; *Cereus peruvianus*, **Peruvian Apple Cactus**, **Pitaya**, are very good white-fleshed, red-skinned fruits; *Echinocereus triglochidiatus*, is a mound-forming cactus with red flowers and fruits rated as strawberry like; and *Espostoa lanata*, **Cacto lanudo**, has red flowers with purple sweet fruits; *Pachycereus pectin-aboriginum*, **Hairbrush Cactus**, gets to the height of a house and has orange-size spiny fruits with sweet flesh, good fresh or cooked; *Trichocereus pachanoi*, **San Pedro**, is a huge cylindrical cacti that can reach tree size, covered with fragrant flowers and edible fruits; *Hamatocactus hamatacanthus*, **Lemon cactus, Turk's Head** are spherical tender cactii with red and yellow flowers followed by lemon-flavoured fruits used raw, in beverages and cakes.

cultivation

Opuntia need a well-drained, open, limy soil and a warm position. They take frost but like warm conditions for fruiting. Check with the local agricultural authorities before planting prickly pear as some species are noxious weeds in Australia. Take care when handling the pads as they are covered with fine barbed hairs.

Ornamental and Wildlife Value
Very decorative and quite a talking point in a garden. They are more reliable under glass and just as attractive. The flowers are good for insects.

Pruning and Training
No pruning is required. When the pads become heavy they may need propping up.

Pests and Diseases
Weed control needs to be good, as these are nasty to weed between. Slugs and snails may develop a taste for the pads.

Propagation
These can be grown from seed, but are slow. Detached pads or pieces root easily and are much quicker.

Harvesting and Storing
This is a thorny task. Wrap a piece of bark round to pick the fruit, which will keep for several days. The peel is best skinned off completely before the fruit is eaten.

other uses

After ensilaging or pulping with salt, prickly pears make a useful animal feed.

Tasty they may be, but the picking and peeling…

culinary

Prickly pears are usually eaten raw in place of drink and are occasionally fried or stewed. The red varieties will stain everything.

Monstera deliciosa from the family *Araceae*

CERIMANS

SWISS CHEESE PLANTS

Herbaceous vine, may ramble or climb to over 12m. Life span: appears perpetual and invulnerable. Fruits: about 2.5 x 22cm, green. Value: some vitamin C.

The Swiss cheese plant is one of the commonest and most enduring house plants, somehow surviving hostile conditions in dark, dry rooms the world over. The leaves are dark green, large and scalloped, and uniquely and curiously, have natural holes in them, presumably to let tropical winds pass with less damage. In its native habitat it is an epiphytic climber, rambling on the forest floor and climbing up vigorously, clothing the trees and throwing down masses of aerial roots. It is a close relation of the arum lily and the flowers are similar. The long, conelike spadix fruit, or ceriman, is green, cylindrical and leathery with tiny, hexagonal plates for skin. The flesh is sweet and richly flavoured, resembling a cross between a pineapple and banana. It is absolutely delicious if completely ripe, otherwise the texture is spoilt by spicules and it is inedible.

Swiss cheese plants are native to Central America, but have been spread worldwide for their attractive leaves and amazing durability. This fruit was discovered in Mexico and was originally known as the Mexican bread fruit. It became known as the shingle plant and classed as *Philodendron pertusum*, then *Monstera acuminata* and now as *M. deliciosa* but is known worldwide as the Swiss cheese plant. In 1874 the fruits were exhibited before the Massachusetts Horticultural Society. The fruits are as delicious as the name suggests, but the spicules make unripe fruits unpleasant, so they have never become widely popular.

'Swiss cheese' originates from holes in the leaves

cultivation

One of the most enduring and robust plants discovered, but will fruit only if given warmth and moisture. It does not need as much bright light as most tropical fruits, and has been grown successfully under glass in most countries.

Ornamental and Wildlife Value

Superb ornamental value almost anywhere frost-free.

Growing under Glass and in Containers

Ideally suited to almost any treatment! For fruits, give better conditions, e.g. copious watering and syringing.

Propagation, Pruning and Training

They can be air-layered or cuttings will root easily. They are happiest climbing up a stout, rough-barked tree or log, or wired on a wall.

Harvesting and Storing, Culinary

When the fruit is ripe the inside appears to swell and the leathery skin plates loosen up; they can be eased off like tiny buttons. Then the flesh can be eaten off the stem. Try it with care – the tiny spicules of calcium oxalate irritate some people's throats but appear harmless. Do not worry about the spicules if you eat only ripe fruits – many people regularly enjoy them. Cerimans are only used as dessert fruit and are widely popular in native markets.

other uses

The vines make a quick-growing screen in warm regions.

Cyphomandra betacea (syn. C. crassicaulis) from the family *Solanaceae*

TAMARILLOS

TREE TOMATOES

Shrubby tree up to 5m. Life span: generally short. Fruits: 4 x 6cm, ovoid, purple. Value: some vitamin C.

The tree tomato is not a tomato but an evergreen, semi-woody shrub from the same family. The leaves are large and lightly felted and smell muskily aromatic. Greeny-pink, fragrant flowers are followed by copious fruits similar to tomatoes but more pointedly egg-shaped and more purple. Each fruit is thick-skinned with two lobes containing about a hundred seeds. They are tasty raw only if well ripened, usually being too acid when they require cooking. The fruits start green and ripen to reddish-yellow or purple. Native to Peru or Brazil, they are widely cultivated in warm zones. They fruit conveniently during much of they year.

varieties

Most so-called 'cultivars' have arisen as a result of grower selection. As plants are easy to grow from seed, any with different characteristics are often named. Because of this they do not have official cultivar status. Yellow-skinned types do not have dark pigment around the seeds and the flesh retains its yellow pigmentation after cooking. **Amberlea Gold**, a medium-sized, yellow-skinned variety, is moderately tasty. **Bold Gold** is a large yellow variety of inferior taste. **Goldmine**, with golden skin sometimes blushed red, is an exceptionally sweet type. **Oratia Red** has large fruit with deep red skin enclosing moderately sweet, well-flavoured flesh. **Red Beau** is oval-shaped, with red skin and an excellent flavour. **Red Delight** is a large, round red-skinned type with moderate flavour.

cultivation

Tamarillos prefer medium to high altitudes in the tropics and demand deep, well-manured soils to produce dessert fruits. For culinary purposes they can be grown anywhere frost-free and are obliging as to soil, preferring well-drained sites.

Pests and Diseases
Tamarillos are very prone to whitefly. Use the predatory wasp *Encarsia formosa*, sticky traps or spray with soft soap. Control aphids with soft soap and red spider mite by maintaining humidity.

Growing under Glass and in Containers
The plants need a lot of light and heat for tasty dessert fruits, but easily give high yields for cooking purposes during the winter months, as they prefer warm days and cool nights.

Ornamental and Wildlife Value
They resemble daturas in many ways, including the smell of the foliage and delicious flowers – much loved by whitefly!

culinary

The fruits are fairly robust until fully ripe and keep for several days. When ripe they are purple and can be eaten raw, but tend to be sour so they are better stewed like tomatoes or plums.

Tree Tomato Jam
Makes approx. 2kg

1kg tamarillos/tree tomatoes
Approx. 1kg light brown sugar
1 small lemon

Stew the tamarillos in a little water until soft. Sieve and return to the heat. Add the same weight of sugar and the lemon's grated rind and juice. Bring to the boil and then bottle in warm, sterilised jars and seal.

Propagation, Pruning and Training
Tamarillos are easily grown from seed or cuttings, fruiting by their second year. They are best trained as a short standard; pruning then is mainly needed to nip out growing points to keep the bush compact.

Harvesting and Storing
In autumn, fruits continue to swell and are ready for picking when brightly coloured, but may not be fully ripe until mid-winter. Pick them at the point where the stem naturally breaks, about 5cm above the fruit. The crop ripens over several weeks.

companion planting

Plant French marigolds alongside to deter whitefly.

TROPICAL AND SUB-TROPICAL FRUITS

Some of these fruits are the tastiest and most luscious in the world. The strong sunlight and hot conditions of northern Australia produce sweeter, stronger flavours (indeed, often excessively so) than in cooler, temperate zones. The natural conditions change little during the year, usually being hot, bright and dry, followed by hot, bright and wet, or by more of the same, rather than the fluctuating heat and light and winter chilling of cooler, southern regions. Tropical plants therefore often set fruit several times a year, or continuously throughout it. Thus tropical fruits are a more reliable source of food than those of cooler areas and less reliance has to be put on storage till the next harvest.

The original species of many tropical fruit have disappeared, to be replaced, even in the wild, by our partially selected stock. This happened far back in prehistory; there is no wild date or banana that corresponds to the cultivated varieties. Many of these long-cultivated plants have been turned into clones, superior varieties propagated vegetatively, often without seed, or not coming true from seed. This handicaps the gardener as only inferior forms can be had from seed; to get better sorts, living plant material has to be obtained.

However, some tropical fruits are still species, little changed from the original, and useful to the gardener, for if the fruits can be obtained, it may be possible to grow the plant. Modern refrigeration and air travel now permit us to enjoy a tremendous range of fresh exotic fruits year round, and the availability and range is being constantly extended.

The first tropical fruits probably reached northern Europe in Roman times, but were then forgotten until rediscovered by late-medieval travellers. To be enjoyed fully, many needed to be ripened longer on the plant than early long-distance transport allowed. The colonisation of the Canary Islands during the Renaissance enabled exotic fruits to be cultivated within reach of the European market, and this was given further impetus by the newly discovered New World fruits.

These new, expensive, luxury fruits were so desirable that owners of large estates in colder countries encouraged their gardeners to try them even though they needed more than a frost-free greenhouse or simple winter protection to grow, let alone fruit. Surprisingly, just as they had succeeded with orangeries, they met with more success; for example, pineapple plants were grown in Britain as early as 1690. However, it required the Industrial Revolution to provide the iron, glass and heat for serious home production.

The stove house was just that – a large glass greenhouse with a massive stove keeping the temperature tropical; different sections were arid and dry or steamy moist. With steam- or water-heated pipes, the stove could be moved to a separate boiler room. The Victorian age saw British-grown pineapples, bananas and mangosteens gracing many a table. Nothing seemed impossible to these horticultural pioneers.

Along with private extravagance, public botanic gardens were built, and specimens were obtained of many plants. Many were successful, but others could not be persuaded to fruit even in extra heat. Now we are more fortunate in cooler regions: with electric light to replicate sunlight we can give these plants the brightness and day length they need. We also have automatic heat and humidity control, so it is easy to grow many exotic fruits ourselves. And if they still will not fruit, they always make attractive house plants.

Ananas comosus from the family *Bromeliaceae*

PINEAPPLES

Herbaceous, 1 x 1m. Life span: short-lived, perennial. Fruits: average 10 x 20cm, dull orange or yellow. Value: rich in vitamins C and A.

Pineapples need little description; they are the most distinctive of fruits – there is nothing else like them. They are Bromeliads, like many houseplants. They resemble common garden yuccas, being nearly cylindrical with a tuft of narrow, pointed leaves emerging from the top. The skin of the fruit is green to yellow, with many slightly raised protuberances. Wild species have serrated, thorny-edged leaves and set seed. Modern cultivars are seedless, with smoother leaves and smaller fruits; those of traditional varieties weighed up to 8kg.

Cultivated and selected from the wild by the people of Central America for thousands of years, the fruits were sensational in 1493 to the crew of Columbus. The first fruit, surviving the voyage back, was regarded as nearly as great a discovery as the New World itself. Pineapple motifs appeared, sometimes distorted, throughout European art – often as knobs on pew ends. By 1550 pineapple was being preserved in sugar to be sent back to the Old World as an exotic, and profitable, luxury. By the end of the sixteenth century pineapples had been spread to China and the Philippines, and were naturalising in Java, and soon after were colonising the west coast of Africa. An enterprising M. Le Cour of Holland succeeded in growing them under glass in 1686 and was supplying plants to English gardeners in 1690. Within a few years there was a craze for pineapples, with noblemen's gardeners growing them under glass on deep hot beds of horse dung and leather wastes as far north as Scotland. British-grown pineapples were sold in the markets at a guinea apiece.

They need a warm, dry sub-tropical climate to fruit. The Victorians raised the cultivation of pineapples to a high level with the regulated heat from steam boilers.

varieties

The **Smooth Cayenne** is the variety most widely grown in Australia. Its leaves do not have the strong serrated edges of many bromeliads. The fruit is a large cylinder with broad flat eyes and very juicy flesh with strong acidity. The rough-leaved varieties have smaller, sweeter fruit with less acid. **Common Rough** and **Ripley Queen** have smaller more prominent eyes than smooth-leaved pineapples. Rough varieties sucker prolifically.

cultivation

A tropical plant, the pineapple needs raised planting beds for sharp drainage, acid soil with pH about 5.5. Pineapples like a dry soil and survive on natural rainfall especially when ripening. Fertilise two weeks after planting, then every 2–3 months. In plantations, pineapples are given a square metre of ground each.

The juice acts as high fibre!

Never let yours chill below 21°C or 'cook' above 32°C. Fruit takes up to two years to mature. Dry plants may survive cold down to near freezing, while damp ones succumb very quickly, then rot. Keep their centre from getting wet in the cold as this is the first to be lost.

Ornamental and Wildlife Value

They are easy to root and grow as houseplants.

Propagation

Suckers from healthy plants are best, fruiting in a year and a half or so. Slips, the shoots produced at the base of the fruit, seeds and even stem cuttings can be used, but take longer to grow and fruit. The crown from a fruit is easily rooted; cut it off whole with a thin shoulder, prise off the shoulder and pull off the lower withered leaves individually. Root over heat in a gritty compost. Suckers are less prone to mould than slips. Once growing, keep foliage moist with regular misting from spring till autumn. From autumn till spring keep dry unless preferred temperatures can be continuously maintained.

Pruning and Training

Pineapples can be grown in containers. Young plants rooted in summer need potting up in spring, growing on for a year and repotting the following spring to fruit that summer or autumn. Pot up annually, and remove superfluous shoots and fruited stumps if you have any. Bury the plants progressively deeper each year – relatively tall but narrow pots are needed. If happy, pineapples may grow and produce for five to ten years.

Weed, Pest and Disease Control

White scale and mealybugs affect potted plants. Outside, crows, rats and wallabies eat fruit.

PINEAPPLES

companion planting

Once the plants are big enough, a dressing of banana skins may encourage them to flower, and again later to help ripen the fruit. A good smoking can also induce flowering.

other uses

Pineapple leaves have a strong fibre used for thread, fishing lines and pinya cloth, used to make the national dress shirt of Filipino men.

culinary

Picked underripe and kept cool, they can be stored for several weeks. They make tasty jam, delicious juice and are best-known canned. Although a fruit, they add sweetness and texture to many savoury dishes, from Chinese to curry, and can even be fried with gammon. Pineapple causes egg whites and jellies not to set and turns milk products bitter unless cooked to above 40°C. If a pineapple is too acid, try eating it with salt – honest, this works!

Pineapple-baked Ham

Serves 4

1 very large tin of ham
1 larger pineapple
garlic (optional)

Carefully empty the meat from the tin in one piece. Sharpen the open end of the can and use it to extract the pineapple from its skin, first slicing off the top shoulder. Leave the skin intact. (Slice and chill the pineapple flesh for dessert, cutting out the tough central core.) Insert the ham in the hole created, pin the shoulder back on to seal, and bake for at least an hour in a pre-heated oven at 200°C/400°F/gas mark 6. (Garlic lovers may rub the ham over before insertion.)

To serve, turn the pineapple on its side to cut circles of ham with a pineapple rind. Serve with puréed sweetcorn and baked sweet potatoes.

Musa species from the family *Musaceae*

BANANAS

Tree/herbaceous plant, 3–9m and nearly as wide. Life span: perpetual as vegetative clones but sterile. Fruits: up to 30cm, green to yellow or red. Value: nutritious and rich in starch.

Banana plants form herbaceous stools of shoots like small trees. Each enormous shoot unfurls sheaths of gigantic, oblong leaves up to 4.5m long. A mature shoot disgorges one flower stalk, which hangs down under its mighty bunch of many combs or hands of bananas. The hands point upwards, sheltered by succulent, purple bracts the size of plates, along the length of the stalk, and a mass of male flowers adorns the end. One bunch can hold about a dozen combs, each with over a dozen fingers. Bananas are the most productive food crop, giving about forty times the yield of potatoes. The fruits are green, ripening yellow, sweet, notoriously shaped and unforgettably scented.

The Ancient Egyptians had the culinary Abyssinian banana (*Ensete ventricosum*), but early travellers from Europe soon discovered sweeter, more edible bananas in most tropical and semi-tropical regions. The hardiest, the smaller Chinese banana, was brought from the East Indies for cultivation in the Canary Islands by 1516 – and, it has been suggested, was introduced to the Americas from there, but evidence of indigenous bananas discounts this. Most cultivated bananas are probably descendants of *M. sapientum*, *M. acuminata* and *M. balbisiana*, wild bananas thought to come from eastern Asia and Indo-Malaysia. *Musa maculata* and *M. rosacea* descendants are popular in parts of Asia and worldwide there exist many other species. In prehistoric cultivation, seed-bearing species were replaced by selected hybrids with big, seedless fruits propagated vegetatively. These superior sorts multiplied and by the nineteenth century there were countless local varieties of bananas in most hot countries. Many of these have now been lost and replaced by a few high-yielding commercial cultivars.

varieties

The banana is an important commercial crop and subject to a number of fatal diseases. The growing of bananas in home gardens is therefore restricted in Queensland, and in New South Wales north of the Hunter region. Queenslanders can only grow **Lady Finger**, a small-fruited type. Tall Cavendish varieties such as **Williams** and **Mons Mari** are relatively resistant to Panama disease. **Dwarf Cavendish** has a smaller fruit but it is prone to 'choke', where the young bunch aborts. Also grown occasionally is **Red Dacca**. None are permitted in commercial banana-growing districts without a permit from the relevant agricultural authority. Plantains are separate varieties, possibly descendants of *M. paradisiaca*, larger and slightly horn-shaped. Plantains are most often used for cooking, not dessert purposes; thus cooking bananas are sometimes referred to as plantains.

BANANAS

No pollination required or wanted

cultivation

In warm climates bananas need a rich, quite heavy, deep, well-drained soil with copious moisture. Freedom from strong winds is also essential. The smallest varieties are usually planted about 3m apart; the larger proportionately more.

Bananas can be grown in containers in cool areas. Elsewhere, they need a frost-free site with good drainage and protection from wind. They are gross feeders and need feeding with potassium and plenty of organic matter in the soil mix. In mild climates, plant suckers in late spring but anytime is fine in the tropics.

Propagation

Some ornamental and inferior varieties grow from seed. The best edible plants are bits of rhizome with a bud or sterile hybrids, propagated by suckers. Viable buds will resemble enormous, sprouting bulbs. They root easily in a gritty compost over heat in a moist atmosphere.

Pruning and Training

Bananas fruit continuously if happy. A stem will flower and fruit in about a year and a half. Only one main shoot and a replacement are allowed; all others should be removed, and once the main shoot has fruited it is cut out. The clump or stool may live as long as a human being, but is replaced commercially every dozen years or so.

Weed, Pest and Disease Control

Panama disease is fatal. The virus bunchy top is spread by aphids and is a notifiable disease.

culinary

Bananas are best matured off the tree and kept in a warm room. Most are at their best when yellow. They can be dried, made into flour or fermented to produce a sweet liqueur. In some countries, bananas are a staple food, being used as a vegetable and a source of flour, as well as a fruit.

Banana Custard Pie

Serves 4

175g digestive biscuits
75g butter
30g strawberry jam
300ml milk
60g honey
15g cornflour
dash of vanilla essence
3 or 4 bananas, sliced and chilled
nutmeg

Crush the biscuits and mix with most of the butter. Press into a pie dish and freeze. Spread the frozen surface with the remaining butter, paint with the jam and refreeze. Heat the milk and honey, mix the cornflour with a drop of water and the vanilla, then pour the hot milk onto the flour mixture. Return to the heat, stirring continuously, till thickened, then allow to cool. Put chilled banana slices into the cooled custard, mix together and pour into the biscuit case. Top with grated nutmeg and chill till required.

other uses

Often used in beauty preparations and shampoos. The foliage will provide good animal fodder.

My plastic tunnel is not quite tall enough

Phoenix dactylifera from the family *Arecaceae*

DATE PALMS

Tree, 25 x 6m. Life span: as long as a human being.
Fruits: just under 2 x 5cm, blue, brown or yellow.
Value: rich in vitamins A, B1 and B2 and some B3.

A tall tree with ferny leaves, the russet dead leaf bases protecting the trunk. Separate male and female plants are required for fruiting, which is prolific. Each tree annually bears several bunches of three or four dozen strings, each string carrying two or three dozen dates, the total weight being up to 68kg.

Dates have been cultivated in the Middle East for at least 4,000 years and all wild forms have disappeared. They have always been one of the staple foods of the Arab peoples, much of whose lives were centred around the oases where the palms were found.

varieties

Date production is new to Australia and restricted to northern Western Australia and the Northern Territory. **Deglet Noor**, the world's most popular variety, is from North Africa. Also grown are **Medgool**, **Barhee**, **Khalal**, **Rutab** and **Tamar**. *P. pusilla/zelanica*, **Ceylon Date Palm**, is smaller and possibly easier to crop. *Bactris/Guillielma utilis*, **Peach nut** or **Pewa**, is a native of Central America, similar to date palms with similar fruit, usually cooked in salty water before eating they taste of chestnuts. The best varieties are seedless. Other relations are **Prickly Palm**, *B. major*, and **Tobago palm**, *B. minor*. *Borassus flabellifer*, **Borassus** or **Palmyra** palm, **Sea Apple** or **Lonta**, is like a tall date palm with shorter fan-shaped leaves. The white flesh is used as a vegetable or a fruit and even canned, the fruits also contain refreshing sap drunk like coconut water. This, and the true sap tapped from the trunk, are boiled down into sugar, Jaggery or fermented into Toddy.

cultivation

One of the few crops to revel in hot, even scorching, dry places, date palms still need irrigation (even with brackish water) to fruit well. Dates need an absence of summer rain, low humidity and heat from flowering (August–September) to fruiting (February–April). They are not fussy about soil types but free drainage is essential. Female flowers need hand pollinating, fruit must be thinned and bird covers applied for good yields. Plants are subject to parlatoria scale.

Propagation
For choice fruit, offshoots or suckers have to be potted up; however, for ornamental use, seedlings are easily germinated but grow slowly. Large trees are easily transplanted with small rootballs. One male will be needed to every fifty females.

other uses

The palms have their sap extracted for sugar or fermenting. They may also be used as lumber.

culinary

Soft dates are partly dried, stoned and pressed into cakes, then exported all over the world. Semi-soft dates are those we find in packs at Christmas. Dry dates are hard, ground to a flour and commonly found only in Arab markets. Dates can be used in cakes, biscuits and confectionery and with curries and savoury dishes. They are also made into wine.

Stuffed Date Chocolates

1 box of dates
1 pack (225g) real marzipan
150g bar of dark chocolate
icing sugar

Stone the dates and stuff with marzipan. Dip in melted chocolate and cool on a tray dusted with icing sugar.

Persea americana* from the family *Lauraceae

AVOCADOS

ALLIGATOR PEAR, VEGETABLE MARROW

Tree, up to 9 x 6m. Life span: short, self-fertile. Fruits: 15 x 8cm, green. Value: rich in fats, proteins, vitamins A, B & C and thiamine.

The avocado is a medium-sized bushy tree with large, green, often rough but shiny, pear-shaped fruits. Each is filled with an enormous stone and a morsel of greeny-yellow flesh next to the leathery skin. (Large avocados are better value than small ones!) The small, greenish-cream, hermaphroditic flowers are especially fragrant. Natives of tropical America, avocados soon spread to India, Australia and other tropical areas. They were naturalised on Mauritius in 1758, but also as north as Florida, California and even Madeira.

varieties

Each tree can yield 500 fruits a year weighing up to 1kg, but smaller ones are preferred in supermarkets. Mexican or Canary varieties generally withstand the lowest temperatures, so use these to grow from stones. **Fuerte** and **Hass** are the commonest varieties.

cultivation

Rich soil, full of humus, and good drainage with plentiful moisture are necessary. Be generous with pot size, but avoid excessively nitrogenous composts.

Growing under Glass and in Containers
If fruits are produced in northern areas, they ripen late, through autumn and into winter, so are best kept under glass. They can be grown in large pots, surviving easily, but are harder to fruit.

Ornamental Value
Avocados are attractive and often grown as houseplants.

Propagation, Pruning and Training
Easily grown from fresh stones kept warm and moist. The best fruiting varieties are layered, or grafted on seedling stock. Little pruning is needed; nip out the centre shoot if you want a more squat shape!

Weed, Pest and Disease Control
Under glass they may get attacks of common pests, but are usually robust.

Harvesting and Storing
The fruit is best picked a week or so under-ripe and ripened in the cool, say at 7°C/45°F. The colour lightens and the flesh softens and becomes like butter. It is very susceptible to bruising.

other uses

The pulp of avocados makes an ideal natural ingredient for face masks and for skin moisturisers.

culinary

More savoury than sweet, an avocado is best with vinegar, pepper and salt, but is usually overwhelmed with prawns and mayonnaise. Containing up to 25 per cent fat, it adds body (and calories) to dips.

Avocado Dip/Guacamole
Serves 6

3 avocados
1 large or 2 small hard-boiled eggs
1 plum tomato, skinned and seeded
1 small sweet red capsicum (I prefer red)
3 spring onions
1 or more garlic cloves (optional)
1 tablespoon lemon or lime juice
dribble of olive oil
salt and pepper in moderation
a little ground coriander
as much chilli powder as you like

Scoop out the flesh of the chilled avocados and blend with all the other ingredients. Chill and serve with crudités.

Mangifera indica from the family *Anacardiaceae*

MANGO

Tree, variable size. Life span: as long as a human being. Fruits: variable in size, flat ovoids, green/ yellow or red. Value: rich in vitamins A, B and C.

Medium to large trees with luxuriant masses of narrow leaves, these carry fruits that weigh anything from a few grams to a kilogram. They have an inedible, tough skin and an enormous, flat stone to which the fibrous flesh adheres.

Mangoes are native to India and exist there in countless variety. Doubtless early Europeans came across them, but they were first recorded by a Friar Jordanus in about 1300. Mangoes have now spread to most hot regions in Australia, especially Queensland.

varieties

The common seedling mango is stringy, not a patch on local cultivars like **Bowen** or **Kensington Pride** and **Banana One**. Others, from Florida, include **Van Dyke**, **Tommy Atkins** and **Kent**. **Nam Doc Mai** is late-ripening for warm climates only, while **Florigon** grows well in cooler areas.

cultivation

Mangoes want a hot, tropical climate and deep, well-drained, rich soils. Excessive rain spoils pollination and drought spoils the quality of the fruit. They want exceptionally deep and wide planting holes dug about 10m apart. Fruit fl y, scale, mango tip borer and weevil borer attack mangoes. Use a suitable control. The fungus anthracnose causes black spots on fruit and loss of the crop.

Propagation

Seedling grown plants are generally stringy and tainted with turpentine. The best table fruit are named varieties either grafted or layered. They will bear in four to fi ve years. They are more expensive but worth every cent.

Young fruits are often pulled – but not this young

Pruning and Training

Remedial pruning of thin and poor growth is necessary once a head has formed, plus root pruning if the tree persists with strong, unfruitful growth.

other uses

The seeds have been boiled and eaten in famines. The wood is poor, but used for packaging crates and firewood.

culinary

Mangoes soften and turn yellow or red as they ripen and do not keep. Picked unripe, they travel well and are fine for culinary use. They are very messy to eat raw! They are widely used for chutneys, jams, tarts, pickles and preserves.

Mango Chutney

Makes approx. 1kg

1kg green mangoes
175g salt
600ml vinegar
75g each peeled chopped garlic cloves; sultanas; chopped dates
50g each chopped fresh ginger; chopped blanched almonds
2 teaspoons hot chilli powder
500g brown sugar

Peel, stone and chop the mangoes, sprinkle them with salt and keep cool overnight. Rinse and drain thoroughly. Mix all the ingredients except the sugar and simmer for several hours till soft. Add the sugar, bring to the boil and bottle in clean sterilised jars.

Store for six months before use.

Carica from the family *Caricaceae*

PAWPAW

PAPAYA

Herbaceous, up to 6m. Life span: very short. Fruits: up to 30 x 15cm. Value: rich in papain, calcium and in vitamins A and C.

Pawpaws (also known as papaya) are small herbaceous 'trees' that resemble palms as they are unbranched with ornate, acanthus-like foliage clustered on top and up to fifty green 'melons' underneath. There are male, female and hermaphrodite plants. The fruits uncannily resemble melons, turning yellow-orange as they ripen. The flesh is usually pink with a central hole full of small round seeds and can weigh up to 2kg.

Although it is indigenous to Central America, the pawpaw has rapidly spread to every warm country. Seeds were sent to Nepal as early as 1626 from the East Indies.

varieties

Pawpaws are either common yellow-fleshed dioecious (needing male and female plants) types or the smaller red-fleshed bisexual types. These Hawaiian or Fijian pawpaws like **Solo** and **Richter Gold** have a different flavour. There are several with sunset or sunrise in the name. **Solo** is a commercial dwarf, but most pawpaws are local varieties selected from seed and varying considerably. Grow them from fruit you like. *Asimina/ Anona triloba*, **Northern Pawpaw**, *Anonaceae*, the **Custard Banana** is a bottle-shaped fruit with fantastic potential. Closely related to the papaya it is much hardier and in its native America is found as far North as Michigan and New York. A large, attractive, long-leafed suckering bush, pest resistant with fragrant purple flowers, it prefers moist not wet soils. Male and female plants are needed, as pollination is by flies. The fruits vary from 5cm to 15cm, are green, ripening yellow to bronze with yellow pulp, big brown seeds and a resinous flavour. Occasionally tasty raw, they are usually best cooked.

cultivation

Pawpaws prefer deep, humus-rich soil, and to be about 3m apart. They need support while young. You should eliminate most males and replace the whole lot every five years.

Growing under Glass and in Containers
They are practical for tall heated greenhouses, and highly ornamental, so also well worth growing as pot plants, but they do not fruit well out of the sub-tropics.

Ornamental and Wildlife Value
Their foliage is very attractive and they're so easy to grow they are worth trying anywhere frost-free and elsewhere as summer bedding!

Propagation
Variable from seed; usually grown by sowing several to a hole and eliminating the poorest seedlings. (Only one male is needed to fifty females, but in fact they can be differentiated only when flowering.) Fruiting occurs within a year.

other uses

Papain, the active ingredient, is used medicinally, and for chewing gum.

culinary

Pawpaws are in season all year, and unripe ones keep for many days. Eaten as dessert or cooked as a fruit or vegetable, pawpaw is delicious, especially the first time. However, most importantly, the fruit and leaves contain papain, which tenderises meats cooked with them.

Pawpaw Breakfast Juice
Serves 2

1 ripe pawpaw
1 small lime
honey or sugar to taste

Scoop out the flesh and sift out the seeds of the pawpaw. Add lime juice and sweetener and liquidise. Serve immediately in frosted glasses with sugared rims as breakfast starters.

Psidium* and *Acca* from the family *Myrtaceae

GUAVAS
AND FEIJOAS

Tree 3–9m. Life span: short. Fruits: 5–8cm, yellow or red. Value: very rich in vitamin A and C, pectin, iron, potassium and calcium.

Guavas are small trees or spreading shrubs with leathery leaves. The bark peels off the smooth, ruddy branches in flakes. Fruits are round, ripening from green to yellow or red, full of acid yellow or red pulp and many hard, round seeds. Native to tropical America, guavas soon became popular the world over and were grown in orangeries. Though Feijoas hail from Brazil, they are now grown prolifically in New Zealand, and have become almost a national fruit.

varieties

There are many species of guavas. *P. guajava* is the commonest, with yellow fruits. Guavas are an acquired taste and variable as well. Named cultivars include **Allahabad**, **Ga11-56-13**, **Hawaiian Pink B1** and **B2**, **Indian White**, **Lucknow** and **Thai White**. Where possible taste each one before buying plants.

For dessert, gourmets choose *P. littorale*, the **Strawberry Guava**. This has a reddish-purple, plum-size, sweeter fruit on a hardier, shaggy-barked tree. *Acca sellowiana* is so similar as to be a variety of guava. It is smaller, with crimson and white flowers and fragrant fruit. It is almost hardy and not self fertile. Feijoas are rich sources of vitamin C.

cultivation

Any good soil and a sunny site is all they require. In a warm climate they are normally planted at about 4–5m apart.

Growing under Glass and in Containers
Acca is most reliable, the **Strawberry Guava** next, but all guavas are easily grown under glass and/or confined in pots. They can be put outdoors during the warmer months of the year.

Pest and Diseases
Guavas are subject to severe fruit fly attack and the fruit serves to overwinter the pest as it ripens in winter. Trees must be sprayed and baited to control them.

Propagation, Pruning and Training
Propagate by seeds for the species but also by suckers, layers or grafts for better varieties. Some plants occasionally produce seedless fruits: note these and propagate from them. Nip out top shoots to promote bushiness, otherwise prune only remedially.

other uses

The heavy wood is used for agricultural implements. The leaves and bark are a native cure for dysentery.

culinary

Guavas are best fresh off the tree, or picked early, as they soften. They are good for dessert, and cooked as tarts, jam and jelly. The burning wood and leaves add a delicious aroma to barbecued and jerked meats.

Guava Jelly
Makes approx. 2kg

1kg guavas
1 large lemon
Approx.1kg sugar

Simmer the washed, chopped guavas for two hours with a little water. Strain, weigh and bring back to the boil. Add the same weight of sugar and the juice of the lemon, reboil, pour into warmed sterilised jars and seal.

Strawberry guava – it really does taste of strawberry!

Artocarpus from the family *Moraceae*

BREADFRUIT
AND JACKFRUIT

Trees up to 28m. Life span: medium. Fruits: up to 20cm diameter, leathery balls. Value: mostly starch.

Both breadfruit and jackfruit are attractive, tall trees with large, deeply incised leaves. From the branch ends hang green, round to ovoid fruits, which have a thin, warty rind and are white and starchy within. Some have about 200 fleshy edible seeds or more, some have none.

Breadfruit are native to the Pacific and East Indies, jackfruit come from the Asian mainland and Indian sub-continent. They were first noted in the voyages of the sixteenth century and soon taken to other hot regions, but never proved really popular. Breadfruit plants being taken to the West Indies played a part in the famous 1787 mutiny on *The Bounty*. When the water supply ran low, the valuable cargo was given water in preference to the crew.

varieties

Artocarpus communis (*incisa* or *altilis*) is the **Breadfruit** proper, bearing a remarkable resemblance, once cooked, to bread. From the West Indies comes the **Bread-nut Tree**, which, when cooked, is claimed to rival a new loaf in both taste and texture. *A. integrifolia* (*heterophylla*) is the **Jackfruit** or **Jakfruit**. The fruit is much bigger, weighing up to 30kg. These largest of fruits strangely spring from older branches and direct from the trunk. When ripe they have a strong odour of very ripe melon.

A. integer, **C(h)empedak** is a similar fruit, even sweeter and pongier, eaten fresh and with more seeds, which are also much prized. Several named varieties of jackfruit are grown in Australia, including **Black Gold, Cheena X** and **Galaxy**.

cultivation

Any reasonable soil and site in a hot and moist climate.

Growing in Containers
The size of the fruiting tree makes it impractical to grow these in pots or under glass except for ornamental value.

Ornamental and Wildlife Value
Very handsome trees, the fruits are valuable to wildlife.

Propagation, Pruning and Training
They can be propagated by seed, but the best varieties come only by root suckers or by layering. Little pruning is required except remedial.

Harvesting and Storing
Breadfruit is eaten fresh after cooking, but used to be stored in pits where the pulp was fermented to make a nauseous soft 'cheese', which would keep for several years. Breadfruits are traditionally stored under water! Jackfruits become the best if a small one on a bent low branch is heavily earthed over before it starts to swell.

companion planting

The jackfruit tree is often used to support pepper (*Piper nigrum*) and as a shade tree for coffee plantations.

other uses

Jackfruit wood is like mahogany, valuable and useful. A yellow dye for clothing is extracted from the wood in India and the East. Breadfruit wood is light and used for box manufacture, and in Hawaii for surfboards.

culinary

Breadfruit are usually eaten roasted, boiled or fried as a vegetable. The edible seeds are often preferred, when they occur. Jackfruit are eaten in the same way and have a stronger flavour. Breadfruit can be dried and ground to a flour offensive to some and may also be eaten raw, in soups or even ice cream.

Baked Breadfruit
Serves 2

Bake a breadfruit in a preheated oven at 190°C/375°F/gas mark 5, until you can push a knife through it easily. Extract the pulp, seeds and all, and serve with curry or a savoury sauce.

Durio zibethinus from family *Malvaceae/Bombacaceae*

DURIANS

CIVET FRUIT

Tree 30m. Life span: fairly long. Fruits: about 25 x 20cm, ovoid, green to yellow. Value: a little protein, a little fat; one quarter to a third is fat and starch.

This is an infamous fruit, banned from airlines and loathed by most people on first acquaintance. It has an aroma similar to that of an over-ripe Gorgonzola cheese in a warm room. The flavour was long ago described as 'French custard passed through a sewer pipe'. The texture is like that of blancmange or custard, and the sweet flavour delicious and addictive. Once bravely tasted, the durian is unforgettable and 'the sensation is worth a voyage to the East'.

The trees are very large and upright with leaves not dissimilar to those of a peach. The fruits are round to ovoid, very large, weighing up to 4–5kg, green initially, yellowing as they ripen, with a long stalk. They are covered in short, sharp spikes and resemble some brutal medieval weapon. The pulp is white with up to a dozen big seeds.

Durians come originally from Malaysia and spread to Southeast Asia in prehistoric times. They have recently been introduced to tropical Australian farms for trial.

varieties

Rare but the clones **Luang** and **Kan Yao** show some promise for cropping in Australia.

cultivation

The large trees need a deep, heavy soil to secure them, but they are not too difficult to please.

Propagation, Pruning and Training

Seeds, if fresh, germinate in about a week and come nearly true. Only remedial pruning work is necessary.

Growing under Glass and in Containers

Their size and their need for tropical heat and moisture make them difficult. They may make good pot specimens if fresh seed can be obtained.

Ornamental and Wildlife Value

Attractive trees in their native climate.

other uses

Durians help get railway compartments to oneself. They are also reputed to be an aphrodisiac.

They can be located by the nose alone

culinary

Durians must be eaten fresh and they quickly spoil due to a chemical change (and the aroma gets worse!). They are best eaten raw but may be made into ice cream or jam, or juiced and drunk with coconut milk. The large, fleshy seeds are boiled or roasted and eaten as nuts.

Durian Delight

Serves 6

225g each unsweetened durian purée, honey, natural set yogurt, cream

Dash of vanilla essence

Mix the ingredients and beat till smooth. Partially freeze, beat again and repeat this two or three times before freezing firm. Keep well sealed until immediately before eating!

Annona* from the family *Annonaceae

CHERIMOYAS

CUSTARD APPLES AND SOUR SOPS

Tree up to 6m. Life span: short. Fruits: variable in size, green and scaly. Value: all varieties rich in vitamins.

A family of small trees, known as custard apples or sour sops, from the flavour and texture of the better fruits. Many have aromatic leaves and/or fragrant flowers. Despite the varying appearance of each species, the common names are often swapped or confused in different countries. The flesh is usually white, sweet and acid, with up to 30 black seeds embedded in it and covered with a thin rind, which breaks off like scales when ripe.

Natives of the Americas, they are most popular there but have spread to other tropical and warm zones. In Australia the cherimoya is revered in the sub-tropics.

varieties

All varieties have leaves with some scent if rubbed, often downy underneath. The odd green tri-petalled flowers are often fragrant, and the fruits resemble artichokes with a banana-cum-pineapple flavour and lots of hard, raisin-sized seeds. *Annona squamosa* is the **Sugar Apple** or **Sweet Sop**, small fruited and knobbly and most common in the West Indies; it's always eaten fresh. *A. cherimolia* is the **Cherimoya**, deciduous and more hardy, growing at high elevations in hotter areas and best for growing under glass in cool countries. *A. muricata* or **Sour Sop** is evergreen with large (up to 2–3kg) green fruits rich in vitamins B and C, with soft spines in ridges and the best flavour but fibrous. Eaten raw as a vegetable, it is made into delicious beverages when ripe. *A. reticulata* is the **Bullock's Heart**, so-called because of the ruddy colour, with firm, sweet, yellow pulp rich in vitamin A numerous other species are grown all over the Americas and especially good are the huge rugby-ball sized **Rollinias**. In Australia, the aptly named **Pinks Mammoth** custard apple produces fruit weighing up to 3kg, while the **African Pride** can weigh up to 800g.

cultivation

They will thrive in poor soils but give better crops with better treatment and prefer dryish, hilly conditions. Trees bear well in the humid tropics once they are three years old.

other uses

Corossol tea was traditionally made from the leaves of *A. muricata*.

culinary

Picked under-ripe they keep for up to a week or so. Ripen wrapped in brown paper; yellowing and scent indicate the time to use – the black bits on the skin are not rot! They are usually eaten raw or used to flavour drinks and ices. They also make excellent ice cream and a really weird cider.

Sour Sop Sorbet

Serves 6

500g sugar
1 large ripe sour sop
60g crystallised ginger

Dissolve the sugar in 450ml boiling water and chill. Squeeze the juice from the sour sop pulp and strain. To each cupful add half a cup of sugar syrup. Partly freeze, beat and refreeze. Repeat twice. After the final beating, mix in the chopped ginger.

Averrhoa carambola from the family *Oxalidaceae*

CARAMBOLAS

Tree up to 11m. Life span: medium. Fruits: up to 5 x 15cm. Cylindrical, star-shaped in cross section, yellow. Value: vitamins A and C.

Averrhoas are small trees with delicate, pinnate (walnut-like) foliage. A profusion of sprays of little white or pinkish flowers is followed by huge quantities of yellow, cylindrical, star-shaped fruits with five prominent angles, which weigh down the branches and give the fruit it's more common name, starfruit.

Natives of Indonesia and the Moluccas, averrhoas are still mostly grown in Southeast Asia and the Indian subcontinent. However, because of their decorative value, and being quite robust, they are now grown in tropical and sub-tropical Australia.

varieties

Carambolas are variable in taste. Some are much better than others, though they are all juicy. I have eaten them from European supermarkets, when they were like yellow soap, and also fresh, when they were amber and a joy. Look for **Kembangan**, **Kary** or **Arkin** varieties. *Averrhoa bilimbi* or **Billings** are similar, resembling gherkin cucumbers, but are used more as vegetables and in curries, and for billings jam.

cultivation

Adaptable to most warm, moist climates and reasonable, well-drained soil. They fruit prolifically with little attention.

Ornamental and Wildlife Value
Burdened with yellow fruit, they are impressive.

Growing under Glass and in Containers
Carambolas are pretty plants, so make good specimens. If they fruit they will put on a terrific show.

Propagation
Usually they are grown from seed, but better varieties are grafted. Only remedial pruning is needed.

other uses

Carambola juice removes stains from linen and can be used for polishing brass. Billings jam also polishes brass.

culinary

They travel fairly well if picked just underripe and then keep for a week or two. The narrow-ribbed carambolas are sourer, the wider fleshier-ribbed ones sweeter. Carambolas are as often used for refreshing drinks as dessert fruits. Their star shape makes excellent decorative garnishes in compotes and fruit salads.

Camaranga or Carambola Jam
Makes approx. 2kg

1kg carambolas
1kg white sugar

Cut the fruit up into finger-thick pieces and discard the sharp edges. Do not discard the seeds, as they improve the flavour of the jam. Add water to cover them and boil till the pieces are softening – about 15 minutes should be sufficient. Add the sugar and bring to the boil again for another 15 minutes, then bottle and seal.

Achras sapota/Manilkara zapota from the family *Sapotaceae*

SAPODILLAS

OR SAPOTAS, NASEBERRIES, BULLY TREES, CHIKKUS

Tree 4–16m. Life span: medium. Fruits: about 6cm, rounded, brown.

Sapodilla makes a medium to big tree with glossy leaves. The fruit is a large, round berry with a rough, brown skin over luscious pulp similar to a pear's, containing a core with up to a dozen seeds much like an apple's – black, shiny and inedible. The tree's milky sap can be tapped in the same way as rubber. Once collected, it is coagulated with heat and the sticky mass produced is strained out and dried to form chicle gum.

Still mostly grown in its native region of Central America, sapodilla is found wild in the forests of Venezuela. Sapodillas were more extensively planted when chicle gum started to be used for a booming new commodity – chewing gum. Now it is an important crop for Mexico and Central American countries. The naseberry is Jamaica's national fruit.

varieties

Local varieties are cultivated for fruit, but there is little commercial demand, as it must be eaten absolutely ripe. However, there is a big demand for chicle gum; varieties selected for sap production can give up to 3kg of gum per year. Varieties grown in Australia include **Sawo Manila** and **Ponderosa** from the Philippines, the **Thai Krasuey** and, from Florida, **Martin** and **Brown Sugar**. *Pouteria/Calocarpum sapote*, **Mamey sapotes** or **Marmalade Plums** are similar *Sapotaceae*, with red fruits used fresh and preserved, and the seed can be made into a bitter chocolate, nearly hardy and grown in many local varieties.

cultivation

Sapodilla prefers very hot, moist climates with rich soil. Young trees are cold tender. Grow 3–4m apart in a slightly alkaline soil with marginal drainage but in full sun. Grafted trees take two to three years to bear and several varieties are available. Trees flower in summer and fruit is harvested next spring.

Propagation, Pruning and Training
Propagate by seed or preferably by grafting for better varieties. Only remedial pruning work seems necessary.

Ornamental and Wildlife Value
Sapodilla has very attractive foliage and the fruits are enjoyed by wildlife.

Harvesting and Storing
Best finally ripened off the tree, when the fruit softens and mellows in a few days to a treacly, gummy consistency. Left on the tree, the fruits become veined with milk, which makes them too acid until bletted like medlars (see page 159).

One of the great unknowns

companion planting

Sapodilla trees are normally grown for the first five years with underplanted legume crops.

other uses

Sapodilla wood is hard and durable, so it is used for handles and tools.

culinary

Perfectly ripened, they are considered superb dessert fruit. The fruits keep up to a month or more in a cold refrigerator. Sapodillas also make a good ice cream and, believe it or not, even an interesting milk pudding with garlic!

Chewing Gum

120g each of chicle gum, glucose, caramel paste, icing sugar
225g sugar
Spearmint or mint flavouring, to taste

Melt the gum carefully in a bain-marie. Meanwhile boil 100ml water, the sugar and glucose to exactly 124°C (255°F). Remove from the heat, add the caramel and boil again. Off the heat, mix the syrup into the melted gum, beating steadily and briskly. Add the flavouring and pour on to a cold surface thickly coated with icing sugar. Roll flat. When cold, cut into strips, wrap and label.

Nephelium lappaceum and *N. chinensis/litchi* from the family *Sapindaceae*

RAMBUTANS AND LITCHIS

Tree up to 18m. Life span: medium to long. Usually not self-fertile; male and female flowers often on separate trees. Fruits: 2.5–5cm, round, reddish or yellow.

Rambutan or ramtum trees are large and spreading, with pinnate leaves, and festooned with hairy, chestnut-like conkers. These fruits are apricot-sized, covered with red or orange-yellow soft spines like tentacles. Underneath the skin the flesh is wrapped around the single, inedible, brown seed. The flesh is sweet, acid, almost like pineapple with a hint of apricot – shame there is so little, as it is one of the best fruits I've ever tried.

Very similar yet more perfumed are lychees, litchees, or litchis. These have a prickly, crackly shell and grow on a smaller tree. Originally from the Malay archipelago, rambutans are greatly appreciated in Southeast Asia where they are often grown in gardens, but, surprisingly, have never proved popular anywhere else. Lychees have long been a Chinese speciality, so they followed their people to many other suitable areas, including Australia.

varieties

Many different varieties of **Rambutan** and **Litchi** are grown in their regions. The **Pulassan**, *Nephelium mutabile/chryseum*, is another species, native to Java; it is similar but covered with fleshy spines instead of tentacles. *N. longana/Dimocarpus* longan, the **Longan**, popular in southern China, is smaller, browny yellow and nearly smooth skinned with similar chewy flesh. Varieties include **Chompoo**, **Haew** and **Duan Yu**. Very similar is *Euphoria malaiense*, **Cat's Eye** or **Dragon's Eye**, though the seeds are huge relative to the flesh. The **Keppel** is an almost mythical fruit that allegedly turns body odours to the sweet smell of violets – it should be compulsory eating before all public events. About 15 varieties of rambutan are grown in Australia, including **Jitlee**, **R156** and **R134**.

Good lychee cultivars for home gardens include **Kwai May Pink, Wai Chee, Tai So** and **Salathiel**.

cultivation

Rambutans need tropical conditions. Lychees prefer lower humidity and sub-tropical climates. Rambutans thrive in temperatures between 15°C and 35°C, as they hate cold. Plant in full sun, 4–5m apart. They flower in spring–summer and fruit summer–winter. Lychees need a dry, cool but frost-free winter and high summer heat. Grafted trees bear after four years. Fruit appears summer–autumn. Longans take cooler conditions.

Propagation, Pests and Diseases

They come nearly true from seed, but the best varieties are budded. Bird and fruit bat damage is a big problem.

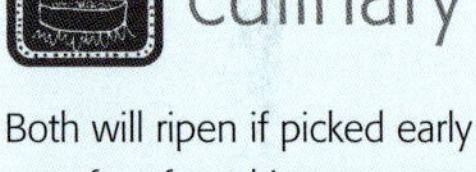

culinary

Both will ripen if picked early off the tree, so they are often found in temperate country shops. Litchis are often preserved in syrup or dried to perfumed 'prunes'. All the fruits are superb desserts. Litchis are often used to close a Chinese meal.

Litchi Sundae

Serves 4–6

1kg litchis
600ml real vanilla ice cream
60g blanched toasted almonds
Nutmeg
30g coarse brown sugar
4–6 glacé cherries

Peel and stone the litchis, then chill them. Layer the fruit in tall glasses with ice cream and almonds and top with a flourish of nutmeg, sugar and a cherry.

Garcinia mangostana from the family *Clusiaceae (Guttifereae)*

MANGOSTEEN

Tree 14m. Life span: long. Fruits: 6cm, round, brownish. Value: small amounts of protein, mineral matter and fat; approx. one-seventh sugar and starch.

The trees are small to medium-sized, cone-shaped and have large, leathery leaves somewhat like a lemon's. The fruits are round, purplish-brown, about apple size, with a rosette of dead petals around the stalk and an odd flower-shaped button on the other end. If you cut the rind around the fruit's circumference, the top can be lifted off to reveal about half a dozen kernels of melting white pulp, tasting between grape and strawberry, tart and sweet, almost syrupy and chewy. There is a seed contained in many kernels, which is not eaten.

Mangosteens are natives of Malaya and were described in detail by Captain Cook in 1770, and with delight. They were introduced to Ceylon (now Sri Lanka) in 1800 and were successfully fruited in English greenhouses in 1855. Widely held to be the world's most delicious fruit, they may be found in tropical gardens everywhere, but are nowhere grown on a commercial scale.

culinary

Use a ladder to climb up and pick mangosteens as they bruise if they fall. They can be picked unripe and kept for a few days or may be made into conserves.

Mangosteen Ecstasy
If you are fortunate enough to have a mangosteen, just eat it!

Not all segments have seeds

varieties

Mangosteens need an equatorial climate with high regular rainfall. They are understorey trees and need shading while young in Australian conditions. They grow around Cairns, Mossman and Darwin (with irrigation). The fruit does not need fertilising and there is little seedling variation. Trees grown from seed tend to be stronger than grafted ones but take up to 20 years to bear fruit.

cultivation

They need deep, rich, well-drained soil, a sheltered site, shade when young, a hot, moist climate. Trees defoliate under 5ºC and need shading for up to ten years in the dry tropics. They prefer a mildly acid, moisture-holding clay loam with plenty of humus. Plant at least 5m apart in the warmer months. Fertilise after cropping (twice a year around December and May).

Propagation
Slow-growing from seed. The best varieties are layered.

companion planting

Mangosteens benefit from light shade, especially when young, preferring tropically bright but not direct light, so they are planted in the shade of taller trees.

TRAVELLER'S TALES TROPICAL FRUITS

There are many more fruits the inveterate traveller may come across in tropical and semi-tropical countries. Some of these are of more practical or commercial interest, such as the spices, while others are of such purely local interest they are rarely if ever recorded. Many may be unknown, as they are unpalatable by 'modern' standards, or they may be delicious but hard to cultivate. As we move into a homogenised world of mass consumption, the numbers of varieties of even the most popular fruits decline. Quaint, diffi cult and unusual fruits have already disappeared from all but local native markets and botanic and private gardens. If you travel far off the beaten track, you may come across the following, and others – but, when choosing to taste them, do not rely on my identifi cation.

Aberia gardneri, **Ceylon Gooseberry**, *Bixineae*

Native to what is now Sri Lanka, this is a small, shrubby tree with large, purple-brown, round berries mostly used for making jams and preserves. Closely related is *A. caffra*, the **Kai**, **Kau** or **Kei Apple** of South Africa, which is yellow and so acid it is used as a pickle, omitting the vinegar.

Baccaurea dulcis/Pierardia motleyana, **Rambeh** or **Rambei**, *Euphorbiaceae*

Found in Malaysia, especially Sumatra, and China, this has long, hanging bunches of large, yellow berries that are reputedly sweet-tasting, juicy and luscious. *B. griffithii*, **Tampoi**, a similar fruit, with buff berries with yellow flesh, and is considered better eating than the Rambeh.

Blighia sapida, **Akee**, *Sapindaceae*

A medium-sized tree from West Africa, grown in the West Indies, especially Jamaica, where the fruit, fried in butter, is considered excellent fare. The fruits are bright red, heart-shaped pods, which burst to reveal three glossy, black seeds the size of peas sitting in a yellowish cup, which is the tasty bit. The seeds are inedible, the pink flesh highly poisonous and even the edible bit is poisonous if under- or over-ripe. One wonders how this ever became popular!

Carissa grandifl ora, **Natal Plum**, *Apocynaceae*

This and *C. carandas* are large, thorny shrubs used as hedges in Natal. They have purple, damson-like fruits tasting of gooseberry which are widely used for tarts and preserves. *C. carandas*, which is also used for pickling, prefers drier areas. *Carissa congesta*, **Kerandang**, is preferred in Malaya.

Ceratonia siliqua, **Carob Tree**, *Leguminosae*, the **Locust Bean** or **St John's Bread**

An edible purple-brown, bean-like pod that tastes so much like chocolate it is ground up and used as a substitute. The seeds themselves are not eaten. The tree is a native of the Mediterranean region, and preserved pods have been found at Pompeii; they are now used as animal feed. Remarkably similar are the closely related **Honey Mesquite**, *Prosopis julifl ora*, and
Honey Locust, *Gleditsia triacanthus*. Often planted as ornamental trees, their pods have a very sweet pulp around the inedible seeds.

Chrysophyllum cainito, **Star Apple**, *Sapotaceae*

Noted by Cieza de Leon in Peru in 1532–50, this is a large, evergreen tree with purple-brown 'apples', which, when cut through, have a star shape in the middle with about half a dozen shiny, brown seeds in a sweet/acid pulp.

Coccoloba uvifera, **Seagrape**, *Polygonaceae*

A coloniser of tropical shores, this is a very salt-tolerant, small, evergreen shrub or tree found from Florida to Venezuela. The 'grapes' are up to half an inch across, mild and sweet. They are eaten raw or jellied. The wood is hard and takes a polish well. It is often used as hedging or for good windbreaks.

Eugenia caryophyllus

TRAVELLER'S TALES TROPICAL FRUITS

Coccoloba uvifera

Eugenia caryophyllus, **Cloves**, *Myrtaceae*

(See opposite) Cloves are the dried flower buds of this Indonesian tree. The **Brazilian Cherry**, **Surinam Cherry** or **Pitanga Cherry**, *E. unifl ora*, has fruits varying from yellow to red and purple; unusually the darker are the more acid. Other *Eugenia* species have bigger juicier fruits though they are often rather bland, such as the **Jambus**, the **Malay Apple**, *Syzygium / E. malaccensis*, the **Water Apple**, *E. aquea*, and the **Rose Apple**, *E. jambos*. *Syzygium paniculatum*, the **Australian Bush** or **Brush Cherry**, has rose-purple fragrant berries used for jellies. *Eugenia dombeyi / brasiliensis*, **Grumichama**, is a red-purple cherry-sized berry very popular in Brazil, fresh and cooked in many ways.

Hovenia dulcis, **Japanese Raisin Tree**, *Rhamnaceae*

I remember having this as a child. Resembling brown candied angelica, it is the dried swollen flower stalk from behind the pea-sized seed of a small attractive Asian tree with glossy foliage. It's eaten as a hangover cure in China, where they also make sugar from the seeds, leaves and shoots.

Mimusops elengi, **Sapotaceae**

This large East Asian tree has fragrant flowers. The 2.5cm yellow berries are eaten when ripe and an oil is expressed from the seed. Other *Mimusops* are also grown for their similar fruits. *M. elata* of Brazil is the **Cow Tree**. Its apple-sized fruits contain a milk-like latex that resembles milk, when fresh, and is drunk with coffee, but soon congeals to a glue.

Pimenta dioica, **Allspice**, **Pimento**, *Myrtaceae*

This small, evergreen West Indian tree has pea-size berries that are dried unripe for their mixed spice flavour.

Piper nigrum, **Pepper**, *Piperaceae*

Black and white pepper are the unripe and ripe (and de-corticated) seeds of this Indian climbing vine.

Spondias, **Spanish**, **Hog** or **Brazilian Plum**, **Otaheite** or **Golden Apple**, *Anacardiaceae*

Distantly related to cashews and pistachios, the Spondias have edible fruits, most of them only when made into preserves, but some are eaten raw. They are purple to yellow, resembling a plum with a central 'stone'. The stone of the **Spanish Plum**, Spondias purpurea, is eaten by some people.

Syzygium paniculatum

Tamarindus indica

Tamarindus indica, **Tamarind Tree**, *Caesalpiniaceae*

This large, handsome tree has brown pods containing very acid pulp used for beverages and in chutneys, curries and medicine.

Vanilla planifolia, **Orchidaceae**

Vanilla is the fruit of an orchid that is native to Central America but is mostly grown in Madagascar. The beanlike pods are cured and dried for flavouring.

Zizyphus jujuba, **Jujube**, **Chinese Date**, *Rhamnaceae*

An East Indian native, this reached China and was improved to dessert quality. In China it is popular dried or preserved in syrup. Jujubes resemble large, yellowish or reddish cherries with thick, tough skin, a hard kernel and a pithy, acid pulp, rich in vitamin C. The thorny, shrubby trees survive in cooler climates and have been in Mediterranean countries since biblical times. Z. *vulgaris*, a native of the Middle East, is similar but less agreeable. *Z. lotus* is like a sweet olive and is thought to be the lotus Odysseus had trouble with.

SHRUB AND FLOWER GARDEN FRUITS

WILD GARDEN FRUITING TREES AND SHRUBS

Many familiar garden plants also bear fruit. Some of these are edible and can add variety and nutritional range to the diet. But first, I must insist that you never eat anything you are not sure of. Have it identified as safe by an expert. Also you must realise that although the fruits of some plants, such as yew, may not themselves be harmful, the foliage and seeds are deadly if ingested in quantity. Various parts may also be an irritant to some people.

However, such warnings aside, there are many familiar plants that have edible, if not actually delicious, fruits. Although they might not seem at first glance very attractive or be popular with many of us today, some of these were once greatly esteemed by native peoples, and others were part of the country fare of our not-so-distant predecessors. With a little care and attention, these plants can provide us with fresh and unusual dishes, far exceeding in vitamins and flavour than those made from the tired and flabby fruits usually offered for sale.

The plants at the beginning of this section are all excellent garden subjects, worthy of anyone's attention, which incidentally bear edible fruit. Some of the other plants with edible fruits are not attractive enough, or grow too big, for most gardens, but are of interest or value to insects or birds, and are more often planted in larger, public or wildlife gardens.

The ideal picturesque garden, often called the cottage garden, is typified these days by extravagant species at flower shows with odd mixtures of flowers, half of them out of season, grown elsewhere in pots and jammed full, with a camouflage of bark. The true cottager's garden was indeed a mixture of plants, but all with a purpose – to provide medicines, herbs, flavourings, fruits and, last of all, flowers.

Fruiting trees and shrubs can be easily cultivated with other plants underneath, and were the backbone of a true cottage garden. A mixture of plants that were found to grow happily together for both production and ornament was sensible, as it produced a mixed ecology, so there were rarely pest or disease problems. In addition, the plants grown in flower, shrub and wild gardens are often innately more reliable than those especially cultivated for fruits, as they are closer to the wild forms, with natural pest and disease resistance.

The biggest handicap for some of these plants has probably been their very attractiveness. If they had been a little less pretty, they might have been developed further for their fruits and have remained part of our diet.

Few of them are palatable raw, at least not to most people's taste, and all are better made into jams, jellies and preserves, but they have appealing and interesting flavours and are of inestimable value to the adventurous gourmet or those wishing to expand their dietary range. And for those interested in breeding, they offer plenty of opportunity for rapid improvement towards bigger, tastier and better fruits.

Amelanchier canadensis from the family *Rosaceae*

JUNEBERRIES

SNOWY MESPILUS, SHADS, SWEET/GRAPE PEARS

Tree/bush up to 6–9m. Life span: medium. Self-fertile. Fruits: 1cm, round, purple-black. Value: rich in vitamin C.

The Amelanchiers are small, deciduous trees or shrubs tending to suckering growth, most noticeable when absolutely covered with white blossoms. The fruits are purplish, spherical and about pea-size, but can be larger. *A. canadensis* is the best species and a native of North America. Though there are relatives in Asia and Europe, these are not as palatable. *A. vulgaris* grows wild in European mountain districts and was long cultivated in England, as much for the flowers as the fruits.

varieties

Amelanchier canadensis was a favourite fruit of Native Americans. It was adopted by French settlers and became **Poires** in Canada and **Sweet** or **Grape Pear** in the USA. It has small, purple berries which are sweet and tasty. *A. alnifolia*, or **Western Service Berry**, is larger and found wild in the states of Oregon and Washington. *A. spicata*, not known in the wild, is a suckering shrub with blue-black berries good for jam or wine. All cultivars are supplied for ornamental rather than fruiting purposes. Juneberries are rare in Australia, where they are also known as **Saskatoon**.

cultivation

Amelanchiers do best in moist, well-drained, lime-free soil. They are slow-growing, tending to sucker.

Ornamental and Wildlife Value

Neat, compact, floriferous, good autumn leaf colours, excellent shrub border plants. Birds like the berries.

Propagation, Pruning and Training

Sow seeds fresh for the species, but graft choice varieties in April on to *Sorbus aucuparia* stock. You may need to remove suckers. Prune only remedially.

Frequently grown as a flowering shrub on lime-free sites

culinary

They can be eaten raw, but are better as jams or tarts, or dried like raisins.

Snowy Mespilus Sponge Cakes

Makes about 10

60g each butter, powdered sugar and white self-raising flour
1 large or 2 small eggs
Dash of vanilla essence
Splash of milk
120g dried amelanchier berries

Cream the butter and sugar, beat in the eggs and vanilla, fold in the sifted flour, then add enough milk to make a smooth mixture. Stir in the berries; pour into greased paper cups. Stand the cups on a metal tray and bake in a preheated oven at 190°C/375°F/gas mark 5 for 20 minutes or till firm.

Growing in Containers

So hardy, they hardly seem worth the space under cover. No particular problems affect these tough plants. They could be delightful small specimens in pots.

other uses

Can be used as rootstocks for pome fruits.

Myrtus communis from the order *Myrtaceae*

MYRTLE

Tree up to 4.5m. Life span: medium. Fruits: 1cm, usually black-blue.

Myrtle is one of sixty small evergreen shrubs which are densely and aromatically leafed, with white flowers.

***Myrtus communis* has long been grown in southern Europe and western Asia. It was highly revered and much enjoyed by the Ancient Greeks, whose mythology held myrtle sacred to Aphrodite, the goddess of love. As all other myrtles are native to South America or New Zealand, common myrtle may indicate a prehistoric link between the continents.**

culinary

Myrtle berries are eaten raw or in tarts and jams or dried. The jam has an aromatic flavour which goes well with savoury dishes. The fresh flowers can be added to a salad. Mediterranean, especially Tuscan, cooking uses the dried fruits and flower buds as a spice. In Chile, **Temo**, *M. molinae*, seed was used to make a coffee.

Myrtle Jam

Makes approx. 2kg

1kg myrtle berries
1kg sugar

Wash the berries and prick them with a darning needle. Simmer them until soft with just enough water to prevent burning. Add the sugar and bring to the boil then bottle in warm, sterilised jars and seal.

varieties

Myrtus communis is grown for fruit and has ornamental forms such as *microphylla* and *tarentina* which are small, rarely reaching more than 60cm high. Their foliage is aromatic when crushed, making them good for small patios or sunny windows, but they rarely fruit well. *M. ugni* is the **Chilean Guava Myrtle**, which has delicious, mahogany red, pleasantly fragrant berries which are used to flavour water. These apparently fruit well in greenhouses. *Luma apiculata,* **Arrayan**, nearly hardy, from Chile, this small evergreen has beautiful leathery leaves, white flowers and then juicy aromatic sweet purple berries, good raw or as jam.

cultivation

Myrtles need full sun and a well-drained soil. They are not averse to lime and are also good by the seaside. *M. communis*, *chequen* and *nummalaria* are the hardiest.

Myrtles come in several species and varieties, though rarely selected for cropping

Ornamental and Wildlife Value

Very attractive evergreens for mild regions. The flowers and berries are attractive to wildlife.

Pests and Diseases

As myrtles are very tough there are no real problems.

Propagation and Training

The species can be grown from seed, or half-ripe cuttings can be taken in late summer with some success. Myrtle is best grown as a bush against a wall for the shelter and warmth. In early summer, clipping is usually preferred to pruning.

Growing under Glass and in Containers

These are very good subjects to have under glass and/or in containers, especially *M. ugni* or *M. communis tarentina*.

other uses

Used in medicine. The dried leaves and wood are fragrant. The flowers are made into perfume and toilet water.

Berberis vulgaris from the family *Berberidaceae*

BARBERRIES

MAHONIAS, OREGON GRAPES

Bush up to 4 x 4m. Life span: short. Fruits: under 1cm, white, yellow, scarlet, purple or black.

The Berberis family contains hundreds of small- to medium-sized, spiny shrubs that have masses of berries in many colours. The leaves of most deciduous varieties turn bright shades in autumn and the wood is usually yellow.

Various species are found all over the world. Our common barberry is now seldom relished, but was once widely popular. Indeed, the settlers in Massachusetts grew so many that in 1754 the province had to forbid further planting.

varieties

Berberis vulgaris is the **Common Barberry**, which once existed in a host of local forms and colours. One found in Rouen was seedless. Other species are enjoyed all over the world: *B. darwinii* is popular; *B. buxifolia*, the **Magellan Barberry**, is large and said to be the best raw or cooked. **Mahonia** is now a separate genus, but is very similar in many ways, only lacking the spines and having pinnate leaves. The flowers are yellow, usually scented, and the blue-black berries of *M. aquifolium* were made into preserves as Oregon grapes.

cultivation

They grow almost anywhere apart from conditions of extreme shade, drought or waterlogging, and are even fairly tolerant of salt spray. Cold hardiness depends on species.

Growing in Containers
They are hardy enough not to need protection, but do make good plants in containers.

Ornamental and Wildlife Value
Some ornamental varieties are very attractive, though not as productive of berries, which are exceedingly well liked by birds. Most varieties are excellent when used for wildlife gardens.

Beautiful in flower and berry, and nice tart jelly

Propagation, Pruning and Training
The species grows from seed, layered or grafted. They can usually be cut to the ground and will recover.

Pests and Diseases
Barberries are an alternate host for wheat rust, so care should be taken not to plant near wheat.

other uses

They make good hedges and game cover. A dye was made from the **Yellow Barberry** wood and roots.

culinary

The berries can be pickled in vinegar, preserved in sugar or syrup, candied or made into jam. The leaves were once used as a seasoning.

Colonel Flowerdew's Bengal Chutney
Makes approx 1.4kg

1kg grated apples
120g each of the following:
dried barberries, soft brown sugar, Demerara sugar, mustard seed, golden syrup
60g each of the following:
chopped onions, chopped garlic, chopped fresh ginger and salt
15g cayenne pepper
600ml vinegar

Mix all the ingredients and simmer till soft, say, 2–3 hours. Bottle in small sterilised jars for six months.

Mespilus germanica* from the family *Rosaceae

MEDLARS

Tree up to 9m. Life span: medium. Self-fertile. Fruits: 2.5–5cm, green to russet.

Medlars resemble pear trees but are smaller, have bigger leathery leaves, single, large, white flowers and fruits like giant, distorted rose hips. The brownish-green fruits have a rough 'leafy' end, which shows the seed chambers. Medlars seldom ripen fully on the tree in cool regions and were eaten 'bletted' – stored till at the point of decomposition. The taste is somewhat like that of rotten pear and they are an acquired taste. Originally from Persia, medlars became naturalised over much of Europe. Theophrastus mentions them in Greece in 300 BC and Pliny refers to the Romans having three sorts. Once very popular, they are now planted infrequently.

varieties

There are only a few left. Generally the bigger the tree, the larger the fruit tends to be. **Dutch** and **Monstrous** are the largest, **Royal** and **Nottingham** the tastiest and smaller. The seedless **Stoneless** has disappeared.

cultivation

Medlars are obliging and will grow in most places, generally preferring a sunny spot in a lawn or grass.

Growing under Glass and in Containers

The tree is hardy, so it is a waste to grow it under cover, but the twisted framework and general attractiveness make it a good specimen plant for pot growing.

Ornamental and Wildlife Value

Pretty flowers, large leaves and gorgeous autumn golds make this a delightful specimen tree, with a twisted and contorted dark framework for winter interest. The fruits are useful to the birds late in winter.

Propagation, Pruning and Training

Medlars can be grown from seed, but are usually grafted on pear, quince or thorn stock. They are best pruned only remedially, as they fruit on the ends of the branches.

Pests and Diseases

Medlars rarely suffer from any problem.

A beautiful small tree in foliage, flower and fruit

culinary

The fruits should be left on the tree till winter and then stored in a cool, dry place till they soften (blet). The pulp was once popular raw, mixed with liqueur and cream, but is better jammed or jellied.

Medlar Fudge

Makes about 2kg

1kg medlars
1 large or 2 small lemons
3 cloves
600ml apple cider
Approx. 1kg light brown sugar
Honey or maple syrup to taste, cream and macaroons to serve

Wash and chop the fruit, add the cloves and cider and simmer until the fruit is soft. Sieve and weigh the pulp. Add three quarters of its weight in sugar and bring back to the boil, then bottle and seal. When required, whip the fruit cheese with honey or maple syrup till soft, spoon into bowls and top with whipped cream and broken macaroons.

Chaenomeles japonica from the family *Rosaceae*

JAPONICA QUINCES

Shrub up to 3 x 3m. Life span: short. Self-fertile. Fruits: 2.5–5cm, round, green/red/yellow.

A tangled mass of dark, occasionally thorny branches covered with red, white, orange or pink blossom in early spring. This is followed later in the year by hard, roundish fruits, green flushing red or yellow.

Often just called Japonica, this shrub arrived in Europe from Japan as late as 1800. It was rapidly accepted and is now widely planted in many varieties and hybrids, for its flowers, not the fruits. There is opportunity for developing a better culinary or even a dessert form.

varieties

The botanical *C. japonica* has orange flowers and is not common. The true **Japonica** is *C. speciosa*. There are many ornamental hybrids and varieties that also fruit. None are worth the trouble of growing for fruit. Just enjoy the flowers of **Sargentii**, **Apple Blossom** and **Falconnet Charlet**.

cultivation

Hardier than **Cydonia quinces**, these are easy almost anywhere, even on shady walls.

Growing under Glass and in Containers

Tough and unruly plants, they are better outdoors. However, I've found them dependable in pots to force for early flowers.

Ornamental and Wildlife Value

The displays of early flowers and long-lived fruit are exceptional, making these valuable shrubs. The flowers come in late winter, benefiting early insects, but the hard fruits often rot before the birds take them.

Propagation, Pruning and Training

Unlikely to come true from seed. Better varieties are easily layered or can be grafted. Winter cuttings may take; softwood cuttings are better but trickier. The shrubs have a congested form and are best left alone or tip-pruned in summer to control their size. I weave young growths like basket work to produce a tight surface that can be clipped.

Pests and Diseases

Fruit fly is a problem.

culinary

Inedible – well, impenetrable anyway – until cooked, when they have an aromatic scent similar to, but different from, Cydonia quinces. They can be used for tarts, baked or stewed or made into cheese or jelly.

Japonica Jelly
Makes approx. 4kg

2kg Japonica quinces
Approx. 2kg sugar

Chop the fruit and simmer in 3 litres water till tender, then sieve and weigh the pulp. Add 500g of sugar per 600ml of pulp and return to the heat. Bring to boil, bottle and seal. Store for three months before use.

Arbutus unedo from the family *Ericaceae*

STRAWBERRY TREE

CANE FRUIT, ARBUTE

Tree up to 6m. Life span: long. Fruits: about 2cm, spherical, red.

***Arbutus unedo* is a small, evergreen tree often with gnarled, shedding bark, rich brown underneath. It has white, heather-like flowers in late autumn as the previous year's crop of spherical fruits ripens. These are stubbly spiky, resembling litchis. The pulp is really no good raw, especially in cool regions, but may be better in warmer climes. *Arbutus unedo* is native to the Mediterranean. The Ancient Greek Theophrastus knew it was edible, but 300 years later, the Roman Pliny did not regard it as worth eating. Ever since, it has been planted for its beauty, yet not really for the fruit, which have remained undeveloped. I gather the descriptive name *unedo* means 'I eat one only'.**

Rubra (above); **Killarney** (top right)

varieties

The ordinary **Killarney Strawberry Tree** is most common and in few varieties; *Rubra* has pink flowers and abundant fruits. Other species are *A. canariensis*, whose berries are made into sweetmeats, and *A. menziesii*. **Madrona**, from California, has cherry-like fruits that are said to have been eaten in the past.

cultivation

A. unedo is, surprisingly, not particular as to soil, but prefers a mild climate or a warm site. Although ericaceous, it does not mind some lime, but does better in a leaf-mould-rich woodland or acid soil. The other species are not as compliant.

Ornamental and Wildlife Value

One of the most highly prized, small, ornamental evergreens. Of slight value to wildlife, though the flowers are handy for insects late in autumn.

Pests and Diseases

Few problems occur.

Propagation, Pruning and Training

Seed of the species comes true, layers are possible and winter cuttings may take. The strawberry tree needs little pruning and usually recovers if cut back hard.

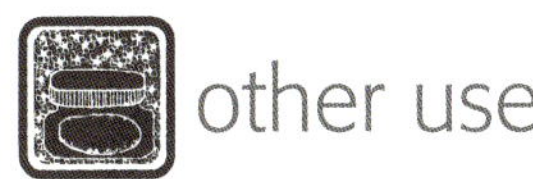

other uses

The hard, tough wood is turned into carved souvenirs of Killarney, especially small cudgels.

culinary

Harvested a year after the flowers, the fruits are made into sweets, confections, liqueurs and sherbets, but rarely eaten raw.

Killarney Strawberry Surprise

Serves 6

225g wheatmeal biscuits
120g butter
120g strawberry jam
225g strawberries
30g gelatine
1 large cup water
Killarney strawberries (arbutus fruits) to garnish

Break up the biscuits and mix them with most of the butter. Press into a tart dish and chill. Once set, rub the biscuit crust with the rest of the butter, line with half the jam, then fill with strawberries. Dissolve the gelatine and the rest of the jam in a cup of hot water, then cool. Pour the jelly over the fruit, swirl and chill. Garnish with Killarney strawberries and serve with cream.

Viburnum trilobum **from the family *Caprifoliaceae***

HIGHBUSH CRANBERRIES

Shrub 4m. Life span: relatively short. Fruits: 2cm, round, scarlet.

A large, spreading shrub with maple-like leaves that give good autumn colour, and scarlet, glossy, translucent berries in mid-summer, very similar to the European Guelder Rose.

Viburnum **is an immense genus of many species, some of which have berries that were once considered highly edible. The Guelder Rose (Snowball Tree, Whitten, Water Elder, *V. opulus*) is now forbidden fruit and as children we are warned how dangerous it is. Though the foliage is poisonous, the fruit was cooked and eaten by the poor for millennia. A native European fruit, it thrives in wet soils and damp hedgerows. Similar conditions suit most species.**

culinary

The berries are not eaten raw, save occasionally after frost, but can be made into sharp-tasting jams and jellies.

American Highbush Chutney
Makes approx. 1.25kg

680g highbush cranberries
300ml distilled vinegar
120g each currants, sultanas, raisins, sugar
15g salt
2 teaspoons each cinnamon, allspice
Pinch of nutmeg

Wash the fruits and then remove each of the stalks. Simmer, with enough water to prevent burning, until soft. Add in the vinegar and the other ingredients, simmer until the chutney thickens. Store in sterlised jars for three months.

varieties

V. trilobum, **Highbush Cranberry**, which is very similar to *V. opulus*, is one of several edible wild North American species; *V. lentago* (**Sweet Viburnum, Nannyberry** or **Sheepberry**) has sweet black berries; *V. nudum* (**Naked Viburnum** or **Withe Rod**) is similar, with a deep blue berry; *V. prunifolium* (**Black Haw**) is sometimes good enough even to eat raw.

V. lentago

cultivation

Very easy to please. Most species do best in moist, humus-rich soil; many, except *V. nudum*, like lime.

Growing in Containers
Tough individuals, these are mostly hardy and mostly need cold conditions, though other viburnums may be grown in pots so that their scented flowers may be enjoyed.

Ornamental and Wildlife Value
Most viburnums are grown for their pretty or scented flowers. The berrying sorts are often as decorative and both fruit and flowers are very useful for attracting insects and birds.

Propagation, Pruning and Training
Species come true from seed but are slow. Most varieties can be layered and some will strike from hardwood cuttings taken in winter.

Pests and Diseases
No common problem, just weeds and bird losses.

Fuchsia* from the family *Onagraceae

FUCHSIA

Semi-herbaceous shrub to 2 x 2m. Life span: short. Fruits: 1cm, round/oval purple-black.

This gloriously flowered plant needs little description, and most of us must have noticed the roundish oval, purple fruits it occasionally sets. As I have always searched for new fruits from far places, I was amused when I first saw fuchsia jelly and learned that I had overlooked these berries, which are so close at hand, often edible and as delicious as many from distant shores.

The first fuchsia was recorded in 1703. Over the following century a few species arrived in Britain from South America with little remark, but in 1793 James Lee astutely launched his *F. coccinea*, the first with impressive flowers, and took the world by storm. Lee claimed he found this new fuchsia in a sailor's window but it was actually supplied to him by Kew (labelled Coccinea) who got it from a Captain Firth in 1788. However, Pere Plumier wrote of *Fuchsia triphylla flore coccinea* in *Plantarum Americanum Genera*, in 1703. What was so 'astute' about launching *F. coccinea* was the way James Lee did it – putting two on display, saying he would only sell one of the pair, for a guinea, which he did, and then replacing it with one of the 300 he had propagated as soon as the client had left. Other species were introduced from New Zealand and now there is an amazing range of colours and forms of hybrids of many species.

culinary

Some are tasty raw, but all are best jellied or in tarts.

Fuchsia Jelly
Makes approx. 2kg

1kg fuchsia berries
Approx. 1kg sugar
Juice of 1 lemon

Simmer the berries with sufficient water to cover. Once they have softened, sieve and weigh. Add the same weight of sugar and the lemon juice. Bring back to boil, then transfer to steralised jars.

varieties

Fuchsia species *corymbiflora* and *denticulata* were eaten in Peru and *F. racemosa* in Santo Domingo. Fuchsia clubs and societies often have jelly competitions. There appears to be no known poisonous variety – and I have tried many. As they are all bred for flowers, the berries are neglected and should be easily improved – there is enough variety to start with! *F. magellanica* is the hardiest, but rarely fruits. The **California Dreamer** series can produce thumb-sized fruits!

cultivation

Even many less hardy species can be grown in cold regions if the roots are well protected, as fuchsias usually spring again from underground to flower and fruit. Make backup plants to be safe and keep these indoors. Fuchsias are amenable to almost any soil but prefer a sheltered, sunny site, protected from the extreme afternoon sun of summer.

Propagation, Pruning and Training
Seed produces mixed results; cuttings are easy to train to any shape. Control growth by nipping out tips in summer; cut back in winter.

Ornamental and Wildlife Value
Fuchsias are appealing. They can support large numbers of unwanted wildlife.

Growing under Glass and in Containers
An ideal plant for a cool or heated greenhouse or conservatory. Can be grown for years in large pots.

Pests and Diseases
They suffer from common pests.

Rosa from the family *Rosaceae*

ROSE HIPS

Clambering shrub up to 9m. Life span: short to medium. Usually self-fertile. Fruits: up to 2.5cm, ovoid, red, yellow or purplish black. Value: very rich in vitamin C.

There can be none of us who does not know roses and few who have never nibbled at the acid/sweet flesh of a rose hip. These are so rich in vitamin C that they were collected on a massive scale during the Second World War to make rose-hip syrup for expectant mothers and babies. Rose stems are commonly thorny with a few exceptions such as the divine **Zéphirine Drouhin**. The deciduous leaves vary from glossy to matt, the flower colour is any you want save black or blue, though wild roses are almost all white or pink. The **Eglantine** rose leaves smell of apples after rain.

Rose hips and flowers are eaten in countries all over the world. The **Brier** or **Dog Rose**, *Rosa canina*, and **Eglantine** or **Sweetbrier**, *R. rubiginosa*, are natives of Europe and temperate Asia. Their fruits have been eaten by country folk since time immemorial, but are now regarded with some disdain. However, eglantine sauce was made at Balmoral Castle from sweetbrier hips and lemon juice and was considered good enough for Queen Victoria. Roses are bred for flowers, not for their hips, so most varieties have small hips. However, a little selective breeding could produce hips as large as small apples within a few generations.

A little breeding and these could be as large and sweet as apples

varieties

The **Brier** and **Eglantine** rose hips are the most common varieties used for hips, though *R. rugosa*, the **Rugosa Rose**, offers larger hips so is more rewarding. *R moyesii* has large flask-shaped hips and *R. omiensis* has pear-shaped, yellow and crimson fruits that ripen early. *R. spinosissima/pimpinellifolia*, the **Scotch** or **Burnet Rose**, is another European native. It has a sweet, purplish-black fruit.

cultivation

Most roses are accommodating, but they prefer heavy soil, rich in organic matter, and need to be kept well mulched with their roots cool and moist, yet not wet.

Propagation

Some species can be grown from seed. Cuttings taken in early autumn are reliable for many varieties and most species.

ROSE HIPS

Ornamental and Wildlife Value
Roses are *the* garden plant. At least one or more can fit into almost any garden anywhere to good effect. Single-flowered roses are valuable to insects and the hips are choice meals for winter birds and rodents.

Growing under Glass and in Containers
Only tender roses such as *R. banksiae* are happy under glass. Hardier varieties tend to become soft and drawn and suffer from pests. They must be kept moist at the roots, well-ventilated and shaded against scorch.

Pruning and Training
This requires a chapter on its own just to list the methods! Basically, for most roses, plant them well apart, prune as little as possible and wind in growths rather than prune. Reduce tall hybrid bushes by a third to a half in height with hedge trimmers annually in late winter.

Pests and Diseases
Roses suffer from a host of common diseases, but provided they are growing reasonably well the only real threat to flower and hip production is aphids. Control these with jets of water and soft soap.

Harvesting and Storing
The berries need to ripen fully on the bush before being eaten raw, but are best taken before they soften for culinary use. All seed hairs must be removed!

Don't forget the petals for salads and garnish

culinary

Hips can be made into jellies, preserves and the famous syrup. The flower petals may be used as garnishes, preserved in sugar or syrup, used for rosewater flavouring, honeys, vinegars and conserves, pounded to dust for lozenges and they make good additions to salads. The leaves of *R. canina* have been used for tea (in desperation, one suspects).

Rose Hip Tart
Serves 6

For the pastry:
225g self-raising flour
150g butter
1 large egg yolk
30g fine brown sugar
Pinch of salt
Splash of water

For the filling:
500g rose hips
60g each fine brown sugar, honey, chopped stem ginger preserved in syrup
1 teaspoon cinnamon
Sprinkling of sugar and grating of nutmeg

Rub together the ingredients for the pastry, making it a little on the dry side, and use it to line a tart dish. Save some to decorate the top. Wash, top, tail and halve the rose hips, extract every bit of seed and hairy fibre, rinse and drain. Mix with the sugar, honey, cinnamon and ginger and spoon on top of the pastry. Decorate with pastry offcuts and sprinkle with sugar and nutmeg before baking at 180°C/350°F/gas mark 4 for half an hour or until the pastry is light brown on top.

companion planting

Underplantings of Alliums, especially garlic or chives, help deter blackspot and pests. Parsley, lupins, mignonette and lavender are beneficial; catnip and *Limnanthes douglassii* are good ground cover underneath roses.

other uses

Strong-growing roses such as *R. rubiginosa, R. spinosissima* or **The Queen Elizabeth** make excellent stock- and people-proof hedges. The flower petals are dried for potpourri and used in confectionery, medicinally and in perfumery. The seeds are covered in hairs that cause itching when put down the back of other children's collars...

Cornus mas **from the family** *Cornaceae*

CORNELIAN CHERRY, SORBET

Tree/bush up to 8m. Life span: medium to long. Deciduous, self-fertile. Fruits: 1cm, ovoid, red.

Cornelian cherry fruits resemble small, red cherries but are generally too sour to eat raw, except for the occasional better one. The trees or large bushes are tall, deciduous, densely branched and suckering, common in hedgerows and old grasslands. The stems are greyish and the leaves are oval, coming to a point with noticeable veins. The flowers are primrose yellow and appear in small clusters early in spring before the leaves.

The Cornelian cherry is one of a genus of about a hundred, mostly small, shrubby plants up to 3m high, but ranging from creeping sub-shrubs to small trees. One of the two species native to Europe and western Asia, *Cornus mas* was once widely cultivated and rated very highly, though now it is rarely eaten even by country folk. There are species from North America and the Himalayas and it seems a shame they have not been cross-bred for better fruits. The Cornelian cherry really is a fruit that has stalled in development and probably would not take much further work to improve immensely.

Cornus capitata

varieties

The variety *C. mas macrocarpa* has somewhat larger fruits and is still available. There used to exist many other improved forms, now apparently lost. In France and Germany there are records of several varieties of Sorbets, as they were called – one that had a yellow fruit, some with wax-coloured fruits, white fruits and even one with a fleshy, rounded fruit. Other *cornus* such as *C. stolonifera*, the **Red Osier**, and *C. amomum*, **Kinnikinnik**, are found in North America and are edible. The former was eaten more in desperation than for pleasure; the latter, found in Louisiana, is said to be very good. The berries of *C. suecica* used to be gathered by Native Americans, who froze them in wooden boxes for winter rations. *Cornus kousa chinensis* comes from China via Japan and is a smaller tree than *C. mas.* The flowers are greyish-purple backed by immense pale bracts; the fruits are more strawberry-like and juicy with better flavour. This species needs a moist, acid soil. *C. macrophylla* and the tenderer *C. capitata* come from Asia and the Himalayas and are eaten raw and made into preserves in India. *C. canadensis (Chamaepericlymenum canadense)*, **Bunchberry** or **Dwarf Cornel**, is a different type altogether. A lime hater more resembling a soft dwarf raspberry in manner of growth, it has white flowers on low, soft shoots with vivid red fruits. These are pleasant enough, if tasteless, and can be added to summer puddings.

cultivation

C. mas is easy to grow almost anywhere but prefers calcareous soil. Some species need acid conditions. Generally they are among the most reliable of shrubs, requiring little attention. They are hardy and need a cool climate to flower. They are spectacularly unsuccessful in warm temperate gardens.

Ornamental and Wildlife Value

Many species are liked particularly for their autumn colour and some species and varieties are grown for their brightly coloured stems. The flowers are early, benefiting insects, and birds and rodents love the

CORNELIAN CHERRY, SORBET

Cornus canadensis

berries. One of the best backbone shrubs of a cool garden.

Propagation
The species come true from seed with some variation, but are slow. Suckers taken in autumn are best; hardwood winter cuttings may take, but layering is more sure.

Pruning and Training
Generally only remedial pruning is needed – though, as these plants sucker, some root pruning may become necessary. Ornamental coloured-stem varieties are best sheared to ground level in early spring.

Pests and Diseases
No common problems bother these tough plants.

other uses

Cornus sanguinea, the **Cornel Dogwood**, **Dogberry** or **Pegwood**, is a common European relation, not really edible, though the fruits were once used for oil and in brewing. *C. alba* varieties tolerate wet or dry situations and can be used to reinforce banks. Dogwoods grow stiff and straight, so were used for arrows.

culinary

In Germany the fruits were sold in markets to be eaten by children (who presumably liked them). They were widely made into tarts, confectionery and sweetmeats, even used as substitutes for olives. In Norway the flowers were used to flavour spirits and in Turkey the fruits were used as flavouring for sherbets. It is noticeable that fruits vary on different bushes and some are more palatable raw than others.

Sorbet Sorbet
Serves 4

1kg cornelian cherries
1 small lemon
Approx. 600g sugar
2 or 3 small egg whites

Wash the fruits, slit the cherries, chop the lemon and simmer them till soft, just covered with water, in a deep pan. Strain and measure the juice, then dissolve 200g sugar per cup of juice. Bring back to the boil, cool and partially freeze. Remove from the freezer and beat, adding one beaten egg white for every two cups of sorbet. Repeat the freezing and beating one more time before freezing until required.

Sambucus nigra from the order *Caprifoliaceae*

ELDERBERRIES

Bush, 8m. Life span: short. Deciduous, self-fertile. Fruits: 7mm, purple clusters. Value: rich in vitamin C.

These well-known, large, many-branched shrubs are loved by children as they have hollow stems good for all sorts of illicit purposes and the strong vertical shoots are easy to break off for mock battles. The plants have a distinctive, rank smell to them and they grow most happily in dank places and on waste ground. The flowers hang in great creamy clusters, varying in smell from sweetest honey to cat's urine. Elderberries themselves are still widely used, but the foliage and stems are slightly poisonous and can be an irritant.

Closely related to the *viburnums*, elderberries are native to Europe and Asia. They have been a resource for the poor, but not loved by many, since pre-history. Elder is almost sacred and surrounded with many superstitions which may have protected it, but cynics believe it was because the berries were useful for making fake 'imported' wine or for upgrading cheap local wines.

varieties

Sambucus nigra is the **common wild elder** with purple fruits. There are several ornamental forms with coloured, filigreed or variegated foliage, though most of these are poor fruiters. **Black Lace** is an ornamental variety with reddish black berries claimed good for wine. *S. nigra fructaluteo* has yellow fruits, but there is no known large-berried form. This is a shame as elder is a prolific fruiter, tough and easy to propagate. There are several related North American species. *S. Canadensis*, **Canadian Elderberry**, was once found good for wine and the unopened flower buds were used as a substitute for capers. The **Blue Elderberry**, *S. caerula*, is from Utah and produces enormous clusters of fruits, rather preferable to *S. Canadensis*, and popular in California for tarts and jellies. Another, *S. mexicana,* apparently bears flowers and green and ripe purple fruits simultaneously in its native land of Mexico. The fruits are said to be as good as blackberries. *S. xanthocarpa*, **Australian Elder**, is reportedly edible. There are several other species that berry. Some of these may possibly be inedible or even poisonous, such as *S. ebulus*, so be careful with identification.

ELDERBERRIES

Sambucus Canadensis

cultivation

Elderberries are too easy for words. They thrive almost anywhere in sun or shade. They prefer a moist spot and rich soil, but then tend to make too much foliage and wood growth at the expense of flowers and fruit.

Growing under Glass and in Containers

There seems no reason to grow elder under glass as it is very hardy. It sows itself in pots of other plants, so clearly also makes a good subject in one!

Propagation

Elder certainly comes up from seed everywhere. The best varieties have to be propagated by cuttings, but this is no problem as they will root like magic.

Ornamental and Wildlife Value

Some of the cut-leafed golden and variegated forms make attractive garden shrubs, but are not generally popular – probably as they grow large quickly and smell rank. In the wildlife garden, the flowers and fruits are

Pruning and Training

Hard pruning in late winter or early spring keeps them confinable, and produces fewer, bigger flower heads and larger trusses of fruit.

Weed, Pest and Disease Control

They do suffer from black aphis attacks, but this is cured with soft soap sprays. Ironically the leaves used to be boiled with soft soap as an aphicide. Bird losses are high unless they are netted.

companion planting

Elder bushes aid composting and should be planted near the bins. They leave a good soil, probably due to leaf litter, if you can lose them.

other uses

Elders make quick but poor hedges and good screens only during summer. Their wood is useful for fishing floats and blow-pipes, and surprisingly long lasting though little used even as kindling or firewood because of superstition. The berries dye things purple. Elder has excellent potential as a biomass crop as they can be coppiced very hard.

culinary

The berries can be dried, used in tarts or jellied. In Portugal large quantities were cultivated for adding a deep red colour to wines, especially to port. The flowers of sweet-perfumed common elderberries can be dipped in batter and fried to make delicious fritters; the berries make an excellent wine..

Elderflower Fritters

Serves 4

120g flour
30g butter
2 small eggs
Up to 1 cup milk
Gallons of fresh elderflowers
Sunflower oil, for deep-frying
Caster sugar, salt and lemon juice, to taste

Mix together the flour, butter, eggs, salt and a little of the milk and stir to a uniform paste. Add the rest of the milk slowly, mixing well. Beat vigorously, then leave in a cool place for an hour. Wash and trim the elderflowers, leaving a long stalk. Using this stalk, dip the flowers in the batter, drain off the excess, then immerse in boiling sunflower oil and deep-fry until tanned. Drain and dry on absorbent paper and remove the stalk. Dredge with caster sugar and a squeeze of lemon juice before serving hot.

Crataegus azarolus **from the family** *Rosaceae*

HAWTHORN AND AZAROLE

Tree/bush up to 8m. Life span: long. Deciduous, self-fertile. Fruits: up to 2.5cm, roundish, usually orange. Value: rich in vitamins C and B complex.

The azarole is a more palatable relation of the well-known hawthorn and is cultivated in many of the Mediterranean countries for its cherry-sized fruits. These are usually yellow to orange, but can occasionally be red or white. They are larger than a hawthorn haw and have an apple-flavoured, pasty flesh with two or three tough seeds. Small, spreading trees or large shrubs, these are typical of the thorn genus, with clusters of large, white flowers that do not have the usual family scent.

The thorn family are remarkably hardy, tough plants for wet, dry, windswept or even coastal regions. They are survivors and various species can be found in almost every part of the world, many of which bear similar small, edible, apple-like fruits. Native to North Africa, Asia Minor and Persia, the azarole, *C. azarolus*, may be the *mespile anthedon* about which Theophrastus wrote. More popular in the Latin countries, it was brought to Britain in 1640. In 1976 it got an award of merit from the Royal Horticultural Society, but it has never really caught on, most probably because other more floriferous varieties and species were readily available.

Crataegus. tomentosa

varieties

The **Azarole** is the more productive of the species and is grown commercially for flavouring liqueurs. It is probably the best choice for a tree for preserves. The Armenian *C. tanacetifolia*, the **Tansy-leaved Thorn** or **Syrian Hawberry**, is another good choice. The berries are almost relishable raw as dessert and have an aromatic apple flavour, which is surprising, as they also closely resemble small yellow apples. They are pale green to yellow, with slight ribs like a melon, and a tassel of 'leaves' at the end. The **Common Hawthorn** or **Quickthorn Haw**, *C. monogyna*, has one seed and is edible but not at all palatable, so is seldom eaten, save by curious children. Reputedly it was eaten raw when fully ripe by Scots Highlanders. The fruits are dark red and hang in immense festoons in autumn. The flowers have a sweet perfume when new, but go fishy as they age – on some trees more than others.

Equally common, *C. oxycantha/laevigata* is very similar, usually with dark red flowers. There are several edible North American species. *C. tomentosa*, **Black Thorn** or **Pear Thorn**, has hard, orange-red, pear-shaped fruits; *C. flava* has yellow fruits; *C. douglasii* is a better species with small but sweet, black berries with yellow flesh. One identified as *C. coccinea* (now *mollis*, sub *mollis, pedicellata* or *intricata*) was very popular with Native Americans, who dried the large scarlet or purple fruits for winter use. Sometimes these fruits were mixed together with chokecherries and service berries before they were dried and pressed into cakes for storage. *C. mollis* also has amazingly big thorns.

cultivation

The thorns are all extremely easy to please and require little skill or attention. They tend to lean in the more exposed situations.

HAWTHORN AND AZAROLE

Common Hawthorn

culinary

The flowers of the **Common Hawthorn** once made a heady liqueur or wine. The young leaves and buds, known to schoolchildren as bread and cheese, had a nutty taste and made a welcome addition to salads. We are now told that both are slightly poisonous. However, the berries of **Azarole**, **Common Thorn**, and especially the Armenian or Syrian, will make excellent preserves, wines and jellies.

Hedge Jelly
Makes approx. 3kg

1kg haws
500g crab or cooking apples
225g elderberries
Approx. 1.5kg sugar

Wash the fruits, chop the apples and simmer the fruits together, just covered with water, for about 2 hours, till softened. Strain and weigh the juice. Add the same weight of sugar to the juice and bring back to a boil. Skim off the scum, jar and seal.

Growing under Glass and in Containers
Because they are so hardy they do not need protection, but several of the ornamental varieties can be grown in pots for forcing to produce early flowers.

Ornamental and Wildlife Value
The shows of blossom and masses of bright fruits make these an excellent choice for larger shrub borders and informal gardens. The flowers, fruit and foliage are useful to all manner of wildlife. Hawthorns have become weed species in cooler parts of Australia.

Propagation
This is more difficult than for many fruits. The haws need stratifying (burying outdoors in a pot of sand) for a year and a half before sowing properly the following spring. They may produce mixed offspring unless they are from a true species grown far from any others. Cuttings are difficult so choice varieties are best budded in May or grafted in April onto common hawthorn stock.

Pruning and Training
Very little is needed. Do not over-thin the branches, as thorns will naturally have a congested head.

Pests and Diseases
Thorns rarely suffer badly from problems, though they are occasionally defoliated by caterpillar attacks. These attacks may be easily avoided by diligent observation and prompt action.

other uses

Thorns make the best and most traditional hedge with a trimmed surface like fine tweed. The wood is heavy and hard and will burn with a good heat.

The spring blossom is cheerful, too

Sorbus aucuparia from the family *Rosaceae*

ROWAN, WHITEBEAM AND SERVICE BERRIES

Tree, up to 15m. Life span: short. Deciduous, self-fertile. Fruits: up to 1cm, spherical, scarlet, in clusters. Value: very rich in vitamin C and pectin.

Rowans are most attractive, small trees with distinctive, pinnate leaves, dark green above, lighter underneath. They have big heads of foamy, cream flowers like elderflowers, but smell unpleasant. In autumn the branches bend under massive clusters of bright red to scarlet berries, which would hang through the winter if the birds did not finish them so quickly. The Latin name *aucuparia* means 'bird catching' and refers to the fruit's early use as bait.

The *Sorbus* family is large and includes dwarf shrubs and large trees. They are spread all over the world and the majority are quite hardy. They colour richly in autumn and are widely grown for their attractive shows of fruits, also in yellow and white. Many new ornamental species were introduced from China during the nineteenth century, but little advance has been made in fruit quality since *S. aucuparia edulis* (*moravica* or *dulcis*) was first introduced in about 1800.

Rowan

varieties

Sorbus aucuparia, the **Rowan** or **Mountain Ash**, has scarlet berries that birds love and which are generally too sour and bitter for our tastes. There are many other ornamental species and varieties, for example *S. aucuparia xanthocarpa*, which has yellow fruits. However, the common rowan is still the frequent favourite choice from the genus and much planted in metropolitan areas. The best variety by far for the gourmand is *edulis* which has larger, sweeter fruits carried in heavy bunches. *S. aria*, the **Whitebeam**, has similar red berries to a rowan and they were once eaten and used for wine. *Sorbus domestica*, the **Service Tree**, is a native of Asia Minor and was also once widely liked, but is now less common. It has smaller clusters of larger fruits of a brownish green, resembling small pears. They need to be bletted like medlars (see page 577) before they are edible. There were pear-shaped and apple-shaped versions; the flavour and texture were improved after a frost and they were commonly sold in London markets. In Brittany they were used to make a rather poor cider. The **Wild Service** or **Chequer Tree**, *S. torminalis*, has smaller, still harder fruits, that would pucker even the hungriest peasant's mouth, but were once eaten by children. Note the seeds contain cyanides and should not be swallowed.

cultivation

Mountain ashes are tolerant of quite acid soils and do not like chalky or limy ones, protesting by being short-lived. They generally prefer drier to wetter sites but, strangely, are commonly seen growing naturally by mountain streams and in wet, hilly country.

ROWAN, WHITEBEAM AND SERVICE BERRIES

Growing under Glass and in Containers
They are hardy and rather too large for growing inside. They can be grown, and fruited, in pots if only a small crop is desired.

Ornamental and Wildlife Value
Almost all the species and varieties are very attractive to us in flower and fruit, turning glorious shades of crimson in autumn, but most unfortunately do lack a sweet scent. Rowans are valuable to the birds and insects and are pollinated by flies and midges.

Propagation
Seed from the species may come true if the tree is isolated, but it must be stratified over winter first. Cuttings are rarely successful, so selected forms are budded in mid-summer or grafted in early spring onto seedling rootstocks. The fruits of rowans are thought to get larger if the trees are grafted on to Service stock.

Service tree

Whitebeam

Pruning and Training
Pruning should be only remedial once a good head has formed, but watch for overladen branches and prop in time. The strongly erect growth of young trees can be bent down and into fruitfulness: pull them down gently with weights tied near the ends.

Pests and Diseases
Apart from bird losses, and being rather short-lived on alkaline soils, the members of this genus need little care and rarely suffer problems. They are thus well liked for amenity planting.

other uses

Rowan bark was used in dyeing and tanning. The wood is strong and was used for handles. Service wood is tough and resists wear well. The berries of the **Wild Service** tree, *S. torminalis*, were also used medicinally.

culinary

Rowan berries make a delicious jelly, almost like marmalade, which goes well with venison, game and fatty or cold meats. They can be used in compôtes, preserves and syrups, and are sometimes added to apple dishes to liven them up. They have been used for fermenting and distilling liquor, and in emergencies the dried berries have been ground into meal to make a substitute for bread. Service fruits were used traditionally in quite similar ways.

Mountain Ash Jelly
Makes approx. 2kg

1kg firm ripe rowan berries
1 small lemon
Approx. 1kg sugar

Wash and de-stem the berries, add the chopped lemon and 425ml water and simmer till soft (for about an hour). Strain and add 450g sugar to each 600ml. Bring back to the boil, skim and jar.

Prunus species* from the family *Rosaceae

SLOES, BIRD CHERRIES, BEACH PLUMS

Tree/bush up to 9m. Life span: medium. Deciduous, self-fertile. Fruits: up to 2.5cm, ovoid, single stone, red to black. Value: rich in vitamin C.

Closely related to orchard plums and cherries, the wild *Prunus* species remain very much tough, hardy alternatives for difficult spots or wild gardens. Sloes are the fruits of the blackthorn, *P. spinosa*, which is a medium-sized shrub, many-branched, very thorny, with blackish bark. The fruits are black ovoids with a bloom that resembles plums, and hard, juicy, green flesh that is usually far too astringent to eat raw. However, like many children, I forever searched for a sweeter one.

Sloes are native to Europe, North Africa and Asia. The stones have been found on the sites of prehistoric dwellings, so they have long been an item of diet. They may be one of the ancestors of the damson and some of their 'blood' has probably got into many true plums. The Bird Cherry is a native of Europe and Asia, especially grown in the north of England. The sixteenth-century herbalist Gerard claimed it was in 'almost every hedge'. Many ornamental *Prunus* species were later introduced in the eighteenth and nineteenth centuries; *P. maritima* was introduced by R. J. Farrer in 1800.

varieties

Prunus padus, the **Bird Cherry** or **Hag Berry**, is a small tree with white, fragrant flowers in late spring; the double-flowered form, *P. padus plena*, is more heavily almond-scented. The leaves and bark smell of bitter almonds and contain highly poisonous prussic acid. *P. maritima*, the **Beach Plum**, comes from the eastern seaboard of North America, from Maine down to the Gulf of Mexico. It is a small, compact shrub with masses of white flowers and red or purple juicy fruits up to 2.5cm across. These can be eaten raw, but are better if preserved. Another North American species is *P. virginiana*, the **Choke Cherry**. This is a tall shrub with glossy, green leaves and variable red to purplish-black berries. The **American Red Plum, Goose, August, Hog** or **Yellow Plum**, *P. americana*, was the Native Americans' favourite and is good for eating raw, stewing or jamming. Neither are generally available or have much to offer gardeners in the southern hemisphere. *P. simonii*, the **Apricot Plum** from China, has large, attractive, red and yellow, scented fruits.

Bird Cherries

SLOES, BIRD CHERRIES, BEACH PLUMS

cultivation

Sloes and Bird Cherries are very hardy and good for making windbreaks. They like an exposed site and thrive on quite poor soils, even one packed with chalk, while *P. maritima* does best in coastal regions, and is happy with salt winds and sandy soils. Do mulch these heavily; water well while establishing on very sandy soils as these hold little water.

Growing under Glass and in Containers
Most of these are hardy and not tasty enough to merit space under cover. *P. americana* may be more fruitful if pot-grown, wintered outside and brought in for the spring through to autumn.

Ornamental and Wildlife Value
All *Prunus* are good at flowering time, but few are worth space in most small, modern gardens. They are more use to the wild garden, as the flowers are early, benefiting insects, while the fruits are excellent winter fare for birds and rodents.

Pruning and Training
Minimal pruning is required and is best done in summer to avoid silver leaf disease. As hedges, blackthorn should be planted at 45 degrees, staggered in two or three close rows, each laid in opposite directions. Most species can be trained as small trees, but leave beach plum bushes alone.

American Red Plum

Choke Cherries

Propagation
The species usually come true from seed. Choicer varieties have been developed for ornamental use and must be budded in summer or grafted in spring. Cuttings do not take.

Pests and Diseases
These wildest members of the *Prunus* family suffer least from pests or diseases.

other uses

Sloes are good hedging plants. Their leaves were formerly used to adulterate tea. Bird Cherries do well in a hedge. Their wood is hard and used for carving and especially liked for rifle butts. Sloe bark was once used for medicinal purposes.

culinary

Sloe berries are much used for liqueurs, especially gin-based ones, and to add colour to port-type wines. All over Europe they are fermented for wine or distilled to a spirit. In France the unripe sloes are pickled like olives. They can be made into juice, syrup or jelly. Bird Cherries have been used in much the same way but are inferior. The American species are used similarly. The Apricot Plum seems strangely under-rated.

Sloe Gin

Sloes
Brown sugar or honey
Peeled almonds
Gin, brandy or vodka

Wash and dry the sloes and prick each several times. Pack the sloes loosely into bottles. To each bottle add 120g brown sugar or honey and a couple of almonds, then fill with gin (or brandy or vodka). Leave for several months before drinking.

Juniperus communis from the order *Pinaceae*

JUNIPER BERRIES

Tree/bush, almost any size. Life span: long. Evergreen, self-fertile. Fruits: 1cm, green ripening black, oily.

The juniper is naturally a small tree or shrub with aromatic, evergreen, needle leaves of blue-green. Many ornamental species and varieties are in cultivation and junipers may now be found as ground cover, specimens or hedging plants.

Juniper is native to Europe, but is being displaced by other more profitable trees. Other species come from all over the world.

varieties

The common juniper berry is used as a flavouring; other species can be more palatable. The berries of *J. scopularium*, the **Rocky Mountain Juniper**, have been eaten raw and boiled, used to flavour meat and even roasted to make a coffee substitute. The **Syrian**

Juniper is dioecious (having separate male and female flowers), columnar-growing, with broad, prickly needles. In its native lands it produces edible, blue-black fruits up to 2.5cm across. A Mexican species, *J. deppeana pchyphlaea*, is said to be sweet and palatable.

cultivation

Found wild on lime-rich hillsides and moorlands, also on heaths and scrubs, juniper surprisingly survives in acid soils and will grow in heather gardens.

Growing under Glass and in Containers

It does not like being under glass, especially in dry air. It can be grown in containers.

Ornamental and Wildlife Value

Valuable conifers for year-round colour and form, junipers will also provide shelter for insects, small creatures and birds.

Propagation

Seed is slow and needs stratification. Autumn cuttings may take, but spring layering is best.

culinary uses

Juniper berries are usually not eaten themselves, but used to flavour meats, sauerkraut and liqueurs. They were used so much for flavouring a spirit made in Holland it became gin, from the Dutch word genever, in turn from the Latin *juniperus*. Dried berries have been used as a substitute for pepper and roasted to make a coffee. In France, *Genevrette* is a beer made from barley and juniper berries.

Porc au Genièvre

Before roasting a pork joint, make incisions all over and push in juniper berries, garlic cloves and black peppercorns. Rub with salt and cook as usual.

Weed, Pest and Disease Control

Junipers have few problems.

Pruning and Training

Trim if needed in early spring.

other uses

Juniper wood and berries were used medicinally, for smoking hams and for making and olive-brown dye. *J virginiana*, the **Pencil Cedar** is used for that purpose. *J. recurva* twigs are burnt as incense in India.

Pinus pinea from the order *Pinaceae*

PINE KERNELS

PIGNONS, PINONS, PINOCCHI

Tree up to 25m. Life span: long. Evergreen, self-fertile. Fruits: up to 1cm long, ivory-white seeds inside a cone. Value: high in minerals and oils.

Pine kernels are more nuts than fruits as we eat the seed and not the surrounding part (in this case, the cone), but they are softer than true nuts. Most pine kernels come from the stone or umbrella pine. It is an attractive, mushroom-shaped tree with glossy, brown cones which expand in the sun, and drop the seeds. Each is in a tough skin which needs to be removed before they are eaten.

The stone pine is indigenous to the Mediterranean region. Loved by the Ancient Greeks, it was dedicated to the sea god Poseidon. The kernels of other species are eaten almost anywhere they grow.

varieties

Pinus pinea grows happily in cooler regions, but without enough sun the cones do not ripen. *P. cembra*, the **Arolla Pine**, is native to Central Europe and Asia and the seeds are a staple food in Siberia. *P. gerardiana*, **Gerard's Pine**, comes from the Himalayas. *P. cembroides* is a native of North America and has pea-sized kernels that taste delicious roasted. *P. edulis*, from Mexico, is the best variety, but unlikely to fruit in Britain. Likewise the **Araucaria Pine** or **Monkey Puzzle Tree**, *A. aurucana*, which has edible kernels and grows but rarely fruits in cool climates. The **Parana Pine**, *A. angustifolia*, from South America, is not hardy and equally is too big for glass-house culture.

Gerard's Pine

cultivation

Stone pines will need shelter to fruit in cold regions. They prefer to grow in sandy soil and acid conditions.

Growing under Glass and in Containers

Most pines grow too large unless confined and are unlikely to crop. *P. canariensis*, however, is a particularly pleasing indoor pot plant.

Ornamental and Wildlife Value

Very attractive if the space is available. Pine kernels will provide excellent food for many species of bird.

P. edulis

Pests and Diseases

Pines need companion bacteria and fungi, so do better if soil from around another pine is used to inoculate new sites.

Propagation, Pruning and Training

They can be grown from seed or grafted (with skill). Pines are best left well alone.

other uses

Pines are a source of turpentine and resin.

culinary

Pine nuts are roasted and salted in the same way as peanuts, and also used in marzipan, confectionery, salads and soups.

Piñon Truffle Salad

Quantities to taste

Pine kernels
Butter
Truffles
Walnut oil
Vinegar
Lettuce

Gently fry the kernels in butter till light brown. Remove from the heat; add finely sliced truffles, oil and vinegar. Cool the mixture and toss it in clean, dry lettuce leaves.

VERY WILD FRUITS

Hottentot Figs

There are many other edible, if not palatable, fruits in gardens and parks, just waiting for breeders to improve them. What could be more gratifying and worthy than to present the world with new and improved fruits that can be grown in almost anyone's backyard? The following are a few of the many that are occasionally eaten by some, but are not widely used. Please remember not to eat anything unless you are 100 per cent sure of it and you have had it identified on the spot by an expert!

Carpobrotus edulis
Hottentot Fig
Aizoaceae

This resembles the mesembryanthemums, with which it was once classed. Native to South Africa, it is a low-growing succulent, that helps bind sandy coastal soils. Large, magenta or occasionally yellow flowers are followed by small, figlike fruits, which can be eaten raw or cooked, pickled or preserved. The fleshy, triangular leaves can be eaten as salad, as can those of the similar *Mesembryanthemum crystallinum*.

Elaeagnus umbellata
Autumn Olive
Elaeagnaceae

A strong-growing, spreading, deciduous shrub from Asia with fragrant, yellow flowers and small, orange or red berries used like redcurrants or dried to 'raisins'. Many species in this genus bear edible fruits, and most of these have fragrant flowers. *E. commutata*, the **Silver Berry**, has pasty, silver berries and silver leaves. *E. angustifolia*, **Oleaster** or **Wild Olive**, has sweet berries, and is still popular in south-eastern Europe. *E. multiflora/edulis*, **Goumi**, from the Far East has very acid, orangey red silver-speckled berries that are good for conserves, beverages and jellies. *E. orientalis*, **Trebizond Date**, was once sold commercially as the fruit was considered very tasty. The plant was more famous for its aphrodisiacal perfumed flowers.

Akebia quinata
Lardizabalaceae

A hardy climber from China with attractive, five-lobed leaflets and scented, chocolate-purple flowers in two sizes. These are followed by weird little purple sausage fruits, surprisingly edible – sweetish but pasty and insipid. This needs a warm spot to ripen the fruits, which have a yellowish pulp full of black seeds. *A. trifoliata* is similar.

Humulus lupulus
Hop
Cannabidaceae

I have to include this strange fruit or I will never be forgiven by my beer-swilling compatriots! A rampant climber closely related to cannabis, this is a hardy native of southern Europe with maple-like leaves. Twining stems produce drooping, green-yellow, aromatic flower clusters that enlarge as they set. These are boiled to add their bitter, aromatic flavour to good ale and make it beer. The youngest shoots can be eaten in the manner of asparagus in early spring.

Taxus baccata,
Yew,
Taxaceae

The foliage is deadly without cure, the seed may be poisonous, but for centuries children have eaten the red, fleshy aril. However, it is advisable not to try this one.

Hippophae rhamnoides
Sea Buckthorn
Elaeagnaceae

Often grown as an ornamental for its silver leaves, this tall, thorny shrub produces acid, orangey-yellow fruits if both sexes are planted. The fruits are too sour for most tastes, but have been eaten in famines and by children and are apparently widely collected in Russia, as they are very rich in vitamin C. They are used as a sauce with fish and meat in France, and in Central Europe they are made into a jelly that is eaten with fish or cheese.

Gaultheria procumbens,
Checkerberry, Teaberry, Ericaceae

A low-growing, evergreen native of North America with white flowers and red berries, needing moist, acid soil and partial shade. The berries are odd raw, but can be cooked for jellies and tarts and were once popular in Boston. Ironically the leaves were once used as 'tea'. *G. humifusa* was also used, as was *G. shallon*, another taller, shrubbier version with great clusters of purple berries which were eaten dried by Native Americans. *Chiognes hispidulum*, **Snowberry** (not the poisonous **Symphoricarpus Snowberry**), is very similar and closely related to *Gaultheria*, with delicious whitish mini-gooseberries with an oil of wintergreen aroma.

VERY WILD FRUITS

Cephalotaxus fortuni, wilsoniana, harringtonia, drupacea,
Chinese and **Japanese Plum Yews** or **Cow's-Tail Pines**

Very much resembling yews, these grow in moist conditions in heavy shade, even on chalky soils. Usually dioecious, the females bear small, plum-size khakibrown olives which bizarrely taste like butterscotch – it could be developed into a superb new fruit!

Lonicera caerula var. *Kamtschtica*,
Honeyberry

The edible berried honeysuckle comes from Siberia and unlike its poisonous relations is a small shrub measuring only a metre each way that resists cold and drought really well. The more cylindrical but blueberry-like berries are effectively seedless and full of anthocyanins. Two plants are required for pollination. *L. angustifilia*, *L. involucrata* and *L. ciliata*, the **Fly Honeysuckle** are other relations with berries once eaten by native peoples – but be careful, most honeysuckle berries are toxic.

Lycium barbarum
Goji also known as the **Wolf berry**, the **Box Thorn**, or the **Duke of Argyll's Tea Plant**

A nearly hardy Solanaceae, this is found from Eastern Europe through to northern India and Tibet. The red berries follow small violet flowers on lax, often spiny sprawling stems. 'More vitamin C than oranges, more beta carotene than carrots and more iron than steak', claims one vendor! Much vaunted as the ultimate healthy fruit, these are not awfully full of mouth appeal but easy enough to grow under cover or in a sheltered garden.

Treacle Berry

Shepherdia argentea
Buffalo berry
Eleaegnaceae

A deciduous hardy shrub with spines, producing small, scarlet or yellow currant-like berries that are tart raw but good for jellies or drying; both male and female plants are needed for pollination. *S. canadensis*, **Soapberry**, is smaller with sour orange berries made into 'Indian ice cream', a froth made by beating them with sweetened water.

Decaisnea fargesii
Lardizabalaceae

A deciduous shrub from the Himalayas grown as an ornamental for the amazing metallic blue pods which surprisingly have an edible white pulp, which is actually sweet and pleasant. Really ought to be improved!

Mitchella repens
The Partridge Berry, Squawberry, Twinberry
Rubiaceae

From North America, this resembles cranberries in many ways but is unrelated. The berries come in pairs, persisting all winter as even the birds find them a bit bland.

Podocarpus macrophyllus
Kusamaki, Japanese Yew
Taxaceae

Apparently Japanese children enjoy these small red to purple fruits raw and cooked. *P. totara* is a dwarf evergreen from New Zealand with a sweet cherry like fruit.

Berberidaceae

Podophyllum peltatum
May Apple
Podophyllaceae

Often grown as an ornamental, this poisonous herbaceous perennial has waxy white flowers followed by small lemon-like fruits that are edible and not unpleasant. *P. emodi* from the Himalayas has larger edible scarlet fruits. Hybridisation could maybe make much improved fruits from these.

Prinsepia sinensis
Cherry Prinsepia
Rosaceae

From Manchuria comes this rather graceful spiny shrub with yellow flowers and juicy fruits, much resembling red or purple cherries. I suspect you need two or more different plants for crops as mine never sets.

NUTS

Nuts are different from fruits. We eat the seeds of nuts and usually not the coverings, though we often find uses for these as well. With fruits, plants are giving us, the animals and birds who consume them, a sweet pulp so that we will, inadvertently, help distribute their seeds. This trade-off is easy for the plant, as the seeds are the expensive items to manufacture and the sugary pulp takes little resource.

However, when we eat nuts, we eat big seeds that are very expensive for the plant to make, as they are rich in oils, minerals, proteins and vitamins. They have a high dietary value to us, but of course this does not serve the plant well. The trade-off is that the plant 'hopes' that if it produces a lot of nuts, some will escape the slaughter and be trampled underfoot or carried elsewhere and hidden but never recovered and thus start a fresh territory.

In northern climes, squirrels are well known for assisting this process by burying nuts, but many other small mammals, particularly rodents, are also involved. Birds similarly hide nuts; there are plausible stories of birds that have filled attics with nuts, popping them in singly throughout the autumn through a small space such as a knot hole.

Because of their high oil content and nutritional value, nuts have long been gathered from the wild. The rise of industry created greatly increased demand for nuts as a source of oils for lighting and lubrication and for turning into margarines, soaps and cosmetics. The pulps that remained were rich animal feeds and helped to fuel the expansion of farming in the nineteenth century. Nuts were no longer wild crops, but had become cultivated crops on a vast scale.

Although nut trees generally require little work, they mostly grow too big for the garden and are best grown agriculturally. (Of course they then suffer from a build-up of pests and diseases – problems associated with all crops if they are grown as monocultures.)

They are slow to come into production, though on the plus side they are mostly long-lived and make good timber. Many nut trees produce very hard or oily wood that lasts well. Walnut is one of the most prized of all timbers, so precious that it is mostly used only as veneer.

Nuts suffer different pests from those that attack fruits. Bigger birds and rodents are more of a threat and, as nuts are larger, they are harder to protect or grow under cover (indeed, except as bonsai, many are almost impossible to keep small). Also, they are unfortunately more tender and susceptible to frost damage than many fruits. This, plus the need for a hot summer and autumn to ripen the nuts, means that most nut trees are best grown in countries warmer than Britain.

One interesting connection between many of the nut trees covered in this chapter is how many of them have catkins and are wind-pollinated, even though these nut trees belong to entirely different families. This also means that they do not generally have scented flowers and give little nectar to insects, but they are, of course, a rich source of pollen.

From a commercial point of view, it is curious how almost all retail nut sales take place at Christmas, a period that serves to outsell the rest of the year put together.

Prunus dulcis/amygdalus from the family *Rosaceae*

ALMONDS

Tree up to 6m. Life span: short. Deciduous. Fruits: 5cm, pointed oval, in brown skin. Value: rich in protein, calcium, iron, vitamins B2 and B3 and phosphorus.

Almond trees resemble and are closely related to peaches, with larger, light pink blossoms appearing before long, thin leaves. Flowering a fortnight earlier than peaches, they are often affected by frost. The wild varieties sometimes have spiny branches. The almond fruit has tough, inedible, leathery, greenish-brown, felted skin with a partition line along which it easily splits. The skin peels off a smooth, hard stone, full of small holes that do not penetrate the shell, containing the single, flat, pointed oval seed. Originally from the Middle East, almonds were known to the Ancient Hebrews and Phoenicians. Long naturalised in southern Europe and western Asia, they are now widely grown in California, South Africa and southern Australia. Almond trees were introduced to England in 1548.

Almond orchards must be well away from peach trees

varieties

Prunus dulcis dulcis is the **Sweet Almond**, *P. dulcis amara*, the **Bitter Almond**. The former is the much-loved nut; the latter is used for producing oil and flavourings and is too bitter for eating. It contains highly poisonous amounts of prussic acid. In Spain, a light-cropping old variety, **Jordan**, is still grown and commercial varieties are available in some regions. The varieties most grown in Australia are **Chellaston**, Johnstone's **Prolific** and **Fugenzo**.

cultivation

Almonds want well-enriched, well-aerated, light soil, and to be planted at least 3m apart. They need no staking after the first year. They want lots of compost and mulches. Usually grown as a bush, they can be planted against walls. They should not be planted near peaches, as they may hybridise, resulting in bitter nuts. Hand-pollination is recommended. They are not completely self-fertile, so several trees should be planted together. Almonds are frost hardy but the flowers can be destroyed by late frosts. They are also drought hardy but will not bear fruit in such conditions. Their low chill

ALMONDS

requirement makes them versatile in a wide range of climates but they prefer a Mediterranean climate.

Growing in Containers
Almonds can be grown in large pots, as they can take heavy pruning if well fed and watered. Pots enable them to be kept under cover during winter and through flowering and then brought out all through the summer, thus avoiding peach leaf curl and frost damage. The flowers must be protected from frosts and so too must the young fruitlets.

Ornamental and Wildlife Value
The almond is a real beauty – the fruiting tree as much as the many ornamental varieties. Cockatoos also love them!

Propagation
Almonds can be raised from stones, but take years to fruit and may produce a mixture of sweet and bitter fruits. Budded on to **St. Julien A**, for example, almonds will normally fruit in their third year. Seedling almond or peach rootstocks are better. Plum rootstocks are sometimes used for heavy soil areas.

Pruning and Training
Almonds fruit on young shoots, like peaches, but need to carry more fruits, so the trees are not pruned as

In the almond the outer flesh is leathery and peels away

Bitter Almond

hard. Commercially, every third year or so a few main branches are cut back hard and the top end of the remaining higher branches is removed to encourage prolific growth from the lower branches and stubs. This is best done in late winter, though it may let silver leaf disease in. It also keeps the bushes lower and more manageable. On walls and under cover, almonds may be fan trained, as for peaches (see page 40). Thinning the fruits is not essential, but prevents biennial bearing.

Pests and Diseases
Almonds' main problem is peach leaf curl; see peaches (page 40) for treatment. Rainy weather in late spring and summer may cause fruits to rot. Dieback and gummosis are symptomatic of poor growth and are best treated by heavy mulching and hard pruning. Borers and beetles often tunnel into the trunk and they can be cleaned out with a thin wire. Shothole, a fungus that affects foliage, needs routine treatment with Bordeaux. Parrots and cockatoos love to eat almonds.

Harvesting and Storing
Once the nuts start to drop, knock them down, peel and dry. Commercially they are hulled, but the nuts will keep better intact. They can be stored in dry salt or sand for long periods.

other uses

The wood is hard and makes good veneers; the oil is used in cosmetics.

companion planting

Almonds are benefited by Alliums, especially garlic and chives. Clover or alfalfa and stinging nettles are also reputedly helpful.

culinary

The nuts are left with the brown skin on, or are blanched to provide a cleaner-tasting product. They may be eaten raw, cooked or turned into a milk.

Sirop d'Orgeat Milkshake
Quantities to taste

Sirop d'Orgeat
Ice-cold full-cream organic milk
Grated nutmeg

To one part Sirop d'Orgeat add approximately seven parts milk, mix well and top with the grated nutmeg.

Carya species from the family *Juglandaceae*

PECAN AND HICKORY NUTS

Tree up to 30m. Life span: medium to long. Deciduous, partly self-fertile. Fruits: up to 5cm, green-skinned, hard-shelled nuts. Value: rich in oils and vitamins B1 and B2.

Pecans are very large, fast-growing trees with pinnate leaves, male catkins and insignificant flowers followed by pointed, rounded, cylindrical fruits. These have a leathery skin that peels off to reveal a reddish, smooth shell enclosing the walnut-like kernel. Hickories are similar, though not as large in tree or fruit, with non-aromatic leaves and peeling bark, while the pecan has grey, resinous leaves. Hickories also prefer more humid conditions than pecans.

These are natives of North America and have been long enjoyed by Native Americans. They are grown in Australia, but rarely crop well elsewhere, though they are widely grown for their timber. The first trees were introduced to Britain in 1629.

Pecans

varieties

Carya illinoensis is the pecan, a fruit much like a walnut in most ways save that the reddish shell is smooth, not embossed, and is also more cylindrical. The trees grow up to 21m high, so are not very suitable for most modern gardens. Burbank developed new varieties of pecan with very thin shells, but these are not widely available. The hickories are similar to the pecan, with more flattened nuts. The trees generally grow up to half the pecan's height again, which is pretty big anywhere. The **Shellbark Hickory**, *C. laciniosa/alba*, and *C. ovata*, the **Shagbark Hickory**, are the more popular and productive sorts. *C. tomentosa*, the **Mocker** or **Square Nut**, has a tasty nut, but is very difficult to shell. *C. cordiformis* is the **Bitternut Hickory**, and *C. porcina/glabra* is the **Pignut**. As their names suggest, these are suitable only for pigs and, of course, hungry children. *C. sulcata* is the **King Nut**, considered the best variety by Native Americans, but not yet developed commercially. Many other minor species are also occasionally eaten from the wild.

cultivation

Pecans prefers a hot, dry, sub-tropical climate; the hickories prefer one that is warmer and wetter.

Growing in Containers

They resent being confined in pots and are unlikely to crop, though they may make good bonsai subjects.

PECAN AND HICKORY NUTS

Bitternut Hickory

Ornamental and Wildlife Value
Given a suitable setting, these are large, attractive trees with decorative foliage that turns a rich yellow in autumn. Their nuts are of significant wildlife value.

Propagation
Normally grown from seed, they are best pot-grown and then planted out as soon as possible in their final site, as they do not like to be transplanted. They are slow to establish and then fast-growing. Improved varieties are grafted or budded on seedling stock.

Pruning and Training
Minimal pruning and training are required. Large specimens need staking for the first few years, as they are slow to take.

Harvesting and Storing
Ripe fruits are knocked down from the tree, peeled (if the peel has not dropped off already) and dried. They do not store as well as walnuts, though they may keep up to a year if they are stored in a cool, dry place. Commercially they are hulled before storage and will keep up to two years at –15°C.

Pests and Diseases, Companion Planting
Very few pests or diseases are problems for the hickories in gardens. The pecan may suffer from coral spot, which needs pruning before it spreads. Twig girdlers, carpenter bugs and longicorn beetles can also be a problem. No companion effects are known about for either tree.

other uses

Hickories are planted for their tough, elastic timber and are renowned as fuel for smoking foods. Hickory bark was used for a yellow dye.

Square Nut

culinary

Pecan nuts taste much like mild, sweet walnuts and to my taste are preferable. They are used raw or cooked in savoury and sweet items, especially cakes and ice cream. Pecan pie is a legendary dessert. Hickory nuts are used similarly and can be squeezed to produce nut milk or oil.

Pecan Pie
Serves 4–6

175g shortcrust pastry
60g shelled pecans
90g brown sugar
3 small or 2 large eggs
225g golden syrup
30g maple syrup
½ teaspoon vanilla essence
¼ teaspoon salt

Roll out the pastry and line a wide, shallow pie dish. Bake blind, weighed down with dried peas or similar, at 190°C/375°F/gas mark 5 for 20 minutes or until cooked. Cool and fill the case with pecans, arranged aesthetically. Beat together the other ingredients till the sugar is dissolved and pour over carefully without disturbing the nuts, which may float. Bake at 220°C/450°F/gas mark 8 for 10 minutes, then reduce the temperature to 180°C/350°F/gas mark 4 and cook for another 30 minutes. Cool and chill well before serving in slices with lashings of cream.

Juglans **species from the family** ***Juglandaceae***

WALNUTS

Tree 40m. Life span: long. Deciduous, partially self-fertile. Fruits: up to 5cm, green sphere enclosing nut. Value: rich in oil; the husks contain much vitamin C.

Walnuts are slow-growing, making massive trees up to 40m eventually, with aromatic, pinnate foliage, silvery bark, insignificant female flowers and male catkins. All parts have a distinct sweet, aromatic smell. The fruits have a green husk around the nut, enclosing a kernel wrinkled like a brain.

***Juglans regia*, the common or Persian walnut, is native to western Asia. Introduced to the Mediterranean basin before the first century BC, it became an important food in many regions and was also grown for timber. Walnuts reached Britain in the sixteenth century, if not in Roman times. The black walnut, *J. nigra*, comes from north-east America and was introduced to Britain in 1686. It is even bigger than the common walnut and widely grown for timber. The nuts are large, very hard to crack and a valuable dietary source of phosphorus.**

varieties

An old Australian variety, **Freshford Gem** is a good choice. It bears early and the tree is a manageable size. **Franquette** is an old but reliable French variety. It flowers late, missing frost and bacterial spot, and is recommended for New South Wales. **Wilson's Wonder** has flavoursome, large nuts but is prone to bird and blight damage. **Chandler** and **Hartley** are recent imports from California; not yet fully tested. **Concord** is a small tree and the nuts are of good flavour. They can grow up to 45m. **Broadview** comes into cropping earlier than most after just three to four years. **Lara** is a French-bred producer of big nuts. **Majestic** is a heavy cropper of big nuts on a very vigorous tree, while **Rubis** produces attractive, different red-skinned kernels. Another American species, the **White Walnut** or **Butternut**, *J. cinerea* is grown for timber and ornamental use. The nuts are strong-tasting and oily. *J. sieboldiana cordiformis* is the **Heartnut** from Japan. Fast-growing, fruiting after only five years or so, it has leaves up to 1m long and small, easily shelled nuts which hang on strings. *Pterocarya fraxiniflora*, **Caucasian Wing-nut**, native to the Caucasus and Persia, was introduced to Britain in 1782. Strong growing relations of walnuts, succeeding in damp places, they have large nonaromatic pinnate leaves, catkins and small edible nuts surrounded with semi-circular wings. They are hardy though sustaining some dieback after hard frosts and could be improved, perhaps by crossing with other species such as the **Japanese Wing Nut**, *P. rhoifolia*, or the large fruited Chinese *P. stenoptera*.

cultivation

Walnuts prefer a heavy, moist soil with cold winters and warm, dry summers. They should not be planted where late frosts occur. As pollination is difficult, it is best to plant several together. If the walnut has damaged bark it produces a more valuable distorted grain in the timber.

Growing in Containers

Huge trees, these can hardly be housed. I've a fifteen-year-old bonsai walnut, but I doubt that it will ever fruit!

Ornamental and Wildlife Value

Very attractive and sweetly aromatic trees, they grow too big for most small gardens. They are not in general very valuable to wildlife, but can be decimated by cockatoos and possums.

Butternut

WALNUTS

Japanese

Propagation
The species can be grown from seed, but are slow. Improved varieties are grafted or budded, and still take a decade to start to fruit, finally maturing around the century. They are best started in pots and moved to their final site while still small, as they resent transplanting.

Pests and Diseases
Rabbits attack young trees. Bacterial blight can cause the kernel to blacken and die. Preventative spraying with Bordeaux helps. Collar rot damages walnut trees.

Pruning and Training
Walnuts must be pruned only in autumn, as they bleed in spring. Minimal pruning is required, but branches become massive, so remove badly positioned ones early. They need no stake after the first years.

Harvesting and Storing
The nuts are knocked down and the sticky staining peel is removed before drying. Walnuts can then be stored for up to a year. For pickling, pick the nuts green when a skewer can still be pushed through.

companion planting

Varro, in the first century BC, noted how sterile the land near walnut trees was. Walnut leaves and roots give off exudates that inhibit many plants and prevent their seeds from germinating. The American species are more damaging than the European and they are particularly bad for apples, *Solanaceae*, *Rubus* and many ornamentals.

other uses

The foliage and husks have long been used as brown dyes and the oil as a hair darkener and for paints. The wood has always been valued for veneers and gun stocks, the more gnarled the better. Walnut trees were often planted near stables and privies, as their smell was thought to keep away flies. The walnut sap has traditionally been boiled to produce sugar.

Black Walnut

culinary

Walnuts may be eaten either raw or cooked, often in confectionery or cakes, and associate particularly well with coffee or chocolate. They yield an edible, light oil. The young fruits may be pickled before the stone forms.

Walnut Aperitif or post-prandial liqueur

Young green walnuts
Brandy
Red wine
Sugar, as required

Wash and prick enough nuts to fill a wide-necked bottle. Fill with brandy, seal and store in a cool, dark place. After a year, decant the brandy into another bottle, refill the original bottle with red wine and reseal. After another year, decant the wine into the brandy, refill the walnut bottle with wine and reseal. After another year decant again, fill the walnut bottle with white sugar and reseal. After a year (making four in total,) discard the nuts and add the sugar syrup to the wine and brandy. Serve in sherry glasses before meals.

Corylus species from the family *Corylaceae*

HAZELS, COBS AND FILBERTS

Tree/bush up to 6m. Life span: medium to long. Deciduous, partially self-fertile. Fruits: up to 2.5cm, pointed round, or oblong oval, brown nuts. Value: rich in oils.

These are shrubby trees, typical of woods and thickets, with dark stems, leaves rounded to a point and magnificent, yellow catkin male flowers in early spring. The gorgeous, carmine-red, female flowers are tiny, sea-urchin-like tentacles that protrude on warm days. The nuts are a pointed round or oblong oval. Hazels and cobs have a husk around the base, while filberts (full-beards) are completely enveloped by the husk. The shell is thin and the kernel sweet. Wild hazels are *Corylus avellana*, but, being wind-pollinated, these have often been influenced by *C. colurna*, cobs, also known as Turkish or Barcelona nuts, and *C. maxima* or filberts.

Hazelnuts of wild species were known in ancient times and filberts were introduced by the Romans from Greece. Pliny claims they came there from Damascus. The Romans may have brought filberts to Britain, but they were not noticed officially till introduced in 1759. Cob nuts were introduced earlier, in 1582, and the American hazelnut, *C. americana*, a similar, smaller nut with a thicker shell and heart-shaped leaves, arrived in 1798. Any appellation no longer signifies true breeding, as these all became interbred during the nineteenth century, giving us most of our current varieties.

Hazel catkins

varieties

The determining factor in hazelnut culture is how trees cope with searing summer heat, winter cold not presenting a problem in Australia. **Cosford Cob** is thin-shelled and a good pollinator of others. **White American** is the most commonly grown, with heavy cropping and good nuts. **White Avelline** bears a small nut and is pollinated by **Turkish Hazel**, **Gunslebert** and **White American**. Newly imported Italian cultivars may in time prove better suited to the Australian climate than earlier English or German varieties.

cultivation

Hazels thrive in stony, hilly ground. A well-drained, loamy soil will do, but heavy, damp, rich soils cause too much rank growth and few female flowers. Hazels need no support and are best planted severally to ensure pollination. They are an immensely easy crop for the lazy gardener, requiring even less effort than most.

Growing in Containers

There seems no reason to grow them under cover and I suspect they would not like it anyway. They survive in pots quite well, looking attractive but seldom cropping.

Ornamental and Wildlife Value

These are not generally noticed, save when their catkins make a welcome display. The **Twisted Hazel** is attractively distorted and deformed and still crops well. The hazels will support many life forms, both large and small, and are also excellent plants for wild gardens.

HAZELS, COBS AND FILBERTS

Propagation
These can be grown from seed but do not come true. Layering or grafting is possible, but root suckers are best, detached in autumn and potted up or planted in situ or a nursery bed for a year before their final move.

Pruning and Training
Traditionally hazels were grown on a low, flat, cartwheel frame. They are probably best trained to spurs on goblets, but are often left to be bushes or thickets. It is worth keeping them on a single trunk, uncongested, and removing the suckers, to prevent losing any of the nuts.

Pests and Diseases
Weedy growth underneath makes it hard to find nuts, so hazels are best planted in grass or mulched. In gardens they suffer few problems on a scale sufficient to damage crops, other than the attentions of birds, rodents, children and especially squirrels.

Harvesting and Storing
The nuts can be eaten a little unripe, but have to be fully ripe to keep. Ideally they should be allowed to fall off, but many are stolen by wildlife. They need to be dehusked and dried to keep well, though I never dehusk my Red-skinned Filberts. They will keep best, and for years, if packed in salt.

Kentish Cob

Kentish Cob

companion planting

Grow chestnuts and other nut trees and plant tansy, catmint or marjoram as a groundcover.

other uses

Hazels make good hedges and windbreaks. The foliage is eaten by many animals, including cows. The stems are tough and flexible, so are good for baskets and hurdles, and forked branches make divining rods. The wood is used for smoking fuel and I smoke my cheese with the shells.

culinary

Hazelnuts of all varieties are used in savoury dishes, but more often in sweet dishes and confections. They are used for liqueurs and can be squeezed to express a light, edible oil.

Hazelnut Macaroons
Makes about 12

120g hazelnuts
120g light brown sugar
1 egg white
Drop of vanilla extract
Whipped cream, to serve

Grind three-quarters of the nuts in a food processor, then add the other ingredients and cream them together. Pour rounds of the mix on to rice paper on a baking tray, place the remaining nuts on top and bake for 15 minutes at 180°C/350°F/gas mark 4. Serve sandwiched with thick or clotted cream.

Castanea sativa from the family *Fagaceae*

SWEET OR SPANISH CHESTNUTS

Tree up to 37m. Life span: long. Deciduous, rarely self-fertile. Fruits: 5cm, prickly burrs containing two or three nuts. Value: rich in oils.

Sweet chestnuts make massive and beautiful trees. They have very large, serrated-edged leaves. The male flowers are long, yellow catkins, different from walnut or hazel catkins, as they are divided like pearls on a string. The fruits are brownish-russet, softly spiny burrs usually containing three brown nuts with thin, tough, leathery shells, flattened on one side and pointed.

Sweet chestnuts are native to the Mediterranean region. They were highly valued by the Romans for food and timber and became widely distributed. They fruit well after hot summers, but are still capable of reaching a large size, so they have been planted for timber and were often coppiced. The major exporter of these nuts has always been Spain, though most southern European countries have their own production, as chestnuts have become a staple food. Madeiran nuts are said to be the biggest and were traditionally served to sustain the peasants for months each year.

varieties

Castanea sativa, the Spanish chestnut, is the only species grown in Australia. In Europe and America, chestnuts have been decimated by chestnut blight, absent in Australia and New Zealand. Local cultivars such as **Flemings Reliance**, **Flemings Special**, **Buffalo Queen** and **Stanley Red** have been developed in the absence of banned imports of bud wood. **Emerald Gem** is a late-ripening nut and **Black Beauty** bears mid-season. Check with local suppliers for the best selection for your area.

Castanea sativa – not for the smaller garden

cultivation

Sweet chestnuts are far too big for most gardens, rapidly reaching 30m or even more. They do not like thin chalky soils, but are not calcifuges and will grow on an alkaline soil if it is also a light, well-drained loam or light, dry, sandy soil. They need no staking after the first year or so. If nuts are required rather than timber, plant on the sunny side of woodlands or windbreaks.

Ornamental and Wildlife Value

Sweet chestnuts make statuesque trees and the large leaves colour well in autumn. The nuts are often rather too useful to wildlife.

Growing in Containers

Chestnuts resent being confined in a pot and they are unlikely to ever fruit in one, but there's a challenge.

Pests and Diseases

Chestnut blight is absent but trees are affected by armillaria root rot and phytophthora. Preventive measures are best such as planting in well-drained soils. Rodents, birds (especially parrots and cockatoos) and possums take the nuts.

Propagation
They can be grown from seed and are fast-growing but still slow to fruit. The best varieties are budded or grafted onto seedling chestnuts.

Pruning and Training
Minimal pruning is required and is best tackled in winter. Chestnuts get very large, so care must be taken to remove unsound branches.

Harvesting and Storing
The nuts are beaten down, the husks then removed and dried. They will keep for a year in cool, dry conditions; longer if totally dried first.

companion planting

Chestnuts are considered healthier when they are grown near oak trees.

The nuts come well protected

culinary

Chestnuts are not eaten raw, but are delicious roasted. They are made into marrons glacés (crystallised chestnuts), ground into flour and then made into porridge, puddings, breads, cakes, muffins and tarts and they are also much used for savoury dishes such as pâtés and in stuffing for meats. Sweet chestnuts are even made into liqueurs.

Chestnut Amber
Serves 4

225g chestnuts
300ml milk
1 lemon
1 vanilla pod
60g breadcrumbs
30g butter
60g caster sugar
2 eggs, separated
120g shortcrust pastry

Roast the chestnuts for 20 minutes, cool and remove the skins. Simmer gently, with sufficient water to cover, until tender, then drain and sieve to a purée. Simmer the milk with the lemon peel and vanilla pod for 15 minutes, then strain on to the breadcrumbs. Blend the butter and half the sugar, mix in the egg yolks and lemon juice and stir in the puréed chestnuts, breadcrumbs and milk. Line a deep dish with pastry and fill with the mixture. Bake at 200°C/400°F/gas mark 6 for 25 minutes, or until firm and brown. Whisk the egg whites to a stiff froth, add a teaspoon of sugar, whisk again and spoon on top of the pie. Sprinkle with more sugar and then return to the oven until the meringue turns a delicious amber.

other uses

Sweet chestnut has long been used for cleft paling. The wood is durable, but has 'shakes' or splits in it. Often used for rough or external timber, such as coffins and hop poles, it makes a poor firewood but superior charcoal. The nuts were traditionally esteemed for the self-service fattening of swine.

Castanea dentata

Pistacia vera from the family *Anacardiaceae*

PISTACHIOS

Tree, up to 9m. Life span: medium. Deciduous, not self-fertile. Fruits: 2.5cm, pointed oval nuts. Value: rich in oil.

Pistachios are small, tender trees with grey bark and grey-green, slightly downy, pinnate leaves. The male and female flowers are borne on separate trees in the wild, but some cultivated varieties may be unisexual. It is hard to tell, as the flowers are inconspicuous though carried in panicles, which later become masses of small, pointed red fruits. These have a thin, green husk covering the thin, smooth, twin-shelled nut, housing a small, oval, green kernel that has a most appealing taste, especially after roasting and salting. Pistachios are one of the most expensive variety of nuts to buy.

Pistachios are natives of the Middle East and Central Asia and, with some close relations, have been cultivated since ancient times. They were grown in Italy in the late Roman period but were not introduced to Britain till the sixteenth and seventeenth centuries and then never proved hardy enough. The seed was distributed by the American Patent Office in 1854 and the trees proved successful in many southern states, where the nuts are now produced in quantity, rivalling the output of the Mediterranean and Turkey. It can also be grown in southern Australia.

varieties

Pistachios, *Pistacia vera*, need an area with a hot, dry summer and a cold winter to set nuts. Cultivation is in its infancy in Australia, and only a few named varieties are available. The old Middle Eastern favourite **Aleppo** is not generally obtainable but the locally grown cultivar **Sirora** or **15/11** was grown from a seedling of the **Syrian Red Aleppo**. It is a prolific cropper with vigorous growth. The other main variety is **Kerman** collected by an American plant hunter from the town in Iran. It performs well along the Murray River.

cultivation

Pistachios are not particular as to soil and are extremely drought-hardy. They are tolerant of flooding, however. They form a very deep tap-root early and care must be taken not to break it off while transplanting. They are useful for growing on poor, dry, hilly soil where other nuts will not thrive. Their greater value commercially also encourages this. One male staminate tree is needed for six female pistillate trees, but as the pollen is shed early it needs to be saved in a paper bag until the pistils are receptive.

Ornamental and Wildlife Value

In warm countries or on a warm wall these are not unattractive, small trees. The unproductive **Chinese Pistachio**, *P. chinenis*, is a small, very pretty and hardy

Mastic Tree

PISTACHIOS

Pistacia vera

shrub. Pistachio nuts are readily taken by maurauding birds and mammals.

Propagation

Although better varieties could be grown, pistachios seem to lack development. Bud stock is grafted onto seedling rootstocks of other *Pistacia* species, usually of *P. terebinthus* or *P. atlantica*. Commercial producers bud in the field because of difficulties planting bare-rooted bushes. Better varieties can be layered, budded or grafted.

Pruning and Training

Only remedial pruning is required and this is best done in mid-summer. Plant in full sun only and in a very warm spot. Train to a vase shape to keep shading to a minimum leaving the centre open.

Pests and Diseases

No common pests or diseases are a problem for pistachios in garden cultivation. Waterlogged soil or humidity can cause rotting of the nuts.

Harvesting and Storing

As these hang severally on panicles, they can be cut off to be dried and husked. They are best stored in their shells, which open automatically if they are roasted.

other uses

P. terebinthus was long ago cultivated for producing first terebinth, the resin which oozes from the tree, and later turpentine. The wood is dark red and hard and used in cabinet making.

Pistachio terebinthus

culinary

Pistachios can be eaten raw, but are most commonly roasted and salted, the shelling being left to the purchaser. They are much used as a colouring and flavouring for a wide range of foods, some savoury and many sweet, including nougat and ice cream.

Pistachio Ice Cream

Serves 6

3 small or 2 large egg yolks
175g honey
1 teaspoon vanilla extract
600ml cream
120g shelled pistachios
Natural green food colouring
Candied lemon slices and glacé cherries to taste

Whisk the egg yolks, honey, vanilla and half the cream. Scald the remaining cream in a bain-marie, add the egg mixture and stir until the mixture thickens. Remove from the heat, cool, chill, then partially freeze. Remove from the freezer, beat vigorously and return. Repeat, but after the second beating mix in the nuts and colouring, then freeze again. Partially defrost before serving the ice cream scooped into glasses, garnished with lemon slices and cherries.

Anacardium occidentale from the family *Anacardiaceae*

CASHEWS

Tree up to 12m. Life span: medium. Semi-evergreen. Fruit: up to 8cm long, unusual. Value: kernels are nearly half fat and one-fifth protein.

Cashews are medium-sized, spreading trees with rounded leaves, related to pistachios. The cashew comes attached underneath the bottom of the much larger and peculiar fruits, cashew apples, which are juicy and astringent. The nut is grey or brown, ear-shaped and contains a white kernel within the acrid, poisonous shell.

Indigenous to South America, cashews were planted in the East Indies by the sixteenth century and are now grown in many tropical regions, especially India and eastern Africa.

varieties

Hybrid selections with upright growth and heavy branching are under trial in north Queensland and the Northern Territory. **KAM2**, **KAM6**, **Guntur** and **9/14** are showing promise.

cultivation

These are best grown by the sea in moderately dry tropical regions and will thrive in any reasonable soil. Cashews need a frost-free tropical climate with distinct wet/dry seasons. Deep well-drained, sandy soils are best. Flowering, nut set and harvest coincides with the dry season. Depending on locality, harvest occurs between August and February. Trees need shelter from wind and irrigation increases yields.

Propagation
Growers propagate their own stock from seed and budwood sourced from agricultural authorities.

Pruning and Training
Only remedial pruning is necessary.

Pests and Diseases
Anthracnose occurs in wet areas. Uncommon cercospora blotch causes spotting and defoliation.

Harvesting and Storing
Once the nuts are picked from underneath the fruits, they have to be roasted and shelled, which, despite mechanisation, is labour-intensive. This is because all the shell must be removed, as it contains an irritant in the inner membrane around the kernel, though this is rendered harmless by heat.

other uses

The shells of the nuts contain an oil used industrially. The 'apples' are then fermented to make a liquor. The sap makes an indelible ink.

culinary

Cashew nuts are popular raw; i.e., already partially roasted, or roasted and salted. They are used in many sweet and savoury dishes and can be liquidised to make a thick sauce. Cashews are fermented to make wine in Goa. The cashew apple is the more valued part and is eaten fresh, preserved in syrup, candied and fermented to wine.

Cashew Tarts
Makes 12

225g marzipan
A little icing sugar
120g cashew nuts
60g honey
1 teaspoon vanilla extract
A little milk
Glacé cherries

Roll the marzipan as pastry and form individual tart cases in a tray dusted with icing sugar. Liquidise the other ingredients, adding just enough milk to ensure success. Pour into the marzipan cases, set a cherry in each and chill them to set.

Macadamia integrifolia (Macadamia ternifolia) from the family *Proteaceae*

MACADAMIAS

OR QUEENSLAND NUTS

Tree up to 18m. Life span: medium. Semi-evergreen. Fruits: up to 2.5cm, grey-husked nuts. Value: over 70% fat.

Macadamia trees are densely covered with narrow, glossy, holly-like, dark green leaves.

The tassels of whitish flowers are followed by strings of small, hard, roundish, pointed nuts in greyish-green husks. The kernel is finely flavoured and of exquisite texture.

These nuts, despite the Greek-sounding name, are natives of north-eastern Australia. They are often consumed in the United States from plantations in Hawaii. They were introduced to Ceylon, now Sri Lanka, in 1868.

culinary

Most macadamia nuts are eaten roasted and salted, but they are also used in certain baked goods and confectionery.

Macadamia Slice

Serves 8–10

120g macadamia nuts
Icing sugar
225g marzipan
1 dessertspoonful apricot jam
30g chopped candied peel

Rinse and dry the macadamia nuts, if they are salted. Dust a rolling board with powdered sugar and roll out the marzipan thickly. Coat thinly with jam and cut into two equally shaped pieces and an approximate third. On one piece spread a layer of nuts and peel, then place one-third of marzipan on top, sticky-side down. Smear the top with jam and add another layer of nuts and peel. Then put the last third on top (also sticky-side down). Carefully press and roll this sandwich flatter and wider until the nuts almost push through. Trim, cut into small portions and sprinkle the mixture with powdered sugar before presenting.

varieties

Two species and several cultivars are grown in Australia.

cultivation

Macadamias prefer tropical or sub-tropical, moist conditions. *M. tetraphylla* is more cold tolerant than *M. integrifolia*, and trees in Melbourne need more sun than those in sub-tropical areas. They are not particular as to soil but need regular water to bear nuts. Trees are drought tolerant but suspend nut production in dry periods. Fertilising with small frequent applications in the growing season increases the yield. Branches are brittle so do not plant in windy locations. Apply a thick layer of organic mulch in summer. Garden trees rarely exceed 10m.

Propagation

Best selections are grafted onto seedlings in autumn or spring. Seedlings readily adapt to new climates.

Pruning and Training

Only remedial pruning is necessary and they will form bushy trees.

Harvesting and Storing

Nuts fall from the tree and are collected so keep the ground clear of weeds. The shells are hard to crack but if heated in a cool oven for a few hours they become brittle. Nuts keep for about one year, though their flavour will deteriorate.

Cocos nucifera* from the family *Arecaceae

COCONUTS

These attractive palms, so typical of dreamy, deserted islands, are spread by their floating, oval-husked nuts. The thick, fibrous husk is contained in a rind and itself encloses a thick-shelled, oval nut with a hollow kernel that is full of milk when under-ripe.

Palm, up to 28m. Life span: medium to long. Evergreen, not usually self-fertile. Fruits: 30cm plus, green-brown, oval husk containing the nut. Value: 65% oil.

Venerated in the islands of the Pacific as a sacred emblem of fertility, coconuts are distributed and known around the world.

Each tree holds a huge weight of small head crushing bombs

varieties

The **King Coconut** of Sri Lanka is esteemed for its sweet juice. The **Dwarf Coconut**, *Nyiur-gading*, of Malaysia has small fruits, but crops when young and at only about a metre high. The **Maldive Coconut** is small and almost round; the **Needle Coconut** of the Nicobar Islands is triangular and pointed.

Definitely not Dorking

cultivation

Coconuts thrive by the sea in moist, tropical heat and rich, loamy soils and are planted about 10m apart. Coconuts may grow in warm temperate spots but rarely fruit even in the sub-tropics. Dwarf coconuts grow to 10m and bear when young. Coconuts can be grown in a container indoors until they grow too large.

Propagation

Ripe nuts that are laid on their side and barely covered with compost will germinate readily in heat.

Harvesting and Storing

Pick the nuts when still green for a refreshing, cold drink or collect ripe fruit as it drops.

companion planting

Coconuts are often grown in alternate rows with rubber trees, and with cacao while young. Climbing peppers, *Piper nigrum*, are grown up the coconut trunks.

other uses

The trunks are used as timber, the leaves for thatch, the husk is coir, used for ropes and matting. The sap makes sugar or is fermented to toddy or distilled to arrack. Dried nuts are copra, used for oil for cosmetics, soaps and detergents. The pressed waste is animal food.

culinary

The milk is drunk fresh or fermented. The nut is eaten raw or cooked, often in the form of desiccated or shredded coconut.

Coconut Biscuits

Makes approx. 10

1 egg white
150g powdered sugar
75g desiccated coconut
Rice paper
Glacé cherries
Crystallised angelica

Beat the egg white until stiff, then beat in the sugar and coconut. Spoon blobs of the mixture on to rice paper on a baking tray. Garnish each with a cherry and angelica and bake at 180°C/350°F/gas mark 4 for 15 minutes or until they are browning.

Bertholletia excelsa from the family *Myrtaceae*

BRAZILS

PARA OR SAVORY NUTS

Tree up to 30m. Life span: long. Semi-evergreen. Fruits: up to 15cm; brown, spherical shell containing many nuts. Value: 65% fat and 14% protein.

These are tall handsome trees found on the banks of the Amazon and Orinoco Rivers. They have large, laurel-like leaves and panicles of white flowers, which drop brown, spherical bombs with thick, hard cases. These need to be smashed to reveal inside a dozen or more nuts shaped like orange segments, each with its own hard shell enclosing the oval, brown-skinned, sweet, white kernel. Natives of Brazil, these are still mainly produced there and also in Venezuela and Guyana. They are grown ornamentally in other countries such as Sri Lanka, but rarely on a commercial scale.

varieties

The tree is rarely grown outside of Brazil but seedlings have shown considerable variation.

You really don't want to climb a Brazil nut tree so you wait till they drop

cultivation

Brazil trees thrive in deep, rich, alluvial soil in tropical conditions.

Ornamental and Wildlife Value
Very attractive trees, but too large and requiring too much heat and warmth for widespread use.

Growing under Glass and in Containers
These can be grown from seed and kept dwarfed in containers, making interesting specimens, but are unlikely ever to fruit.

Harvesting and Storing
The individual nuts are obtained by cracking the spherical containers, which are sealed with wooden plugs. Inside their shells the nuts will keep for up to two years.

Pruning and Training
These need no special attention, but are slow. They are often not cultivated, but are gathered from the wild, as they take fifteen years to start fruiting.

Propagation
The nuts can be started off in heat, but actually take months to germinate.

other uses

The oil expressed from the kernels is used industrially; bark once caulked ships.

culinary

Most often Brazil nuts are eaten raw at Christmas time, but are also widely used in cooking, baking and confectionery.

Treacly Brazil Pie
Serves 6

225g shortcrust pastry
75g Brazil nuts
60g breadcrumbs
75g golden syrup
Juice and grated rind of 1 lemon
Cream, to serve

Roll out three-quarters of the pastry and line a pie dish with it. Use dried peas to weigh it down, and bake blind at 190°C/375°F/gas mark 5 for 10 minutes. Remove the peas and put a layer of nuts around the base of the case. Mix the other ingredients together and pour on top. Decorate with strips of pastry and then bake for 20 minutes at 190°C/375°F/gas mark 5. Serve the pie with lashings of whipped cream.

Arachis hypogaea from the family *Leguminosae*

GROUNDNUTS OR PEANUTS

Herbaceous, 60cm. Life span: annual. Self-fertile. Fruits: 1cm small oval seeds. Value: rich in oil, protein and vitamins B and E.

Peanuts are always known and used as nuts, although they are in fact the seeds of a tropical, pea-like, annual plant. After pollination of the yellow 'pea' flower, the stalk lengthens and pushes the seed pod into the ground, where it matures. The light brown husks shell easily to reveal a few red-skinned, whitish-yellow seeds.

Natives of tropical America, peanuts were brought to Europe in the sixteenth century and remained curiosities until the nineteenth. Useful for oil, animal feed and 'nuts', they are now grown worldwide.

varieties

Virginia and **Runner** peanuts are low, bushy plants with two large seeds per pod. **Spanish** and **Valencia** peanuts are smaller and more upright. **Red Spanish** and **Virginia** are commonly grown in Australia. Similar in several ways to peanuts are **Tiger Nuts**, *Cyperus esculentus*, *Cyperaceae*. Also called **Ground-Almond** or **Chufa**, these are also not a nut at all but edible underground rhizomes of a small perennial grass-like sedge grown in dry sandy soils, mostly in western Asia and Africa.

cultivation

Peanuts prefer loose, dry sandy soil. Cool, wet summers are unfavourable. Even in southern Australia, they will produce light crops in the home garden. They need 120 to 150 days to mature in spring and summer. Grow in rows with 6–10 plants per metre.

Ornamental and Wildlife Value

Too pea-like to be attractive, they have curiosity value. The seeds are only too valuable to wildlife!

Pruning and Training

These require no care. The old, runnering varieties were more difficult.

Pests and Diseases

Peanuts suffer from few pests though a fungus, mites and thrips can occur.

Harvesting and Storing

Lift plants in late summer when leaves yellow and leave nuts to dry for a few days before eating to eliminate a mild toxin in freshly dug pods.

Propagation

Sow in pots in heat for growing on in large pots to fruition, or planting out in favourable areas. In warm countries they are grown outdoors, sown 8cm deep, about 60cm apart each way.

Growing in Containers

For novelty, peanuts can be grown in a deep container on a sunny deck in cooler areas. Start in spring and add a light dressing of lime before planting then feed with complete fertiliser.

culinary

Peanuts are commonly roasted and salted, and are much used in baking and confections, savoury sauces and for their butter and edible oil. They should be kept dry until required.

Roast Peanuts
Makes 1kg

1kg peanuts
30g garlic
1 x 50g can anchovies
7g oregano

Boil the peanuts for 2 minutes and slip off their skins, then dry the nuts. Blend the garlic, anchovies and oregano. Coat the peanuts with this mixture and roast at 180°C/350°F/gas mark 4 for 10 minutes or so. Stir and cool.

companion planting

Peanuts have been grown with rubber and coconuts.

other uses

Peanut oil is used industrially.

Grow them in the ground, not pots

OTHER NUTLIKE FRUITS

Araucaria araucana
Monkey Puzzle or **Chile Pine**
Auracariaceae
These well-known trees, with spiny, overlapping, dark green leaves festooning the long, tail-like branches, rarely fruit in the UK, it seems, as they are usually planted singly. Where they have been planted severally, as at a school in Sussex, they reportedly set seed and the nuts were shed most years. In Chile the seeds are eaten raw, roasted or boiled. Closely related trees are also grown in Brazil and in Australia.

Brosimium alicastrum
Maya Breadnut is a tall Caribbean tree with round yellow fruits containing a large edible seed. Not to be confused with the Breadnut which is the seedy form of the normally seedless Breadfruit, *Artocarpus*, see p 561.

Canarium ovata
Pili Nut
Burseraceae
This is the legendary and rare Pili nut frustratingly rated as the best tasting of all nuts by those fortunate enough to have found it.

Castanospermum australe
Moreton Bay Chestnut
Leguminosae
These poisonous Australian nuts are relished by native Australians, who leach them in water before drying and roasting the nuts to render them edible.

Coffea arabica
Coffee
Rubiaceae
Small, evergreen trees, which once grew wild in Arabia and are now cultivated in most hot countries. Coffee 'beans' are seeds from the cherry-like berries, roasted to oily charcoal, then leached with hot water.

Terminalia catappa
Geranium tree, **West Indian Almond**
Has red geranium-like flowers followed by small flattened walnut-like fruits containing a very hard-to-get-at edible kernel much resembling almond.

Fagus sylvatica
Beech
Fagaceae
A well-known tree that can reach 30m and chokes out everything underneath with heavy, dry shade. Although parts of the tree are poisonous and have been used medicinally, an edible oil can be extracted from the seeds and they have been eaten raw and roasted to make 'coffee'. In sheer desperation, beech sawdust has been boiled, baked and mixed with flour to make 'bread'. A worthy subject for parks on acid or alkaline soil, but far too large for most gardens! The **American Beech**, *F. grandiflora*, is similar.

Ginkgo biloba
Maiden Hair Tree
Ginkgoaceae
This 'prehistoric' plant is grown ornamentally for the strange, leathery, fan-shaped leaves, which turn bright yellow in the autumn. The gingko rarely sets fruits, which resemble unpleasant-smelling, yellowish plums, as it is usually planted singly whereas both male and female forms are necessary. In the Far East the seeds, which are like round, vaguely fi shy almonds, are eaten, especially by the Chinese at weddings.

Myristica fragrans
Nutmeg
Myristiceae
These nuts are only ever used as a spice. They are natives of the Moluccas Islands in Indonesia and are commercially grown in few other places save Grenada in the West Indies. The trees reach 18–21m and have fruits resembling apricots or peaches which split, like almonds, revealing a nut surrounded by a reddish yellow aril. This is the spice, mace. Inside the thin shell is the brown nutmeg kernel which rattles when ripe. If still alive, they will germinate in heat after three months or so.

Quercus species
Acorns
Fagaceae
Although acorns are not edible raw these have been ground, leached and cooked in times of hardship, some varieties were apparently relished, and with huge numbers of species these have great potential for breeding a new tasty nut or oil source. Acorns fatten swine but can kill horses! *Q. macrocarpa*, **Bur Oak**, has the biggest acorns, they also have a low tannin content and are easily made edible. The **Cork Oak**, *Q. suber* also bears more edible acorns.

Simmondsia chinensis
Goat Nut, **Jojoba**
Grown mainly for the oil which is odourless and does not go rancid, the small nut-like fruit can be eaten if desperate.

Xanthocerus sorbifolium
Bob's Nuts
Sapidaceae
From China comes this pretty slow growing, very hardy tree much resembling a rowan with sprays of almost orchid-like flowers followed by green, smooth, small apple-sized capsules with thick hard walls that split and peel back to drop about a dozen or so black shelled nuts. These much resemble macadamias when roasted. Very good!! Apparently the flowers and foliage were also cooked and eaten.

THE FRUIT GARDEN

PLANNING THE FRUIT GARDEN

Planning your fruit garden means deciding on your priorities – what do you want most? A little thought beforehand can save you a lot of wasted effort and ensure you actually get what you are after. With vegetables and bedding plants we have the luxury of burying our mistakes annually; with our trees and bushes we need to be more certain.

Although most of us acquire our garden fortuitously with our house, we usually have quite a wide choice of what we actually do with it, though the tendency is rarely to make radical changes. However, if we spend as much time and effort planning and remaking the garden as we do on decorating and furnishing the rest of our home it will turn out a mighty fi nc placc!

Obviously, the soil, climate, large trees, buildings and the rest of the hard landscape have to be worked around. But with skill and cunning, and modern materials, we can have almost any fruit we desire. Ultimately, the fruits we choose to grow must depend on our budget as much as our climate. Growing fruit in the open garden is easiest and cheapest but a heated greenhouse allows for growing many more.

I think the fi rst criterion for choosing fruit must be taste. After all, if you are growing for yourself, there is no point having poorly fl avoured varieties or ones that are widely available commercially. Go for those with fl avour and sweetness even if they are poor croppers. If you fi nd you especially like a particular kind, you can always grow more.

The Greater Plaited in his native surroundings

Vine arches add a productive aesthetic

Freshness is invaluable and one's own fruits are the most truly fresh. It makes sense to choose fruits and varieties that are best eaten straight off the plant and thus rarely found in shops. Likewise, dessert types are preferable to cooking varieties as we eat them with all their vitamins and fl avour intact while culinary fruits lose some of their goodness in the cooking.

Of course, growing your fruit yourself guarantees freedom from unwanted chemical residues, and applying plentiful compost will ensure a good internal nutritional balance in the fruit. However, when choosing fruits, bear in mind that their dietary value can vary as much with variety as with type or growing conditions. For example, **Golden Delicious** apples contain a third or less vitamin C than **Ribston Pippin** while **Laxton's Superb** has only one-sixth!

Economy must always be considered. Fruit growing requires higher investment initially than vegetables but running costs are lower. Similarly, soft fruit plants are cheaper than tree fruits individually, but require netting from birds, fruit bats and possums in many areas. For maximum production, tree fruits produce as much weight from fewer plants per hectare and usually require less maintenance, but are slower to crop and live longer. Likewise, vine fruits and cordons require more posts, ties and wires than trees or bushes. Any form of greenhouse or cover is costly, requiring upkeep, and of course heating uses much expensive energy.

Seasonal implications and the time taken to maintain different fruits also need to be considered, although in general fruit requires much less labour per yield than vegetable production. Initially the preparation and planting are heavy demands on time and energy but afterwards the workload is light, for the amateur if not for the professional. Fruit trees and bushes generally need mulching, thinning, picking and pruning, which are all light tasks and can be done upright in pleasant conditions. Growing the fruit is only half the battle though. After picking we need to process and store the fruit and this takes more time than the growing! Don't plan to grow fruits that mature just when you go away on holiday!

SOIL, SITES, PREPARATION AND PLANTING

Preparing a good seedbed is the same for vegetables or for fruit seedlings, and the cats never help

Most old gardening books started off with instructions to make a garden on a well-drained, south-facing slope with rich, loamy soil. If only we had such choice! We must often take what comes. And as we get small gardens with modern houses we rarely have much choice of positioning within.

Shelter is the best help we can give our plants – good hedges, fences, windbreaks, warm walls, cloches, plastic sheets and even old curtains on frosty nights. But be careful not to overdo it, as this will make the air around the plants stagnant.

To a limited extent we can control our soil. This is preferably as friable, moist and rich as we can make it for most fruiting plants. Of course, it is very difficult to alter the basic soil type; a clay soil is always going to be heavy and a sandy soil will always be well-drained and hungry. The best cure for most soil difficulties is to incorporate more humus from compost, green manures, mulches and well-rotted muck.

Excessive fertiliser, organic or chemical, is not required and can be detrimental, causing soft, rank growth and poorly ripening wood. Lime is needed by many plants and is often of more value in old gardens than more manure!

The natural acidity of the soil must be taken into account. A few fruits, such as blueberries, require acid conditions. On the whole, though, we have unwittingly selected plants that grow happily in the average soils most of us have in our gardens, which are mildly acid to slightly alkaline.

Drainage is occasionally necessary to prevent waterlogging, as no fruiting trees or bushes survive with drowning roots. But for most gardens, water is more often a problem in its absence. Growing on raised areas is preferable to draining away the water, in areas with dry summers.

In regions of high summer rainfall some fruits, such as cherries and strawberries, rot rather than ripen. In hot, dry areas fruits, such as apples, may fail to swell or ripen too quickly and have poor flavour and texture. The temperature may get too cold in winter and freeze unprotected plants to death, or just enough to destroy fruit buds. Areas with late frosts can regularly have complete blossom loss, or the growing season may be too short or too cool for a plant to complete its cycle or ripen the fruit. We can get around this by growing many plants under glass.

A more difficult climatic problem to solve comes in mild maritime regions where there are too few cold days to make the plants go dormant. Without this dormancy period some plants fail to thrive or fruit successfully. This need for dormancy is why it can be difficult to grow some plants under cover. Others may be sensitive to day length. For example, strawberries can be persuaded to grow happily throughout the year but are difficult to fruit when the days are short and nights are long.

Whatever they are, they're too many and need spacing!

Watermelon under a cloche

However, we commonly grow the plants we do because they are so easy and reliable. It is only when you venture to explore the more exotic that you start to encounter some of the more varied and interesting difficulties.

Preparation and planning are everything. The more you can plan in advance and the more carefully you prepare the site, the better the results and the more pitfalls avoided. Always work out schemes on paper. Draw a map of existing features and plan how you will fit in the new. Then imagine walking round after five years when all the plants have grown up.

Remember that once the planting is done the future is determined. So do a good job and do not skimp on the digging or preparation of the hole. In this case, bigger is always better! Mix in garden compost with the soil and, whatever the final intention, do not allow a weed or blade of grass within a circle as wide as the tree or bush is high, for three years.

A small tomato seedling will put on a lot of growth in very few weeks

For trained, tall and lax subjects, the stakes or supports must be strong enough to do the job and must last for a reasonable number of years. It is false economy to be mean on these, as they will be hard to correct when the plants are fully grown.

Do not bury plants too deep. Almost all wish to be planted at the same depth as they have grown, and keep their roots in their respective and different layers. Do not force them doubled up into a cramped hole and never pack them all down in a flat layer unless they grew like that. Gently pack soil around the roots, filling and firming as you go. It is better to over-firm than otherwise! Then attach the support if needed.

I prefer to mulch heavily from the second year, making the roots go down initially by regular hoeing. However, a plastic sheet or carpet mulch is equally good at retaining moisture and suppressing weeds. Generous watering in dry spells for the first year is absolutely crucial.

A bit of the good stuff

BUYING PLANTS AND PROPAGATION

To fill an average garden with plants does not require an immense investment, but the outlay is still quite enough to warrant care and budgeting. If you plan and choose carefully, a wide variety of good plants can be found. Specialist mail order nurseries usually provide a greater choice, and often more cheaply as well, than most local suppliers. They also generally give excellent service and are convenient. Get several catalogues and compare them carefully before ordering, and do so in good time.

Buying plants has the advantage of ease and speed over growing them yourself, but is relatively costly and incurs a high risk of importing weeds, pests and diseases, especially with pot-grown specimens. I prefer bare-rooted plants to pot-grown for all but difficult subjects as they are easier to inspect. I do not trust the hygiene of potted specimens and now always investigate them carefully. Bare-rooted subjects are dormant, so they are much easier both to inspect and clean.

The root systems on well-grown, bare-rooted trees are usually more extensive than those of pot-grown plants. Furthermore, for larger-growing trees, I believe it is unsafe to plant pot-grown specimens with the first metre of each root coiled round in a ball! However, for most smaller subjects, containerised plants are more convenient and will give good results from reputable suppliers.

Tease plantlets apart after soaking their roots

Each grapevine makes loads of cuttings every year

Propagating your own plants is very satisfying, often cheap, hygienic and can give excellent results, but for some fruits it is a long, slow process, and with others, difficult or impossible.

Some plants are remarkably easy to multiply. Most suckering and clump-forming, fruiting plants can be divided in spring, as can most herbaceous plants. Strawberries and raspberries throw new plants all the time and we do well to prevent their waste of resource by removing them early on. The blackberry tribe root their tips anywhere they can in autumn, and many plants will root where they touch the ground to form natural layers, which easily detach with roots in autumn.

Many of our annual fruits, such as tomatoes and melons, are quickly, easily and usually grown only from seed. Indeed almost all fruits can be grown in an original wild form or as a semi-improved form from seed. However, no plant will fruit until mature, and if started from seed this can take many decades for most trees. Until the fruit is produced there is usually no way of telling what it will be like – and it may not be very good.

Almost all the best varieties of fruiting plant are not species that come true from seed but need growing from a bit of an existing specimen. If you can get a live piece of a desired plant with a bud on it, it can usually be grown into another fruiting plant, commonly by taking cuttings, or by layering, grafting or budding.

Many fruiting plants can be grown from a hardwood cutting, a piece of their dormant wood stuck in the ground. For some, such as blackcurrants, this is nearly infallible; others need more care. Ideally, push cuttings into a slit trench lined with sharp sand in moist ground, firm well and keep them weed-free and protected from drying winds – a cloche is usually advantageous. Most success is had with new wood that has not flowered, is well ripened and is cut and set in autumn when it is full of sap. The lower cut is usually made through or just below a joint and a piece selected which has a healthy bud at the top, and spindly pieces can be cut off. Usually all buds below ground level are removed to leave the main stem – i.e. it's best to have two to five buds above the ground level with none underneath.

Layering is most successful. Select a shoot as for a cutting, damage the bark and then surround it by moist, sterile, gritty compost. This can be as simple as weighing down the stem and burying a bit of it in compost under a heavy stone. A year or so later it will probably have grown roots and can be detached and grown on elsewhere. Many evergreens and difficult subjects are thus easily propagated. Alternatively, a plastic bag or pot of moist compost can be made to enclose a section of shoot which is likewise detached when rooted – handy for vines and tall, stiff plants.

Softwood cuttings are usually taken in mid-summer, short, soft tips in leaf, though most removed. They need a shaded cloche or a coldframe, preferably with bottom heat, to do well. Many plants may be multiplied in this way, especially evergreens. It requires more skill, but more plants can be produced from less material than with hardwood cuttings.

Some plants are only propagated by grafting or budding small pieces on to more easily grown rootstocks; however, often these are done with special rootstocks simply to influence growth or to get the maximum number of plants from limited material. Budding and grafting techniques, although apparently simple, are profoundly difficult to master without much practice and are beyond the scope of this book. (I'm not being patronising, just try it for yourself, if you doubt it!)

Do wear gloves, if not gauntlets, when pruning gooseberries

GROWING FROM SEED

Clay pots are better for many plants

Growing from seed is the most rewarding method of propagation. Almost every fruit you buy has seed within, though it may not always be viable. Specialist seedsmen offer rare and unusual seed and, provided regulations do not forbid it, seed can be obtained from friends or travel abroad. (There are several criminal penalties for importing non-commercial seeds and plants into the UK!!) Seed may be slow to germinate, may require warmth or a period of cold first, but sooner or later, given the right conditions, viable seed will germinate, free of pests and disease. Given growing conditions reasonably like the original, eventually it will flower and fruit, though you may need a male and female for this result!

The drawbacks are that plants grown from seed do not come true and can take many years to grow to maturity and fruit, and by then they are often far too big. Grafting the seedling on to a dwarfing rootstock is beyond the skill of most of us. However, we can constrain many plants by growing them in containers, which prevents their forming extensive root systems and thus limits their top growth. Most seed, however you obtain it, should be sown as soon as possible. Seed that is fresh, with fruit attached, is usually cleaned first, but occasionally it may need the pulp to be fermented away before sowing.

A tray of water may keep the compost too wet: be careful

Most seedlings do better with a bit of heat

Although some seed may succeed best in a seed-bed, more reliable results come from sowing in pots in a coldframe. For seeds from warmer climes, a heated propagator is needed. Do not cook them, though. A few seeds germinate best if they are chilled for a period first, though they rarely need freezing. Similarly, most seeds need to be soaked to germinate, but few can stand waterlogging for longer than an hour or two.

The compost in which you sow the seeds is important. Sterile compost is the best if the seed is small or slow to germinate. Most seeds do best in a gritty, well-aerated, humus-rich compost but some have special needs. Obviously use an ericaceous compost for plants that dislike lime. Most seeds do not want the initial compost to be very rich in fertiliser as this burns their tender roots. Indeed they often germinate better in a mixture of sharp sand and leaf mould.

Do not sow too densely or too deeply. Be patient. Remember that some seeds naturally take a long time to emerge. When all else fails, reread the sowing instructions. Once seeds do germinate and emerge they should be divided and repotted as soon as is practicable. Also, you should repot plants regularly as they grow to fill each pot, or they will be dwarfed prematurely.

CONTAINER CULTURE

Blueberries in a bath go well in front of a vine on a wall

Many plants which would be difficult otherwise can be grown in containers. Containers cramp their root system and thus prevent them growing too big or too quickly. Allied with pruning, this allows us to dwarf plants we would find too large to handle. Often this restriction is resented by the plant, and perversely, may result in earlier fruiting.

With attention to feeding and watering, almost any plant can be coaxed to grow in a container, although it may not be persuaded to bear fruit, or at least not prolifically. Grapevines in the ground are rampant growers that crop heavily. In a large tub they are far less vigorous, but can still be expected to give several bunches. Many different varieties can thus be squeezed into the space otherwise occupied by one, allowing greater variety and a longer season.

Containers are particularly useful for plants that would not survive in the ground. If you have a chalky soil, the lime-hating plants can be grown in containers of ericaceous compost. Don't forget to water the plants with rain water, not tap water, as the latter is often as limey as the soil.

Conveniently, plants in containers can be taken under cover during hard weather and kept growing over a longer season. This makes it practical to grow more tender plants than would otherwise be possible. Likewise, plants in fruit can easily be moved under cover for more secure protection from birds or damp.

Watering plants in their containers is very important. Most plants need moist soil but drown if waterlogged and wilt if dry. If you cannot be sure you can maintain religious watering devotion, install an automatic system of irrigation. Stand the plants on capillary matting, or at the least stand them in drip trays of gravel.

No matter how good the compost originally, with time it gets used up. Re-potting into a larger container is usually the best solution, but eventually this becomes difficult. The alternatives are top dressing with an enriched mix of compost and organic fertiliser, or feeding with a diluted liquid feed such as fish emulsion or comfrey and nettle extract. It is invariably better to administer these additions little and often rather than all in one go.

The container itself is important to some plants. Normally plastic pots are as good as porous earthenware, but the latter are preferred by some plants, such as citrus. Indeed, plants which prefer really well-aerated soil do best in lattice timber or basketwork containers, though these may not last long and may be prone to drying out the compost.

Apricots can be cropped in big buckets

GROWING IN GLASSHOUSES AND CONSERVATORIES

There is no substitute for walk-in cover, which is more valuable if heated and frost-free, and even more so if kept warm or even hot. If maintained as warm as a living room all year round, many exotic fruits and vegetables become possible from oranges to eggplants. It is not only summer crops that benefit. Lettuce, spinach and other hardy winter salads produce more tender, better-quality crops in an unheated greenhouse than outside.

I grow exotics such as guavas under cover as they would not crop otherwise. The extra heat ripens the fruit and also the wood, which often cannot ripen outdoors. Some plants take many months to crop each year and without cover they would never ripen before frosts come. Extra warmth and shelter allow us to have tender or delicate plants that would not survive in the open, and mean we can have the same crop earlier than outdoors – for example, strawberries or tomatoes.

Grapes benefit from being indoors, away from the birds and weather

Tomatoes are reliable under cover

Often it is best to grow plants in containers that are to go under cover as this allows for more variety in the same area, though each plant will necessarily yield less than if it was in the ground. Containers not only control the vigour of the plants but also make them portable, so they can be moved under cover and outside as convenient. This suits many fruits such as the citrus, which really prefer to be outside all summer but need frost protection in winter. By contrast, many varieties of grapevine are best under cover for an early start and for ripening, but need to be chilled in winter to fruit well. This is why some plants are difficult. They need hot summers and warm autumns and also cold winters to go dormant. Without dormancy they do not ripen wood or fruit well and often just fade away. It is quite easy to chill a greenhouse in a cold area for the couple of months required, but not, of course, if other tender plants are kept there also.

The other requirement may be for extra light. Many plants need more light than can be had in winter through dirty glass. The physical barrier reduces light intensity by half. Fortunately, artificial lights are cheap to fit and run – compared to heating anyway. Some plants are very demanding; not only do they want more light and heat but they want enough hours of complete darkness every night as well. This requires the fitting of blinds to exclude daylight and light from any nearby streetlights, too! Similarly, some plants find bright light too intense and need shading. Fortunately most exotics are remarkably easy to grow. The biggest problems are usually the cost of heating and the eventual size of the plants.

FRUIT CAGES

Fruit cages are cover with netting. They are necessary to protect soft fruit in areas with many birds. The most troublesome birds, such as blackbirds and pigeons, can be excluded with coarse 2.5cm mesh, while smaller, insectivorous birds, such as wrens and bluetits, can still gain access. If all the net is wire, squirrels and rodents can also be stopped. If a finer mesh, down to about 1cm, is used then bees can still enter, but large moths and butterflies are excluded.

Fruit cages have other advantages. The netting itself makes a more sheltered environment enjoyed by the plants. Light frosts are kept off, and chill winds are reduced. In very hot regions, denser netting gives welcome shade and cooler conditions.

A fruit cage can even be reversed, in principle, to enclose all of a small garden and to confine ornamental seed- and insect-eating, but hopefully not inadvertently fruit-eating birds. On a more prosaic level, it is practical to grow plants on a tall leg and then run chickens underneath for their excellent pest control. It is sensible to arrange it so that, if you have chickens, they can at least be running in the cage during most of the year when the plants are not in fruit.

Fruit cages can be hand-crafted from second-hand materials; easily assembled custom-made ones are also available. In areas of high wind, obviously, the most substantial materials have to be used. Permanent sides of wire mesh and a light net laid on overhead wires for the roof are most practicable. Make sure you can remove the roof net easily if snow is forecast as a thick layer on top will break most cages.

Most fruit cage plants are natives of the woodland's edge and do not mind light shade, but few of them relish stagnant air, so do not overcrowd them. Fruit is sweeter if ripened in the sun. A few fruits such as grapes must have full sun to ripen at all well, so give these a prime position. You should always provide plants with more space than seems reasonable.

Because most fruit cage plants grow naturally at the woodland's edge, they also prefer a richly mulched, cool, undisturbed and often shallow root run. Most of them will respond well to thick mulches and summer pruning to improve the fruit quality and stop the plants growing too large. Generally fruit cage plants do not like having vegetables around them if this involves digging or hoeing. However, some companion flowering plants such as *Limnanthes douglassii* are invaluable.

Redcurrants and no cage = no redcurrants

ORCHARDS

Orchards are devoted to the production of top or tree fruits, such as apples, pears and plums. Some fruits are less common, only being widely grown in suitable areas – for example cherries are never grown in wetter coastal regions but are common in drier inland zones such as Young, in New South Wales.

Orchards were always grassed down for convenience and soil preservation, though recent practice has been for bare cultivation, but this has been shown to be irresponsible. Initially weed-free conditions must be maintained in the orchard, but in general the preservation of bare soil is counterproductive. Most home orchard fruits will be best with a heavy mulch, ground cover or companion plants, or rough mown lawn.

For comfort and least cost, private orchards are still customarily planted with standard or half-standard trees on strong rootstocks. Though more intensive plantings with more dwarfi ng stock are more productive, they also require much more pruning and training and are difficult to mow underneath!

Grass clippings are an excellent mulch if put on in thin layers, and are a good fertilizer if allowed to mulch down. However large rural orchards should not be composed solely of grasses, as these compete strongly for resources in the topmost layers and do not contribute much to the mineral levels. Include clovers, lucerne and chicory seeds in your sowing mixture. Special blends are now available ready mixed.

Traditionally orchards were combined with grazing livestock. Though no longer done on a commercial scale, the practice is still useful for amateurs. Running chickens underneath adds interest and fertility, and almost guarantees freedom from most pest problems. Cynics might add, 'especially if you do not overfeed them!' Ducks control slugs and snails better than hens and do not scratch and damage so much, and the drakes do not crow so they are preferable from that point of view. Geese are superb lawnmowers, converting grass into fertilizer and eggs as well as being the most noisy watchdogs. Be warned though, as geese may severely damage young plants with thin bark if they are hungry.

Other forms of livestock are more dangerous to the home orchard. I suggest that no four-legged herbivorous animals are allowed anywhere near valued plants unless each is individually and securely fenced and protected.

Orchards are also an enticement to two-legged rats and most are surrounded with a thick fence or barbed wire in country areas. This, and a narrow verge of long grass and native plants, simultaneously provides a good background ecology to help control all the other pests of the orchard.

A better way of staking

ORNAMENTAL FRUIT GARDENS

A Doyenne du Comice pear espalier is also decorative

Trained fruit trees and bushes which can be bought ready-made in a host of interesting and architectural forms, such as espaliers and fans, create interest out of season as the framework of the plants becomes revealed. Attention to the appearance of the supports is essential as they are also disclosed for much of the time. Neatness and uniformity are thus of the greatest moment. Pergolas can look as beautiful clothed in grapevines as they do with any climber and even a fruit cage can be fashioned ornamentally from the right materials.

It is important in a fruit garden to allow for plentiful light and air – more than perhaps might be granted with a shrub garden. Wide paths aid such design and can be of grass sward where wear is light. Gravel is next choice for practicality and economy, and concrete or stone flags where the area is small or budget large.

More colour and interest, with benefit to the main planting, is obtained by having suitable companion plants to provide shelter, ground cover, flowers for nectar and pollen for the beneficial insects, and sacrificial plants that give up their fruits that others may not be eaten. However, vegetables are not easily mixed in. They do not grow well surrounded by vigorous competitors such as fruiting plants, but most of the culinary herbs can be grown to advantage and use.

Wildlife Fruit Gardens

Although these may be as stylised and neat as any purely decorative garden, an accurate description of many so-called wild gardens is 'unkempt'. Indeed, the term is often used to justify total neglect.

However, if the aim is truly to provide more and better habitats for endangered native flora and fauna, then neglect is not enough. A wild garden needs to be managed so that we maximise the number and forms of life supported. The more fruiting and berrying plants we include, the more wildlife we attract, and we need to ensure other basic necessities for wild creatures. The fruit helps immensely but shelter for nesting and hibernation, water and peace are also required. Dense brambles, shrubs and evergreens are mandatory, but do ensure the gardener can still gain access. Paths should be maintained to permit various tasks, but of course excess traffic will soon drive away most creatures.

Many garden soils are too rich for the more appealing wild flowers. To establish these it is frequently necessary to start them in pots and plant them out into sites prepared by removing the turf. Thus they should be kept away from the fruiting plants which require richer conditions.

Fruits do well with flowers underneath

MAINTAINING THE GARDEN

We prune for two main reasons: to remove diseased, damaged and ill-placed growths and to channel growth into fruit production. We may also prune to reduce the size of the plant as it becomes too large for the space available, which is really cause for replanning.

Excessive pruning, especially at the wrong time, is counterproductive. In general, pruning even moderate amounts from a tree or bush in autumn and winter stimulates regrowth, proportionately as much as the amount removed. This is usefully employed when the plant is young and we wish to form the framework by stimulating the growth of some young and vigorous replacement shoots.

However, such autumn and winter pruning is not so suitable for more mature fruiting plants whose structure is already formed and from which we wish to obtain fruit. Most respond much better to summer pruning, which is cutting out three-quarters of every young shoot, bar the leaders. This restricts the growth and causes fruit bud production on the spurs or short sideshoots formed. These may be further shortened and tidied in the winter, but then, as only a little is removed, vigorous regrowth may be avoided.

The majority of our perennial, woody, fruiting plants can be trained and pruned to make a permanent framework which carries these spurs, preferably all over. Growing just one such single stem, branch or cordon on a weak rootstock allows us to squeeze many varieties into the same space as one full-sized tree. Obviously such single-stemmed cordons do not produce very much fruit, especially as it is hard to make them longer without going too high.

Growing two, three or more branches is a better compromise. These can be arranged as espaliers (in tiers), fans (where they radiate from the centre), or gridirons of almost any design. However, for the vast majority of trees and bushes, the actual shapes most commonly employed are the expanding head, and the open bowl or goblet arrangement, on top of a single stem or trunk.

If you give a woody plant space and freedom, it tends to make an expanding mounded head like an upturned bowl or vase of dense growth on the surface and an almost empty space inside. This is least work and looks after itself, but it keeps getting bigger, and much of the fruit grows in shade. For the best fruit it is necessary to maximise the surface area of fruiting growth exposed to the sun and air. To do this, you should try to invert the natural bowl or vase shape by removing the main leader from the middle and training the branches as a bowl with a hollow centre open to the sky. The number of main stems is customarily about five or six, which divide from the trunk and redivide to form the walls of the goblet. The stem or trunk may be short, as is common with gooseberries, or taller, which is often more convenient.

Where the branches of a tree divide from the trunk on a short trunk they are termed bushes: at waist to shoulder height they are called half-standards, and standards where they will start higher still. Bushes, especially those on the more dwarfing stocks, tend to be too low to mow underneath but can always be mulched instead. Half-standards grow large, depending on stock, and are tall enough to mow underneath. Full standards make very big specimens and are usually planted only in parks and meadows.

Young, unformed plants (maidens) can be bought more cheaply than those with a good shape already trained by the nurseryman. It is very satisfying to grow your own espalier or gridiron from a maiden, but the result will depend on your skill and foresight. These may be better used elsewhere. Therefore buy your trees ready-made, unless you feel gifted. Soft fruits are quicker to respond and more forgiving, so are worth trying for yourself.

Some fruits need to be pruned on the renewal principle. Whole branches or shoots are continually replaced as they reach a year or two old and after they have fruited. Raspberries are typical, the old shoots being removed at ground level as the young are tied in.

Grapevines can be constrained to two young branches emerging from the trunk, replaced each year. Peaches on walls similarly have young shoots tied in and old fruited ones removed. Blackcurrants have a third of growths from the ground removed each year.

A few plants are pruned only at certain times of year. Hollow-stemmed, tender and evergreen plants are pruned in spring once the hardest weather is over and Prunus are pruned in summer to avoid disease. Although it may seem complicated, pruning is easy once you have done it a few times. Provided that you do not get carried away and remove excessive amounts, you are unlikely to do much harm to the plant. Be sure to use clean secateurs which have been sterilised with alcohol; rarely use a saw and cover any large wounds with a proprietary sealant to stop any water getting in.

Work on steps requires two people, or beware...

Remember, prune ruthlessly

FERTILITY AND WATER MANAGEMENT

Good stuff for the compost heap

Fruiting plants need sufficiently fertile soil and water to grow and yield well, but ordinarily most are not as demanding as vegetable crops. Provided they are thinned, fruit yields can be surprisingly good in soils and seasons when many vegetables fail. Indeed, excess fertility or moisture will frequently result in too much vegetative growth and little, or poorly ripening fruit as a result.

The main advantage of the majority of fruiting plants is that they are perennial. Growing in open ground, they make extensive root systems which find the water and nutrients required. Annual and short-lived crops generally need much more attention to soil fertility and water provision because they have limited root systems. Plants in containers similarly require much care, and because of the confinement they will also readily suffer from any excess.

Fertility is best provided organically from materials that slowly convert to a useable form in the soil. Well-rotted farmyard manures, good compost, seaweed meal, hoof and horn meal, or bone meal and fish emulsions are all suitable materials for mulches.

Weeds being kept down with old carpet, neatly

Sieving the compost makes it cleaner and more useful

If mineral shortages are suspected, ground rock dusts provide cheap, slow-release supplies; potash, phosphate, magnesium (dolomitic) limestone, calcified seaweed and lime are all widely available, cheap and pleasant to apply. Wood ashes are extremely valuable to most fruiting plants. Seaweed extracts sprayed on the foliage can give rapid relief from mineral deficienicies.

Bulkier materials such as well-rotted manure and compost also provide much humus which is essential for the natural fertility of the soil, its water-holding capacity and its buffering action (preventing the soil being too acid or alkaline). The humus content is conserved by minimal cultivation and refraining from using soluble fertilisers.

More humus can be provided by growing green manures. These occupy the soil when other plants are dormant throughout winter. Nutrients and water that would have leached away are combined with winter sunlight to grow dense covers of hardy plants. These also protect the soil surface from erosion and rain impaction. When the weather warms up, green manures are incorporated in situ by digging in or composting under a plastic sheet. Or remove and add to the compost heap.

Organic mulches such as well-rotted manures, composted shredded bark, leaf mould, mushroom compost, straw or peat are all advantageous to most plants. They rot down at the soil's surface, aiding fertility and humus levels, and suppress weeds if they are thick enough, but most importantly they help to conserve soil moisture.

For most gardeners a shortage of soil moisture is more of a problem than low fertility. With sufficient moisture, fertility can be created by the soil life; without moisture the soil cannot even use a fertiliser supplied. Every effort must be made to capture every drop of rain and store it till needed. Water butts can hold only so much, while the humus in the soil can hold much more, as it soaks water up like a sponge.

Once the winter rains have drenched the soil a mulch prevents it evaporating away again. Any mulch helps, but the looser and thicker, the better. Less than 5cm is ineffective; add more after a few months as the initial applications will pack down.

When organic material for mulching is in short supply, use inorganic ones. Sharp sand and gravel make good moisture-retaining mulches and are cheap and sterile. Grass clippings are an excellent mulch, if applied in thin layers – though if applied too thickly in wet conditions they may make a nasty, sticky mess. Clippings provide a rich source of nitrogen and encourage soil life. They soon disappear and need topping up. Continuous applications slowly make the soil less alkaline and more acid, which is often advantageous.

Despite mulching and enriching the humus content, watering is often required. It is essential for new transplants until they have been established for at least a year, particularly for evergreens which cannot drop their leaves if under stress and survive dormant. Water before it is too late; if a plant is wilting it is already suffering badly!

Soak one plant's roots each day on a rota rather than give a daily splash to each one. It is bad practice merely to wet the soil surface. This draws the roots up to form a surface mat, while much is wasted by evaporation. A good soaking descends and draws the roots after it; thus they become deeper and more able to find other soil moisture on their own.

Remember that watering should be done well or not at all. If you bury a length of hosepipe with the roots of a tree, you can inject the water right where it is needed during the critical first few years. Likewise a pot or funnel pushed in nearby is a useful aid. When time is limited and cash more abundant, it is wise to invest in automatic watering equipment. Drip feeds and seeping hoses will allow a constant and even supply of water without the gardener's constant attention, and soon repay the investment.

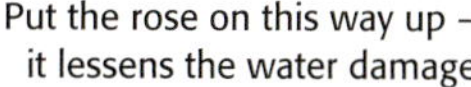

Put the rose on this way up – it lessens the water damage

WEED AND GRASS MANAGEMENT

Weeds compete with our crops for space, water and nutrients, and they are better at it! Worse, they harbour pests and diseases. For maximum growth, all our plants require weed-free conditions, especially when they are small, not well established and only just sown or planted.

Keep all weeds from appearing within a radius of about each plant's own height as this is the area most densely filled with their root systems. For perennials, this clear circle should be kept clean of all weeds for three years before planting companion plants, ground cover or grassing down. We often start trees off in a small circle of bare soil a mere 30cm or so across, cut into a neatly cropped lawn; a bare circle a couple of metres across will do some real good.

Complete elimination of all weeds from an area before planting is invariably worthwhile. It can be by several cultivations with plough, harrow or simply spade and rake. It is less effort to use sheet mulches of plastic or carpet, or even, once off, a 'safe' weed killer if you are non-organic. Whichever of these you choose, it is much easier than trying later to weed among the plants. Once the established weeds are all gone we have only to control new ones coming from seed. Such weeds are easily prevented from germinating in bare soil by covering it with several centimetres of mulch.

Weeds in the sward just add variety under fruit trees

Weeds in a patio or on a seedbed are a problem; flame-gunning is one answer

As mulches are also useful for adding humus and retaining water, they are the most sensible way of controlling weeds under most fruiting plants. However, occasionally we want bare soil. In these areas the weeds are best controlled with a sharp hoe. Use a hoe weekly when weeds are a problem and fortnightly when they are thought banished.

When woody perennial plants are mature, they are less badly affected by general weed competition but still suffer, especially where the weeds are allowed to grow over them and steal light and air as well. In order to prevent weeds we can use mulches, but they do not create a very good garden ecology, so instead we tolerate ground-cover plants. These occupy the ecological niche to advantage and with less detriment than the weeds they prevent.

The most convenient ground cover is usually grass sward. Once they are well established it is traditional and often convenient to grass down underneath most fruit trees and between the more vigorous soft fruits. Grass competes vigorously, especially if kept closely mowed as a lawn. However, grass sward is simple to maintain, ornamental, hygienic and prevents worse weeds. Turf is durable, it resists wear well and soon repairs damaged patches. If mulches spill over grass sward, and so yellow the leaves, it soon recovers. The clippings themselves are a free source of mulching material, and can contribute much fertility to our plants.

Grass sward produces most useful clippings when the grass is cut often and not too closely. Long grass grows more quickly, is more drought-resistant and suppresses turf weeds better than if it is closely cropped. Of course, if you let it get too long, it becomes wet to walk on and is brown underneath when you cut it short again. However, cut your grass regularly and frequently with slightly greater height of cut, and you soon see a better sward resulting. The longer, more vigorous grass soon chokes out most weeds.

Traditionally orchard grass was allowed to grow long and flower in late summer and autumn when the fruit was ripening. The grass took up nitrogen, other nutrients and water and prevented the trees making late, soft growth. The low nitrogen level in the soil also helped the fruit to keep well and turned the apples redder.

A daisy grubber eliminates many other weeds too

When grassing down, it is sensible to include clovers in the grass seed mix as they have the advantage of fixing nitrogen from the air to aid the grasses. A clover and grass mixture also stays greener for longer in hot, dry summers and, if left to flower, the clovers attract bees and other insects that are beneficial.

Provided you are not growing ericaceous plants or fine, bowling-green grasses you should lime all your turf every fourth year, even if you have lime in the soil. Most swards slowly become acid in the topmost layer, and this encourages mosses and acid-loving weeds. If such weeds – for example, daisies – are increasing, you need to add more lime: up to a couple of handfuls per square metre per year. You probably also need to raise the height of your cut. If weeds that like wet, acid soils such as buttercups appear, lime is desperately needed and probably better drainage as well.

Although four-legged livestock may be too risky to our plants in a garden, they are fine lawnmowers in meadow orchards with well-fenced trees. For the private gardener, geese are the safest option. They graze grass closely and soon eradicate favourite snacks, so are usefully borrowed to remove buttercups, dandelions and clovers rapidly – even if you do not want to have them full-time.

The rest of the hot water can be poured on weeds; they soon give up

PEST AND DISEASE CONTROL

The aim of this is to preserve the yield or appearance of our crops, but we must ensure that the costs incurred in the process do not outweigh the gains. Commercial apples are, ironically, sprayed to prevent scabby patches on their skin, which is now peeled and discarded to avoid the very residues left by many such sprays.

For the home gardener the main causes of fruit loss in most years is the weather. If we grow crops that are, on average, successful only in good years in our area, such as grapes in central England, we must accept that in other years we will do badly. There is very little we can do to make the sun come out, the wind stop or the rain fall.

The second cause of loss is probably the gardener. We all leave action too late, skimp preparation and routine tasks, put plants in less than their optimum positions, and then overcrowd them as well. What we must remember is that our plants 'want' to leaf, flower and crop. They are programmed as tightly as any computer. If we give them the right input, they must produce the right output for us.

A soft soap or seaweed spray solves most problems

Red spider mite is best controlled with the predators you buy in and release

If we give our plants the right conditions, they are also healthy and vigorous enough to shrug off most pests and diseases. Healthy plants grow in a well-suited site and soil, with shelter and water when they are small, and are not overfed. Excess fertiliser makes plants flabby and prone to problems. Keep them lean and fit with well-made compost and mulches. Many pests are like wolves, eliminating the sick and weak, ignoring the healthy.

Disease is most efficiently prevented by vigilance and prompt action combined with hygienic pruning and healthy air circulation. Spraying diluted seaweed solution once a month throughout the growing season acts like a vitamin pill. It makes plants more resistant to diseases, and many pests. This is probably because seaweed contains minute amounts of almost every element and thus corrects for soil deficiencies.

However, our plants will still be attacked by some pests and diseases that do require action. Most of the time these do not take all of a crop and often we do not truly need all of it in any case! All we have to do is to achieve what we want with the minimum interference, and any surplus can be left for the wildlife anyway.

The most effective way to control pests is to persuade others to do it for you. The natural ecology always controls them in the long run. We can help it quickly reach a balance of more ladybirds, thrushes and frogs and fewer aphids, snails and slugs. Our allies require shelter, nest sites, food out of season, water and companion plants. If we provide these, they increase in number and thus the pests decrease.

With careful selection of which cultivars we grow, we can have resistant varieties that do not suffer as much from a given problem. There are varieties of most fruits that are more or less resistant to many of their common diseases, such as scab with apples and root rots with strawberries and tomatoes. Resistance to pests is rarer as they soon adapt and overcome the host's resistance. However, the white- and yellow-fruited forms of normally red fruits will escape while the birds wait for them to turn. Timing can be of service. For example, late raspberries usually escape the depredations of their fruit maggot. Having many fruits which ripen at the same time also reduces damage. When successive plants ripen they are picked clean by small numbers of pests which are overwhelmed by a glut, as may be the gardener!

The simplest method of protection is to use a barrier to prevent pests or disease reaching the plant. For example, strong netting will generally stop birds, and plastic sheet umbrellas over peach trees during winter prevent peach leaf curl.

Yellow sticky traps indicate what's about

Copper rings may be expensive, but work

An impenetrable woven or plastic sheet mulch fitted tight to a tree trunk prevents pests emerging from underground reaching the open and equally prevents them crawling down to the roots. Provision of fine holes must be made in plastic sheets to allow both air and water to pass freely. Their appearance can easily be improved by adding thin mulch on top.

Traps of corrugated cardboard, carpet or old sack can be made by rolling strips around trunk or stem. These attract pests by replicating creviced bark. They hide within and we unwrap and dislodge them in winter. Non-setting sticky bands applied to aluminium foil wrapped tightly around trunk, branch or stem stop pests climbing up and down. Do remember to paint the support as well.

Sticky traps can be bought which lure flying pests to them with pheromone sex attractant 'perfumes'. Others use the smell of the fruit or leaf to entice the pests to a sticky end. Jars of water with lids of foil containing pencil-sized holes trap wasps when baited with fruit juices or jams (not honey).

Putting down mulches in late winter seals in the spores of many diseases before growth starts. Raking mulches aside in early winter will reveal pupae of over-wintering pests which can be left to the birds.

Only when the preventative measures and traps have failed should we turn to direct action. The most ecological spray of all, in fact, is simply a powerful jet of water. Although many pests may clamber back they are unlikely to if shot halfway across the garden. Obviously project them to an area without plants on which they can survive – the open lawn is best.

Soap sprays kill most small insect pests by suffocation and are remarkably safe for us and the environment. People used to employ ordinary household soap flakes, but some improved soft soaps are now sold specifically for pesticidal use. Ordinary household baking soda, sodium bicarbonate, contained in almost every cake and patent medicine, was similarly used as a safe fungicide. Bordeaux mixture is another old-fashioned fungicide. It is wholly chemical, being made from copper sulphate and lime, but it is allowed to organic gardeners if used in moderation.

Derris, nicotine and pyrethrum, insecticides made from plant products, were allowed to organic gardeners, degraded rapidly and killed pests immune to soft soap. They are now being withdrawn and where permitted must be used only according to instructions. Please spray at night when the bees have gone home!

A friend indeed

Birds

Birds are the cause of most loss in many areas. Netting is the answer. If the whole plant cannot be enclosed or moved under cover, then protect each fruit or bunch with waxed paper or netting bags. These can be made from sections of nylon stockings. Lengths of stocking or hosepipe painted like snakes, fake spiders and cats of fake fur are all good bird-scarers but have to be moved often to fool them for more than the first day. Things that flash, such as pieces of foil and humming tape, all work but likewise for a short time. Scarecrows rarely work at all! Sacrificing some fruits and leaving these on the ground, or better still on a table, is easier than keeping birds away entirely!

Brushing on alcohol or soft soap can clean off many problems

Aphids

Aphids are more often an inconvenience than a real problem for established perennial plants. With some, such as redcurrant leaf blistering aphis, no harm is detectable. Indeed, they are performing the equivalent of summer pruning for us. However, heavy aphid infestations may require a soft soap spray. Usually ants are involved in these infestations as well, needing simultaneous extirpation.

Ants

A minor problem on their own, ants farm aphids and scale insects, making these more of a threat. Put out some sugar, watch where they take it home, then pour boiling water down their hole.

Wasps

Wasps are valuable allies early in the summer when they control caterpillars and other pests. Later on in the year, they turn to fruit and need trapping with jars half full of water and jam. Dusting them with flour enables you to follow them home. Nests can be destroyed with proprietary killers puffed in the entrance when wasps return in the evening.

Slugs and Snails

These are attracted to real beer in a saucer, which entices many to drown themselves. (Ground beetles, which are useful allies, may also come. Put a few twiggy sticks in the saucer to give them a way out.) Slugs and snails can be spotted with a torch on warm, moist evenings and can be destroyed.

Well, some things are sent to keep us on our toes

A bottle of old wine dregs will attract many flying pests

Scale Insects

Scale is most troublesome on plants under cover and on walls. Hand-pick minor infestations and spray them with soft soap. There are now also some commercially available predators.

Red Spider Mites

These are a serious threat under cover and on walls and even in the open. Spraying water and keeping the greenhouse air humid discourages them.

Attract them on to plants of broad beans, which are then composted, spray with soft soap, and introduce the commercially available predator *Phytoseuilis persimilis*.

Wood lice are best caught with a mini vacuum cleaner

Hens soon get rid of vine weevil infestations

Whitefly

Whitefly are mostly a problem under cover. Thin out flying adults with a vacuum cleaner, spray plants with soft soap and introduce the commercially available predator *Encarsia formosa*.

Vine Weevils

The adult weevil is dark grey, beetle-like, 1–2cm long, with a very long snout. It takes rounded bits out of leaves, but most harm is done by the grubs, which are up to the same size, with a grey/pink body and brown head. They destroy the roots of many plants. Adults can be trapped in rolls of corrugated cardboard, in bundles of sticks or under saucers, where they hide during daytime. Chickens running underneath tall crops can ensure that no adults survive long enough to lay eggs. The grubs can be destroyed by watering on the commercially available predatory nematode/eelworm.

Rabbits

Only netting the area will keep rabbits out. In case they get in, have a plank ramped against the fence so they are not trapped inside and eat even more. If the perimeter cannot be secured, surround or wrap each plant in wire netting. If this is impossible, feed the rabbits when snow stops them finding their own food and before they bark your plants! Just the smell of a ferret or its droppings will drive them away.

POLLINATION AND COMPANION PLANTING

Almost all our fruits require their flowers to be pollinated. Many are self-fertile and can set by pollinating themselves, but crop better if cross-pollinated. Some of these – for example figs – have varieties that will produce fruit parthenocarpically, without pollination; thus they are often seedless. A few fruits, such as **Conference** pears, are partly parthenocarpic: if not pollinated by another variety, their fruits are different and oddly shaped.

Some fruits do not have male and female flowers on the same plant and so we have to grow a non-fruiting male to pollinate every half dozen or so females. Kiwis and grapevines are good examples. For convenience, we have bred varieties that carry both sexes.

Some fruits and many nuts are wind-pollinated, others by bees and other insects. Under cover, neither of these natural pollinators exists and we have to assist. A rabbit's tail, a cotton ball or piece of wool lightly touched on each flower should suffice. We can lure more insects to help by growing attractant companion plants and this can add a bit of colour and life as well. Commercial tomato growers even buy cardboard nests of bumble bees to pollinate for them.

Outdoors early in the year there are few insects about and for the earliest flowerers pollination is risky. Again, hand pollination is effective, but tedious. It is better to ensure insect pollination by increasing the numbers. Planting companion plants as attractants helps; taking up bee-keeping makes an enormous improvement.

To pollinate each other, not only do varieties have to be compatible, but they also have to flower at the same time. All reputable catalogues have a choice of suitable cross-pollinators indicated. When in doubt, choose the wild species, which is often the best pollinator for most of its varieties. Alternatively, simply plant more varieties. This is especially true for a few fruits which are not good pollinators themselves. For example, the apples **Cox's Orange Pippin** and **Bramley's Seedling** never crop together, but if you add a **James Grieve**, all three fruit.

Companion planting is of immense benefit to most fruiting plants as it brings in and supports pollinating and predatory insects, and maintains them throughout the rest of the year. We must aim at having a continuity of flowers throughout the year as it is these that provide nectar and honey for the bees, hoverflies and other beneficial insects.

Of particular usefulness is *Limnanthes douglassii*, the

There are three water butts hidden here

poached egg plant, which is a low-growing, self-seeding, weed-suppressing, hardy annual. I find it especially beneficial under soft fruit and gooseberries. *Phacelia tanacetifolia*, *Convolvulus tricolor*, pot marigolds and clovers are all very good for beneficial insects.

Other plants can be good companions to our fruiting plants by repelling pests. French marigolds are one of the strongest and their smell will keep whitefly out of a greenhouse. Planted about the fruit garden, they disorientate pests sniffing for their quarry. The aromatic herbs such as rosemary, thyme, sage, southernwood and lavender are all excellent companions as they not only camouflage the air with their perfume but they are long-flowering, also benefiting the various pollinators and predators.

Alliums are valuable companions. Their smell deters many pests, yet their flowers attract beneficial insects. They help protect the plants they grow with from fungi and are even claimed to improve the scent of roses. Garlic and chives are the easiest to grow and use in quantity at the base of the most fruit trees and bushes.

Many companion plants help access nutrients and make them available for our fruiting plants. Clovers,

Strawberries hitch a ride with the grapes and peaches

Hand pollinating should be called brush pollinating, really

lupins and the other leguminous plants are especially good as they fix nitrogen from the air and the surplus will feed our crops. Alfalfa/lucerne is exceptionally deep-rooted and brings up minerals from depths other plants cannot reach. It should be included in the seed mixture for orchard and wild garden swards. Similarly a few thistles and docks can be tolerated in those areas for the same purpose. Clovers and chicory should be included whenever grass is seeded as the sward that is produced will be both richer and lusher.

In grass at the base of trees, dense shrubs and hedges, bulbous, spring-flowering plants can be fitted in with no difficulty. These areas can remain uncut till the bulbs' foliage dies down and their flowers will be a rich source of pollen and nectar for the earliest pollinators and predators. Some ivy in the hedges will provide late flowers to feed the insects in autumn before they hibernate.

Ground-cover plants provide habitats for ground beetles and many other useful creatures, but may also harbour slugs, snails and over-wintering pests. On the whole it is better to have such habitats kept as far as possible from soft fruit and seed beds – after all, the beetles, frogs and hedgehogs can walk further than slugs and snails!

Some plants are specifically helpful to others and a few hinder. These are noted with the entry for that particular fruit. For example, the Romans noticed that oaks were bad for olives, and cabbages were not good companions for vines, but rue benfited from the presence of figs.

HARVESTING AND STORING

They'll be gone soon, then what will you do?

Picking and Ripening: Fruit Stores

Without doubt most fruits are best, and certainly are enjoyed most, when they are plucked fully ripe off the tree or vine. Only a few, such as melons, are improved by chilling first. The majority are tastiest fresh and warmed by the sun. Some, such as pears, have to be very carefully nurtured till they are fully ripe. They then need to be picked early and brought to perfection, watched daily, in a gently warm, not too dry, dim room. Medlars are similarly picked early and are then ripened, or bletted, to the point of rotting.

The best date for picking will vary with the cultivar, the soil, the site and the season, which can only be determined by experience as these factors will all vary considerably. Of course, it will generally remain much the same in relation to other fruits nearby which are also subject to the same conditions, i.e. in a late year, most fruits are late, which is pretty self-evident anyway.

On any tree, the sunny side ripens first. In the northern hemisphere, this is usually the south eastern corner, as the morning sun is stronger than the afternoon, because the air is clearer. Fruit will also ripen earlier where any extra warmth is supplied, so that growing sites next to a wall, window, chimney or vent, or just close to the soil, are favourable places for finding early fruits. Likewise, when all the rest have gone, you may still find some hidden away in the shade.

If you want to store the fruits for home use they need to be at just the right stage. Most fruits store best when picked just under-ripe. They may keep longer if picked even younger, but this is at the cost of both flavour and sweetness.

Although we occasionally store some fruits, such as pears, for a period to improve their condition, predominantly we store fruit to extend the season so that we can enjoy them as long as possible. On the commercial scale tremendous advances have been made with gas, humidity and temperature-regulated cool rooms. Many fruits can be stored for months, some even a year or more, in these conditions. Of course, we amateurs cannot duplicate these, but nonetheless we can keep most fruits for longer if we treat them well.

To be stored, all fruit must be perfect. Any blemish or bruise is where moulds start. It is no use trying to store anything that has any real damage. Use it up straight away or process it into juice, jelly or purée. Choose varieties that are suitable for storing – many early croppers are notoriously bad keepers! Waxing fruits is undoubtedly good for extending their life but could help shorten yours! Some fruits will keep as well if they are wrapped in oiled paper. Another early, successful method of mould deterrence was to dip each fruit in a solution of sodium bicarbonate and then dry it before storing. This worked well, but it could leave a powdery appearance.

Common, long-keeping fruits such as apples and quinces can be stored at home for months, or even up to a year. The major problems, apart from the moulds, are shrivelling through water loss and the depredations of rodents and other bigger pests. A conventional store is too large for most of us and the house or garage is too warm, too cold or too dry. I find dead deep freezers and refrigerators make excellent compact stores. They are dark, keep the contents at the same constant temperature and will keep out night frosts easily. Most useful of all, they are rodent-proof, and they can even be locked to deter two-legged rats!

Harvest and then process and store

Jam is the usual answer

Some ventilation is needed and can be obtained by cutting holes in the rubber door or lid seal. If any condensation occurs, it usually indicates insufficient ventilation, but too much draught will dry out the fruits. The unit can stand outdoors, as it needs no power. In a shed it is out of sight and better protected against the cold, but may then get too warm. In the UK, have it outdoors in the shade or in a cool shed. Extra frost protection is simply ensured, in extreme conditions, by putting a sealed bottle of warm water inside the unit each night and morning. To save space, provided the water table is low, a dead chest freezer can be sunk into the ground and the lid painted over.

When putting fruits in the store it is usually best to leave them to chill at night in the trays and to load them into the store in the morning when they have dried off, but before they have warmed up again. Similarly it is helpful to chill and dry off the fruits initially by leaving the store open on chill, dry nights and closing it during the day for a week or two after filling.

Most types of fruit are best removed from the store some time before use, so any staleness can leave them. Care should be taken not to store early and late varieties together or any that may cross-taint. Obviously it is not a good idea to site your store in the same place as strong-smelling things, or substances such as onions, paint or creosote! Likewise, although straw is cheap, convenient litter, it taints the fruit if it gets damp. Shredded newspaper is safer, though is also has a slight whiff. Dried stinging nettles are reckoned good but dangerous to handle.

Always inspect stored fruits regularly. They can go off very quickly. Remember, if only one in ten goes off every month, you have to start with two trays just to have one tray left after six months. So do not store any fruit long just for the sake of it, but store well what you will use.

Juicing

I find juicing to be the very best way of storing fruit, other than turning it into wine, but that's another book! Not all fruits can be juiced, but the majority can be squeezed to express the juice, or heated or frozen to break down the texture and then strained. Sugar may be added to taste as it improves the colour, flavour and keeping qualities. When the juice remains unheated, honey may be substituted, though it has a strong flavour of its own. Sweet juices such as apple can be mixed with tart ones like plum.

Fruit juices may be drunk as they are, added to cocktails, drunk as squashes diluted with water, and used in cooking. They take less space in a freezer than the fruit itself and are fine for use afterwards. I freeze mine in the wax cartons and plastic bottles milk comes in, leaving a little space for expansion.

Grapes are the easiest to press and the most rewarding, and you can ferment the pips and skins afterwards. Such wine tastes no worse than most of my regular home-made brews, though that is not difficult! Grapes are best crushed first to break the skins. Most of the currants and berries can be squeezed in the same way. Apples and pears must be crushed first and then squeezed: they will go through the same juicing equipment as grapes, but more slowly than the more juicy fruits.

Pulpy firm fruits such as blackcurrants and plums are best simmered with water till they soften; then the juice can be strained off. If you repeat the process and add sugar to the combined juices, you also have the basis for jellies. Raspberries, strawberries and fruits with similar delicate flavours are best frozen, then defrosted and strained, to obtain a pure juice which is unchanged by heating.

Suitable equipment for processing large amounts of fruit is widely available if the quantities are too large for kitchen tools. Many different presses and crushers are sold and hired for home and small-scale wine-makers. Commercially juices are passed through microfine filters or flash-pasteurised. At home they will ferment rapidly in the warm, last longer if kept cool in the refrigerator, and keep for months or years deep frozen. I have two freezers, one for juices, and one for everything else, as I want to drink at least a pint of apple, grape or strawberry juice a day.

Early Sulphur gooseberries

Small fruits can be made into jam, well marmalade here

Jellying and Jamming

These methods preserve the fruit in sugar gel. Jelly is made from the juice only, without the seeds and skins, while jam is made with and often also contains whole fruits or pieces thereof. A conserve is expensive jam, usually implying more fruit and less sugar or filler. (Freezer jams are conserves made with so little sugar they go mouldy quickly unless kept frozen and then used from the refrigerator.) Almost any fruit can be jammed or jellied and many fruits are palatable only if so treated. The fruit is cooked to the point when the cells break so that the juices run. The juice is then turned to a gel with sugar which acts as a preservative as well. Most fruits need to have up to their own weight of sugar added to them to make a settling gel.

With jellies, the juice is often meanly and foolishly augmented with the squeezings of the fruit pulp reheated with some water. This thinner part then requires proportionally more sugar to set. Jellies are made from the strained juice and these washings, so they set clear and bright and are appreciated by many as there are no seeds, etc. It is easy to pick and prepare fruits for jellies as the odd sprig, hard or under-ripe fruit or bit of leaf will be strained out.

Many prefer the texture (and don't forget the nutritional value) of jams with the seeds and skins, and so on. But these do require much more careful picking and preparation. My solution for, say, blackcurrants, is to pick the very finest berries carefully first, and then more roughly pick the bulk of the fruit to jelly. As the bulk is going to be strained there is no need to be so careful to keep out the sprigs. The bulk is simmered down to a juice, strained and then before it is set with the sugar the finest berries are added.

White sugar is usually needed for jamming and jellying unless a strong flavour is required. Honey is not really successful as the flavour is strong and it goes off when heated as much as is needed for jam. Similarly, concentrated juices can add too much flavour. The amount of fruit can always be increased and the sugar decreased if your technique is good and you can eat the jam quickly!

Ideally, you should simmer down the fruit with the absolute minimum amount of water. Strain if it is for jelly, add the sugar and bring to the boil. Skim off any scum and then pot in sterile conditions. Hot jars and clean lids that are put on immediately will improve results. Store, once cold, in a dark, cool place.

Some fruits are difficult to set, particularly strawberries in a wet year. Add chopped apples to the jelly fruits or their purée to the jams to supply the pectin needed to make any jam set. Extra acidity for a pleasing tartness which brings out the sharp flavour of some jams is often achieved using lemon juice. Whitecurrant juice is a good substitute and redcurrant even better, especially where the jam colour is important. Adding whitecurrant or redcurrant juice also aids the setting of difficult jams. Their flavour is so tart yet mild that their jellies make good carriers for more strongly flavoured fruits in shorter supply, especially for raspberries and cherries.

Finally, here is an important tip. It is quicker and easier to make three 2.4kg batches of jam than one 5kg batch.

The result is always better. Large batches have a low heating and evaporating surface compared to their volume and take much longer to process, so the fruit degrades more. Remember: quickly simmer down to a pulp, add the right amount of sugar, bring back to the boil, skim and pot. No standing around watching some great cauldron bubble all day!

Drying

Many fruits can be dried if they are sliced thinly and exposed to warm, dry air. Sealed in dark containers and kept cool and dry, they may be stored for long periods to be eaten, dried or reconstituted, when required. However, in the UK and much of maritime Europe and North America, the air is too humid and so drying process is not quick enough. Nor is it helped by the low temperatures in these regions. Solar-powered dryers, simple wire trays under glass, with good ventilation, allow fruit to be dried to a larger extent, but in regions of the highest humidity the fruit may still go mouldy before it dries. Flies and other insects must of course be excluded!

I find that slicing the fruit thinly and hanging the pieces, separated by at least half their own diameter, on long strings over my cooking range provides the dry warmth and ventilation needed to desiccate most within a day or two, or even just overnight for the easier ones, such as apple. Oven-drying with artificial heat is risky as it can cook the fruit, destroying the value, texture and keeping properties. However, it is possible if the temperature is kept down and the door kept partly open. It may be more convenient to finish off partly dried samples in the cooling oven after you have finished baking. The dying heat will desiccate the fruit well and incurs little risk of it caramelising.

Wine is another answer

Freezing

Most fruits freeze easily with little preparation, unlike vegetables, which need blanching first. Obviously only the best are worth freezing as few fruits are improved by the process! Most fruits turn to soggy lumps in a pool of juice when defrosted, which is not quite as appetising as the fine-textured fresh product. However, they are still packed full of sweetness, flavour and vitamins, so are well worth having for culinary use, especially in tarts, pies, sauces and compotes. A mixture of frozen fruits is marvellous if they are partly thawed but not totally defrosted, so they retain their frozen texture like pieces of sorbet, served with cream.

For most fruits, merely putting them in sealed freezer bags or boxes is sufficient. However, they tend to freeze in a block, making it difficult to use them piecemeal later. If you freeze them loose on open wire drying trays or greased baking trays, they can be packed afterwards and will stay separate. Fruits that are cut or damaged need to be drained first or, if you have a sweet tooth, they can be dredged in sugar, which absorbs the juice before they are frozen. Stone fruits are best de-stoned before freezing as otherwise the stone can give an almond taint. The tough skin of some fruits, such as tomatoes or plums, is most easily removed after freezing and before use, by carefully squeezing the frozen fruit under very hot water; the skin will then slip off easily.

Fruits lose value slowly in the freezer. The longer they are frozen, the less use they are nutritionally, but they do not deteriorate as badly as vegetables or meat and fatty products. Although a freezer is an electrical expense and a capital cost, it is wonderful to have the choice of your own fruits and their juices throughout the year – just whenever you fancy some.

THE YEARLY CALENDAR

These are reminders of the essential tasks for the majority of amateur fruit gardeners. Obviously the exact timing varies with locality, site and soil. If you grow some of the more unusual exotica, there are other requirements.

Late Winter

- Check stores; remove and use any fruits starting to deteriorate before they go over and infect others.
- Spread a good layer of compost or well-rotted manure under and around everything possible, preferably immediately after, but not just before, a period of heavy rain.
- Spread a good layer of mulch under and around everything possible, preferably immediately after a period of heavy rain.
- Lime most grass swards one year in four, more often on acid soil, but not among ericaceous plants or lime haters!
- Once ground becomes workable, plant out hardy trees and shrubs that missed the autumn planting.
- Sow very earliest crops for growing under cover.
- Ensure good weed control, make sure no weeds are getting away, hoe fortnightly or add some extra mulch on top.
- Do major pruning work to trees and bushes missed earlier or damaged in winter (but not stone fruits or evergreens).
- Prune autumn-fruiting raspberries to the ground.
- Spray everything growing with diluted seaweed solution at least once a month, and anything with deficiency even more often.
- Spray peaches and almonds with Bordeaux mixture against peach leaf curl.
- Make a health and hygiene check and examine each plant in your care for pests, diseases and dieback.
- Apply sticky bands and inspect the sacking bands on apple trees, and others if they have suffered from many pests.
- Check straps and stakes after the gales.
- On still, cold nights protect the blossoms and young fruitlets from frost damage with net curtains, plastic sheet or newspaper.

Early Spring

- Spread a good layer of compost or well-rotted manure under and around everything possible, preferably immediately after, but not before, heavy rain.
- Plant out evergreens and the more tender hardy plants.
- Protect them from frost and wind the first season.
- Sow plants grown under cover or for later planting out about now.
- Ensure good weed control, make sure no weeds are getting away, hoe fortnightly or add some extra mulch on top.
- Cut the grass at least fortnightly, preferably weekly, returning the clippings or raking them into rings around trees and bushes.
- Spray everything growing with diluted seaweed solution at least at monthly intervals, and anything with deficiency symptoms more often.
- Spray peaches and almonds with Bordeaux mixture against peach leaf curl.
- Spread wood ashes under and around plants, giving priority to gooseberries and culinary apples.
- Make a health and hygiene check and examine each plant in your care for pests, diseases and dieback.
- Prune back tender plants and evergreens and protect the new growth against frost afterwards.
- Pollinate early-flowering plants and those under cover by hand.
- On still, cold nights protect the blossoms and young fruitlets from frost damage with net curtains, plastic sheet or newspaper.

Mid Spring

- Ensure good weed control, make sure no weeds are getting away, hoe weekly or add extra mulch on top.
- Cut the grass at least weekly, returning the clippings or raking them into rings around trees and bushes.
- Sow seed for plants grown under cover or for later planting out.
- Plant out more tender hardy plants under cover or with protection.
- Spread a good layer of mulch under and around everything possible, preferably immediately after a period of heavy rain.
- Spray everything growing with diluted seaweed solution at least at monthly intervals, and anything with deficiency symptoms more often.
- Spread wood ashes under and around fruit trees, giving priority to gooseberries and culinary apples.
- Water all new plants established within the previous twelve months whenever there has been a little rain.
- Deflower or defruit new plants to give them time to establish themselves.
- Pollinate plants under cover by hand.
- Tie in new growths of vines and climbing plants.
- Make a health and hygiene check weekly and examine each plant in your care for pests, diseases and dieback.
- On still, cold nights protect the blossoms and young fruitlets from frost damage with net curtains, plastic sheet or newspaper.
- Make layers of any difficult subjects that you possess.

Late Spring

- Ensure good weed control, make sure no weeds are getting away, hoe at fortnightly intervals or add extra mulch on top.
- Sow plants grown under cover or outdoors.
- Plant out tender hardy plants under cover or suitable protection.
- Pollinate plants that are under cover by hand.
- Cut the grass at least fortnightly, preferably weekly, returning the clippings or raking them into rings around the bottoms of trees and bushes.
- Water all new plants established within the previous twelve months, especially whenever there has been a little rain.
- Deflower or defruit new plants to establish them.
- Spray everything growing with diluted seaweed solution at least at monthly intervals, and anything with deficiency symptoms more often.

Raspberry canes bent down and interwoven

Tubs are convenient

- Make a health and hygiene check twice weekly and examine each plant in your care for pests, diseases and dieback.
- Tie in new growths of vines and climbing plants.
- On still, cold nights protect the blossoms and young fruitlets from frost damage with net curtains, plastic sheet or newspaper.
- Make layers of the most difficult subjects.
- Protect almost every ripening fruit from birds and other greedy creatures.

Early Summer

- Ensure good weed control, make sure no weeds are getting away, hoe at fortnightly intervals or add extra mulch on top.
- Plant out tender plants now, or move them out for the summer.
- Cut the grass at least fortnightly, preferably weekly, returning the clippings or raking them into rings around trees and bushes. Raise the height of cut of your mower.
- Spray everything growing with diluted seaweed solution at least at monthly intervals, and anything with deficiency symptoms even more often.
- Water all new plants established within the previous twelve months, especially whenever there has been a little rain.
- Make a health and hygiene check twice weekly and examine each plant in your care for pests, diseases and dieback.

Summer Pruning, Part One of Three

- From one third of each plant, remove approximately half to three-quarters of each new shoot, except for leaders. This applies to all fruit such as redcurrants and whitecurrants, gooseberries and all trained apples and pears. Prune grapevines back to three or five leaves after a flower truss.
- Carefully tie in fragile, new growths of vines and other climbing plants.

Fruit Thinning, Part One of Three

- Remove every diseased, decayed, damaged, misshapen, distorted and congested fruitlet. This applies to all apples, pears, peaches, apricots, quality plums, dessert grapes, gooseberries and figs, especially to trained forms.
- Compost or burn rejected fruitlets immediately. Of course, usable ones, such as the larger gooseberries, may be consumed.
- Take soft cuttings if you have a propagator.
- Make layers of the most difficult subjects.
- Protect almost every ripening fruit from birds and other animals.

Midsummer

- Ensure good weed control, make sure no weeds are getting away, hoe at fortnightly intervals or add extra mulch on top.
- Cut the grass at least fortnightly, preferably weekly, returning the clippings or raking them into rings around trees and bushes. Raise the height of cut of your mower.
- Spray everything growing with diluted seaweed solution at least at monthly intervals, and anything with deficiency symptoms even more often.
- Water all new plants established within the previous twelve months, especially whenever there has been a little rain.
- Make a health and hygiene check twice weekly and examine each plant in your care for pests, diseases and dieback.
- Tie in new growths of vine and climbing plants.

Peaches crop well in drier warmer areas

A stocking support helps the melon grow bigger, and stops it dropping off

Summer Pruning, Part Two of Three

- From the second third of each plant remove about half to three-quarters of each new shoot, except for leaders. This applies to all redcurrants, whitecurrants, gooseberries and all trained apples and pears. Prune grapevines back to three or five leaves after a flower truss. Blackcurrants may have a third to half the old wood removed after fruiting. Stone fruits are traditionally pruned now to avoid silver leaf disease.

Fruit Thinning, Part Two of Three

- Remove every diseased, decayed, damaged, misshapen, distorted and congested fruitlet. This applies to all apples, pears, peaches, apricots, quality plums, dessert grapes, gooseberries, figs and especially trained forms.
- Compost or burn rejected fruits immediately. Of course, it is always nice to consume useable ones.
- Take soft cuttings if you have a propagator, root tips of the black and hybrid berries.
- Protect almost every ripening fruit from the birds.

Late Summer

- Ensure good weed control, make sure no weeds are getting away, hoe at fortnightly intervals or add extra mulch on top.
- Plant new strawberry plants, if you can get them.
- Cut the grass at least fortnightly, preferably weekly, returning the clippings or raking them into rings around trees and bushes. Lower the height of cut of your mower.
- It is a good idea to spray everything that is growing with diluted seaweed solution at least once a month, and anything that has deficiency symptoms even more often.
- Water all new plants established within the previous twelve months, especially whenever there has been a little rain.
- Sow green manures and winter ground cover on bare soil that is not mulched; grass down orchards.
- Make a health and hygiene check and examine each plant in your care for pests, diseases and dieback.
- Apply insect traps like sticky bands and sacking bands to apple trees, and other fruit trees if they suffer from many pests.

Summer Pruning, Part Three of Three

- To last third of each plant remove approximately half to three-quarters of each new shoot, except for leaders. This applies to all redcurrants, whitecurrants, gooseberries and all trained apples and pears. As before, prune grapevines back to three or five leaves after the fruit truss.

Fruit Thinning, Part Three of Three

- Remove every diseased, decayed, damaged, misshapen, distorted and congested fruitlet. This applies to all apples, pears, peaches, apricots, quality plums, dessert grapes, gooseberries, figs and especially trained forms.
- Compost or burn rejected fruits immediately. Of course, the useable ones may be consumed.
- Protect almost every ripening fruit from the birds.
- Root the tips of the black and hybrid berries.

Early Autumn

- Ensure good weed control, make sure no weeds are getting away, hoe at fortnightly intervals or add extra mulch on top.
- Plant out any pot-grown specimens also, as well as those that can be dug with a decent rootball or moved with a little disturbance.
- Cut the grass at least fortnightly, preferably weekly, returning the clippings and fallen leaves or raking them into rings around trees and bushes. Lower the height of cut of your mower.
- Sow green manures and winter ground cover on bare soil that is not mulched; grass down orchards.
- Spray everything growing with diluted seaweed solution at least once a month, and anything with deficiency symptoms even more often.
- Make a health and hygiene check and examine each plant in your care for pests, diseases and dieback.
- Apply insect traps like sticky bands and sacking

Courgettes unpicked become marrows – you want marrows?

bands to apple trees, and to others if they suffer from many pests.

- On still, cold nights protect ripening fruits from frost damage with net curtains, plastic sheet or newspaper.
- Protect first the tops then the stems and roots of more tender plants before the frosts come.
- Bring indoors tender plants in pots or protect them.
- Take cuttings of plants as soon as they start to drop their leaves.
- Prune early-fruiting raspberries and hybrids, and blackcurrants and other plants as soon as they start to drop their leaves.
- Protect almost every ripening fruit from the usual hordes of hungry pests.
- Root tips of the black and hybrid berries.

Mid Autumn

- Ensure good weed control, make sure no weeds are getting away, hoe at fortnightly intervals or add extra mulch on top.
- Plant out bare-rooted hardy trees and bushes if soil is in good condition and they are dormant.
- Cut the grass at least fortnightly, preferably weekly, returning the clippings with the fallen leaves or raking them into rings around trees and bushes.
- Spray everything growing with diluted seaweed solution at least once a month, and anything with deficiency symptoms even more often.
- Make a health and hygiene check and examine each plant in your care for pests, diseases and dieback.
- Top up the sticky bands and inspect the sacking bands on apple trees, and on others if they suffered from many pests.
- Check straps and stakes before the gales.
- On still, cold nights protect ripening fruits from frost damage with net curtains, plastic sheet or newspaper.
- Take cuttings of hardy plants as soon as they start to drop their leaves.
- Prune early-fruiting raspberries and hybrids, and blackcurrants and other plants as soon as they start to drop their leaves.
- Protect first the tops then the stems and roots of more tender plants before the frosts come.
- Check stores; remove and use any fruits starting to deteriorate before they go over and infect others.
- As before, protect almost every ripening fruit from the birds.

Late Autumn

- Ensure good weed control, make sure no weeds are getting away, hoe at fortnightly intervals or add extra mulch on top.
- Plant out bare-rooted hardy trees and bushes if soil is good and they are dormant.
- Cut the grass at least fortnightly, collecting the clippings with the fallen leaves or raking them into rings around trees and bushes.
- Make a health and hygiene check and examine each plant in your care for pests, diseases and dieback.
- Look at the traps; top up the sticky bands and inspect the sacking bands on apple trees, and on others if they suffered from many pests.
- Check straps and stakes before the gales.
- Spread a good layer of compost or well rotted manure under and around everything possible, preferably after, but not immediately before, any heavy rain.
- On still, cold nights protect ripening fruits from frost damage with net curtains, plastic sheet or newspaper.
- Take cuttings of hardy plants as they start to drop their leaves.
- Prune late fruiting raspberries, hybrid berries, currants and vines, trees and bushes as the leaves fall.
- Protect first the tops then the stems and roots of more tender plants before the frosts come.
- Check stores, remove and use any fruits starting to deteriorate before they go over and infect others.
- Protect almost every ripening fruit particularly from the birds.

Early Winter

- Ensure good weed control, make sure no weeds are getting away, hoe at fortnightly intervals or add extra mulch on top.
- Plant out bare-rooted hardy trees and bushes if soil is good and they are dormant.
- Collect the fallen leaves and use for leafmould or rake them in rings around trees and bushes.
- Make a health and hygiene check and examine each plant in your care for pests, diseases and dieback.
- Top up the sticky bands and inspect the sacking bands on apple trees, and on any others if they suffered from many pests.
- Check straps and stakes before the gales.
- Spread a good layer of compost or well rotted manure under and around everything possible, preferably after, but not immediately before, any heavy rain.
- Prune late fruiting trees and bushes as the leaves fall and do major work to trees and bushes (but not to stone fruits or evergreens).
- Check stores, remove and use any fruits starting to deteriorate before they go over and infect others.

Mid Winter

- Make a health and hygiene check and examine each plant in your care for pests, diseases and dieback.
- Check straps and stakes before the gales.
- Check stores, remove and use any fruits starting to deteriorate before they go over and infect others.
- Take it easy and look back over the successes and mishaps of the previous year, enjoy the fruits of your labours and plan for even more fun and endeavour in the coming seasons.

Pears may need propping

FURTHER TRAVELLER'S TALES FRUITS

Adansonia digitata
Baobab, **Monkey Breadfruit,** *Bombacaceae*
This large African tree has a swollen trunk often hollowed by age. The leaves are eaten as a vegetable and the fruits, up to 30cm long, are fat, cylindrical, dark and hairy. They have a floury white pulp that reputedly tastes like gingerbread, with small black seeds that have been ground and eaten in times of famine.

Antidesma bunius
Bignay
Coming from the Far East and Northern Australia, this tropical evergreen tree – originally from India – produces grape-like bunches of multicoloured berries which are relished raw, though sour, and made into jams or eaten with fish.

Billardiera longiflora
Appleberry, *Pittosporaceae*
An acid-loving, nearly hardy climber from Australasia, which has oblong dark blue berries with a pleasing taste. Many similar species are eaten by the native Australians.

Bouea macrophyla
Gandaria
This is just like a small mango gone very wrong. However, many in the Far East become addicted to its odd, though very juicy, taste.

Butyrospermum parkii
Shea Butter Tree, *Sapotaceae*
A native of central Africa, this small stout African tree has white fragrant flowers followed by plum-like fruits with a thick pericap that bleeds when green. Once fully ripe, this has some pulp, which is sweet and perfumed, but the fruits are gathered more for their seeds which have a high fat content and are used to make shea butter. The wood is resistant to termites.

Canarium edule/Dacryoides edulis
Safu, *Burseraceae*
The fruit is a large violet drupe that is too bitter to be eaten raw, but is fatty and nutritious once cooked. It is popular in West Africa.

Canarium commune
Chinese olive, **Java almond**
This is a closely related, rather attractive tree from South-east Asia, which is grown for the tasty kernel.

Casimiroa edulis
Casimiroa, *White Sapote or Zapotl*
From South America (but not a Sapota or Sapodilla), this plant looks pretty much like an apple crossed with a mango, buttery custardy, tasting a bit like pear flesh, with white seeds and a bitter papery skin that must be avoided. Chill before eating and they will not keep long, going rock hard to too soft in days. Claimed to have medicinal values as well as vitamins A and C.

Cecropia peltata
Trumpet Tree, **Monkey's Paw**, *Urticaceae*
This stinging nettle relation is the tropical equivalent of elderberry as a weed; from South America, it takes over old human habitations. The small apple-sized fruits are watery and fig flavoured.

Cicca acida
Malay Gooseberry, *Euphorbiaceae*
A small tree resembling a Carambola but with bunches of small greeny yellow berries, each with a hard seed and sour acid flesh eaten fresh but more often made into pickles.

Cynometra cauliflora
Nam-Nam, *Fabaceae*
Popular in Malaysia, this tree relation of the beans has odd, wrinkled, kidney-shaped, small apple-sized pods concealing juicy yellow, sour, flesh wrapped around a big seed.

Bixa orellana

Dillenia indica
Chulta, **Elephant Apple**, *Dilleniaceae*
This is a tree with huge leathery leaves and strange fruits a bit like globe artichokes with acidic pulpy bits and is rather stringy. It is used for sherbets, curries, jelly, making vinegar and, apparently, as treats for elephants.

Emblica officinalis
Indian Gooseberry, *Euphorbiaceae*
The fruits are small marbles of yellow or green. They are too acid to be eaten raw, but are amazingly rich in vitamin C, containing three hundred times as much as orange juice. They are often jammed and pickled and used to treat scurvy.

Euterpe oleracea
Acai Palm, *Palmaceae*
From the Amazonian basin, this plant has acid berries that are claimed to be incredibly health giving and so these are now appearing in smoothies and other tonic beverages.

Gnetum gnemon
Gnemon, *Gnetaceae*
A primitive plant from Java, this has what are technically cones, though not resembling a pine's; from these swell green 'fruits' that are really seeds. When these turn orangey-red the skin or rind is edible and most often used in cakes and confectionery.

Grewia asiatica
Phalsa, **Pharsa**, *Tiliaceae*
This is a shrubby reddish tree from India and the East Indies, which has many small red berries that are too acid and dry to eat many of. However, they make the most delicious sorbets and syrups, and are very popular in northern India.

Harpephyllum caffrum
Kaffir Plum
A dark red fruit, used for jelly, on a house-high tree with glossy leathery leaves and an un-pc name.

Heteromeles arbutifolia
Christmas Berry, **Tollon**, *Rosaceae*
This is an easy-to-grow, attractive pot plant closely resembling a holly with white scented flowers and red, holly-like berries. It is a unique plant, found only in California, where it makes a shrubby tree 9m in height. It may also be hardy enough to grow on a wall in southern Britain.

Irvingia gabonensis
Duika, **Wild mango**, *Irvingiaceae*
This is a large central African tree which has an inferior mango pulp, but the seed is oily and is used for cooking and soap-making. It is also used in Gabon chocolate or *pain de dika*.

Bixa orellana
Annatto, **Lipstick tree**, *Bixaceae*
This is a small evergreen tropical shrub-cum-small tree that has heart-shaped leaves with panicles of peachy flowers followed by heart shaped pods with seeds embedded in a coloured flesh used as a lipstick, for dyeing hair and clothes and used commercially as the colouring Annatto.

Lardizabala biternata
Zabal Fruit, Aquiboquil, *Lardizabalaceae*
These are sold in Chilean markets: a climber with dark evergreen leaves, clusters of purple black flowers are followed by finger-length purple sausages full of sweet pulp. Nearly hardy, this is a superb conservatory or cold greenhouse plant or even for the warmest garden.

Lansium domesticum
Langsat, **Dokong**, **Longkong** or **Duku**
Meliaceae
These are a tribe of small yellowish berries with parchment-like skins hanging like slim bunches of grapes from large Far Eastern trees. The Duku is the preferred choice, though has a bitter seed to be avoided; the kongs are not big ape relatives but bigger sweeter Dukus.

Malpighia glabra/ punicfolia/ emarginata Acerola
Barbados Cherry, *Malpighiaceae*
Big evergreen tropical shrubs with pink or red flowers followed by thin-skinned juicy red berries with a very high vitamin C content that are mouth puckeringly acid, so are used in drinks and tonics with much sweetening.

Mammea americana
Mammey Apple, *Guttifereae*
This is a large evergreen tropical tree with an orange- to grapefruit-sized russeted yellowish fruit; this contains one to four big seeds in firm juicy flesh which is best eaten stewed, though some eat them raw if very ripe.

Morinda citrifolia
Dog Dumpling, *Rubiaceae*
This is a handsome glossy foliaged, small tropical tree which almost continuously flowers, attracting hummingbirds whilst dropping strange, off-whitish, macabrely pineapple-like fruits which make ripe Camembert seem like fresh air. Yet these are believed to be very healthy medicine, especially if fermented first. The leaves are also used as poultices for pain, fever and headaches and the roots widely used for dye.

Owenia acidula
Australian Native Nectarine, *Meliaceae*
This is a small, tender, ornamental tree with pinnate foliage, white flowers and bluish black fruits with very acid red pulp, which is good for drinks, juices and jellies. The large stony seed is used for jewellery.

Parinarium curatefolium
Mupunda, *Chrysobalanaceae*
There are a number of other closely related fruits found in Africa. This is considered the best, with reddish-brown or greyish plum-sized drupes on a shrubby bush.

Parmentiera aculeata
Cucumber Tree, *Bignoniaceae*
A Central American small tree, this bears flowers directly from the trunk which turn into very cucumber-like fruits used raw, roasted and cooked.

Pereskia aculeata
Rose Cactus, **Barbados Gooseberry**, *Cactaceae*
These very floriferous plants closely resemble small trees with woody stems and deciduous leaves and are the least succulent of the cacti family. The highly perfumed flowers vary from orange to white through yellow and the fruits resemble orange or yellow cherries. They are popular for preserving in the West Indies.

Randia formosa
Raspberry Bush or **Blackberry-jam Fruit**, *Rubiaceae*
This South American tender shrub can be grown in a frost-free conservatory to fruit in a large pot. The white flowers are followed by woody shelled fruits with a jam like sweet, sticky centre. GOOD!

Salacca zalacca
Snakefruit, Salak, *Palmaceae*
Another palm tree fruit; coming in bunches of a couple of dozen, the 'nuts' are an inch or so across and covered in what looks just like snakeskin with flesh tasting like a mixture of banana and pineapple all wrapped about a brown seed.

Sicana odifera
Musk Cucumber, **Casabanana**, **Curuba** or **Coroa**
Cucurbitaceae
This South American climbing vine resembles a lushly grown and prettier cucumber plant, but its tendrils really serve to glue themselves at the tips as well as twine. A perennial in Brazil and Ecuador, it can be grown very easily in more northern climates as an annual or conservatory subject. A very vigorous plant, it has yellow flowers and yellowish-red fruits with a sweetish flavour, but which are strongly fragrant – too strong for many. The fruits can be eaten young as vegetables and ripe as fruits, most commonly in jams.

Theobroma cacao
Cocoa, *Sterculiaceae*
The nibs are not eaten raw but fermented, dried and ground to make our chocolate. The trees are small natives of the Americas but now mainly grown in West Africa. The melon-like pods are green, ripening to red or yellow, and spring directly out of the trunk and main branches of the tree, following delightful fuschia-like pink flowers. Their pulp is sweet and edible also. Closely related is **Pheng Phok**, **Chinese Chestnut,** *Sterculia monosperma*, of which the nuts are much esteemed by the Chinese, who eat them boiled or roasted.

Yucca Baccata
Eve's Date, *Liliaceae*
This is closely related to our **Adam's Needle**, the spiky garden perennial which flowers but rarely sets fruit. *T. baccata* is too tender, or rather too loathing of damp, so needs to be grown under cover. The flowers need hand pollinating, then purple peach-sized, stubby cylindrical fruits form which have an aromatic bitter-sweet taste. The native Americans were fond of them fresh or dried and also ate the flowerbuds roasted or boiled.

Theobroma cacao

USEFUL BY-PRODUCTS

Wood Turning, Natural Dyes, Scented Firewoods and Smoking Foods

Most fruit trees and some bushes and vines produce thick branches and trunks which may have value as timber once the productive life of the plant is over. However, most is burnt on bonfires or in the grate without considering any of the other uses.

Treen is the term used for any small object made from wood. Many different and useful implements, and especially kitchen utensils, can be fashioned out of home-produced fruit woods once they have seasoned for a year or two. Platters, bowls and jam spoons, rolling pins, egg cups, pestles and mortars, nutcrackers, lemon squeezers, cruet sets, napkin rings, moulds, bobbins and children's blocks and toys are easy to make and well within the reach of any of us. Grape stems are traditionally turned into corkscrew handles. Fruit woods have fine colour and grain which enhance such objects and also make them suitable for inlay and marquetry work.

Barks, fruits and leaves were used for dyes long before our modern bright chemical colours were invented. Many prefer the muted colours and pastel softness of such dyes, which visually blend more easily than their vibrant modern counterparts. Apple, pear and cherry barks yield dyes in shades of yellow, as do the roots and stems of berberis, while reddish-yellows come from pine-cones. Walnuts stain everything they touch and need no mordant to help fix their dye, which can be obtained from the roots, leaves and husks. In the past walnut dye was used to give a suntan to pale Gypsies, as a hair dye and a floor stain. Elder bark with an iron mordant gives a black dye, the leaves with an alum mordant give a green dye and the berries produce shades of purple, blue and lilac, often used as hair dyes. Rowan berries give a black dye, plums and sloes a blue dye and their bark yields a red-brown colorant, while junipers give an olive brown.

Scented leaves and flowers, especially citrus ones, can be used for perfumes and pot-pourri. Most are at their best collected in early morning, once the dew has dried and before the heat has parched their scented oils away. The soluble perfume may be collected and concentrated into fats and oils or the plant material can be dried and used as it is. Quinces are particularly aromatic and were once very popular bases for pomanders.

Dyeing things is fun, but don't make me wear it

Many types of the wood from orchards and their hedges are useful fuels, though others are less so, as this traditional rhyme puts well:

Logs to burn, logs to burn.
Here's a wood to make you wise.
Logs to spare the coal a turn.
Listen to my woodsman's cries.

Beech wood burns bright and clear,
the Hornbeam blazes too
if the logs are kept a year,
seasoned through and through.

Oak logs they'll heat you well
once they're old and dry.
Larch logs like Pine do smell
and their sparks do fly.

Pine itself is good as Yew
for warmth on bitter days.
Beware the Poplar, Willow too
long to dry and short to blaze.

Birch logs they burn too fast
Alder, Elder, scarce at all.
Chestnut logs the best to last
if they're felled in fall.

Holly logs will roar like wax
you can even burn it green.
But Elm like smouldering flax
will never flame be seen.

Pear's wood and Apple logs
they will scent your room,
Cherry logs across the dogs
smell like flowers in bloom.

But worth their weight in gold
are Ash logs, smooth and grey,
burn them young or burn them old
buy all that come your way.

Not only do these fruit trees give a burnable wood, but a sweet scent is also produced from their burning logs which is much esteemed by those with open fires. When choice wood like this becomes available, it is often saved for celebrations and special occasions.

Major pruning or felling of trees is done in autumn and winter but the timber must be dried before it can be burned efficiently. Generally the older and drier the wood, the better for heating: for scenting, though, it is best one year old. Timber should be sawn into logs while fresh and green as it is cut most easily then. The logs should be stacked horizontally so air can pass through and water cannot soak in, ideally covered over the top to keep rain off.

All prunings from the orchard that are too small for logs can be used for kindling, once dried. Smooth clean prunings can be used to make wildlife shelters, and if you have a shredder they can be processed and then composted. However, to prevent any build-up of diseases and pests, all infected and diseased material should be burnt straight away. It is also usually sensible to burn thorny material, such as bramble stems.

Bonfires burn best if started with a little good tinder and then fed with material piecemeal. Ideally, support the fire off the ground on old bed irons or similar so air can get underneath. This reduces pollution and makes the fire roar upwards instead of smouldering and drifting. Once the fire is finished and cooled, the ashes should be collected for use as fertiliser or for making soap.

Oh no, it's my birthday present!

Smoking with sawdust and nut shells in my woodstove

The smoke from burning many fruit woods can be used for smoking foods. This is a traditional way of preserving foods such as fish and meat, and/or improving their flavour, as with cheese. It is not unusual either: cheese smoked with applewood is on sale in almost every delicatessen and supermarket so there is obviously a demand for it.

Smoking foods is not difficult. They are often hot-smoked for immediate consumption, but generally most are smoked in cool temperatures, as this prevents the fats going rancid. Most meats and many fish are pre-treated with salt, by pickling, marinating or part-drying before smoking. For safety, please refer to specialist books for more precise details. However, in principle the smoking process is very simple. The food is hung from racks or suspended in a container through which the cool smoke from sweet-burning woods passes for several hours. After this it is matured for some time to let the flavour permeate throughout the food.

I make my own apple, peach and pearwood-smoked cheese in the chimney of my house. It is unused and cool during the summer so I hang the cheese down inside the chimney and light a small, cool, smouldering fire of fruit-wood sawdust and prunings in the stove underneath. The fire is kept smouldering overnight and in the morning the cheese is beautifully smoked. In theory the cheese should mature in a cool place for a month before it is used, but in my house it rarely stays uneaten that long!

PAST GLORIES

Victorian and Edwardian gardeners were fascinated by the wide range of tropical fruits available from the countries of the British Empire. These truly magnificent pineapples were grown in England at the end of the nineteenth century. They are examples of what could be achieved without the use of modern chemical pesticides and fertilisers. The greenhouses were usually south-facing to make the best use of the sun's heat. Steam and hot water pipes were used to generate internal heat and keep the greenhouses at the optimum temperature. The results, as shown above, were quite remarkable. May the growers of the past inspire your own efforts!

SOME INTERESTING BOOKS

These are a few of the many worth looking for. Although they are not all directly concerned with fruit, they contain useful and relevant advice. Some are now out of print and need unearthing from libraries.

William Cobbett
The American Gardener: A Treatise On the Situation, Soil, and Laying Out of Gardens, On the Making and Managing of Hot-Beds and Green-Houses; and On the Fruits, and Flowers
1821

E. A. Bunyard
Anatomy of Dessert
1929

E. A. Bunyard
A Handbook of Hardy Fruits
Picton, 1994

The Diagnosis of Mineral Deficiencies in Plants
HMSO, 1943

Richard Mabey
Food for Free
Fontana/Collins, 1972/75

Whealy & Thuente (eds.)
Fruit, Berry and Nut Inventory
Seed Saver Exchange, 1993 (ISBN 0-882424-51-4)

L. D. Hills
The Good Fruit Guide
Henry Doubleday Research Association

E. A. Bunyard
A Handbook of Hardy Fruits
Picton 1994

E. A. Ormerod
Handbook of Insects Injurious to Orchard and Bush Fruits
Simpkin, Marshall, Hamilton & Co., 1898

Hillier's Manual of Trees and Shrubs
David & Charles

Thomas Rivers
The Miniature Fruit Garden
1860

Werner Schupan and C. L. Whittles
Nutritional Value in Crops and Plants
Museum Press, 1965

Thomas Rivers
The Orchard House
1859

R. B. Yepsen (ed.)
Organic Plant Protection
Rodale, 3rd printing 1976

The Oxford Book of Food Plants
Peerage Books, 1969

Brillat-Savarin (trans. M. F. K. Fisher)
The Physiology of Taste
Knopf, 1949

Henry W. Beecher
Plain and Pleasant Talk about Fruits, Flowers and Farming
Derby & Jackson, 1895

Plant Physiological Disorders
ADAS, HMSO, 1985

Hardy Plant Society
The Plant Finder
1987

Anthony Huxley
Plant and Planet
Allen Lane, 1974

Henry Phillips
Pomarium Britannicum
Horticulture Society London, 1821

George E. Brown
The Pruning of Trees, Shrubs & Conifers
Faber & Faber, 1972

Long Ashton Research Station
Science and Fruit
University of Bristol, 1953

Sir John Russell
Soil Conditions and Plant Growth
Longmans, 8th edition 1954

U. P. Hendrick (ed.)
Sturtevant's Edible Plants of the World
Dover Publications, 1972

William Forsyth
Treatise on the Culture and Management of Fruit Trees
1803

Oleg Polunin
Trees and Bushes of Britain and Europe
Oxford University Press, 1976

Macmillan, Barlow, Enoch & Russell
Tropical Planting and Gardening
Macmillan, 1949

Robbins, Crafts & Raynor
Weed Control
McGraw Hill, 1942

L. Junius Moderatus Columella
12 Books on Husbandry
Printed for A. Miller, 1745

INDEX

PHOTOGRAPHIC ACKNOWLEDGEMENTS

KEY
A: Alamy
BAL: Bridgeman Art Library
BF: Bob Flowerdew
FY: Fran Yorke
GAP: GAP Photos
GH: Geoff Hayes
GPL: Garden Picture Library
GWI: Garden World Images
LL: Lisa Linder
MG: Michelle Garrett
PC: Pete Cassidy
WH: Will Heap

Introduction
Page **1** BF; **2** PC; **7** PC; **9** 'The Arabian Nights', 1895/ Private Collection/Roger Perrin/BAL; **10** Robert Harding Picture Library Ltd/A; **11** Vegetable and Flower Market (oil on canvas), Muyser, Arnout de/Alinari/BAL

Orchard Fruits
Page 12 PC; **14** PC; **16** BF; **17** top PC, bottom BF; **18** left GH, right PC; **19** PC; **20** top and left BF, bottom right PC; **21** MG; **22** top Mark Bolton/GAP, bottom Christina Bollen/GAP; **23** top Sally Maltby, centre Jonathan Buckley/GAP, bottom MG; **24** PC; **25** left BF, right FY; **26** left FY, right PC; **27** WH; **28** top Dave Bevan/GAP, bottom Juliette Wade/GAP; **29** top Juliette Wade/GPL, bottom MG; **30** top Emma Lee, bottom Andrea Jones/A; **31** top MG, bottom David Askham/A; **32** top PC, bottom Christina Bollen/GAP; **33** left John Glover/GAP, right MG; **34** left imagebroker/A, right PC; **35** MG; **36** Arco Images GmbH/A; **37** left GPL, top right blickwinkel/A, bottom right MG; **38** top Christie Carter/GPL, bottom FY; **39** left Maddie Thornhill/GAP, top right MG, bottom right BF; **40** PC; **41** left FY, right BF; **42** top BF, bottom FY; **43** MG; **44** top Trevor Sims/GWI, bottom BF; **45** left Holmes Garden Photos/A, right MG; **46** top CuboImages srl/A, right John Swithinbank/GWI; **47** left Sine Chesterman/ GWI, top right MG, bottom right Nic Murray/A; **48** top BF, bottom FY; **49** MG; **50** Dave Bevan/GAP; **51** left Frederic Didillon/GAP, right MG; **52** top Holmes Garden Photos/A, bottom BF; **53** left Susie McCaffrey/A, top right MG, bottom right GardenPixels/A

Soft, Bush and Cane Fruits
Page 54 PC; **56** adrian davies/A; **57** left BF, top right PC, bottom right MG; **58** top Jonathan Buckley/GAP, bottom BF; **59** top left PC, top right MG, bottom Howard Rice/GAP; **60** BF; **61** top Michael Howes/GPL, bottom left and right MG; **62** top BF, bottom Organica/A; **63** left FhF Greenmedia/GAP, bottom MG; **64** right Botanica GPL, left BF; **65** MG; **66** John Glover/GAP; **67** left Phil Degginger/A, top right MG, bottom imagebroker/A; **68** top Juliette Wade/GPL, bottom BF; **69** top PC, bottom MG; **70** top BF, bottom FY; **71** top FY, bottom left BF, bottom right MG; **72** top PC, bottom BF; **73** left Paul Debois/GAP, top and bottom right MG; **74** top blickwinkel/A, bottom BF; **75** MG; **76** FY; **77** top Paul Debois/GAP, bottom Dufour Brigette Dit Noun/GPL; **78** left Paul Debois/GAP, right Howard Rice/GPL; **79** MG; **81** top BF, bottom Michael Howes/GPL; **82** top James Baigrie/ GPL, bottom Dave Bevan/GAP; **83** MG; **84** top Juliette Wade/GPL, bottom Michael Howes/GPL; **85** left Arco Images GmbH/A, right MG; **86** PC; **87** left BF, right MG; **88** BF; **89** top Juliette Wade/GPL, bottom MG; **90** BF; **91** top Christie Carter/GPL, bottom MG; **92** PC; **93** BF; **94** BF; **95** top MG, bottom Rita Coates/GWI

Annual Tender Fruits
Page 96 FY; **98** left BF, right PC; **99** top left and right PC bottom right WH; **100** Howard Rice/GAP; **101** left PC, right WH; **102** top PC, bottom BF; **103** top Maxine Adcock GAP, bottom WH; **104** Paul Debois/GAP; **105** BF; **106** PC; **107** left BF, right WH; **108** left Graham Strong/GAP, right BF; **109** left GH, bottom BF, right PC; **110** top BF, bottom Pernilla Bergdahl/GAP; **111** left Juliette Wade/GAP, centre Friedrich Strauss/GAP, right WH; **112** left Olivier Asselin/A, right amana images inc./A; **113** top WH, bottom Nigel Cattlin/A; **114** Eelco Nicodem/A; **115** top BF, bottom Bon Appetit/A; **116** BF; **117** MG; **118** left John Glover/A, right BF; **119** top BF, left PC, right MG; **120** top BF, bottom Arco Images GmbH/A; **121** top PC, bottom MG; **122** top and bottom right PC, bottom left BF; **123** PC; **124** left Andrea Jones/GAP, right Dave Bevan/GAP; **125** left Lynn Keddie/ GAP, right MG

Perennial Tender Fruits
Page 126 Inga Spence/A; **128** BF; **129** top BF, bottom John Glover/GAP; **130** top left PC, top right FY, bottom BF; **131** top left FY, top right PC, bottom MG; **132** Emma Lee; **133** top GH, bottom MG; **134** PC; **135** top and bottom left BF, bottom right MG; **136** top BF, bottom Susanne Kischnick/A; **137** left BF, centre Tim Gainey/A, right MG; **138** top Arco Images GmbH/A, bottom left Nigel Cattlin/A, bottom right MG; **139** top ImageGap/A, bottom MG; **140** top Arco Images GmbH/A, bottom MG; **141** BF; **142** left blickwinkel/A, right BF; **143** Douglas Fisher/A

Tropical and Sub-tropical Fruits
Page 144 GH; **146** GH; **147** left MG, right BF; **148** GH; **149** top left and bottom BF, top right MG; **150** top GH, bottom MG; **151** imagebroker/A; **152** top Nigel Cattlin/A, centre Photoimagerie/A, bottom MG; **153** left Arco Images GmbH/A, right MG; **154** left BF, top right MG, bottom right PC; **155** top GH, bottom left BF, bottom right MG; **156** left Courtney Turner/GPL, top MG, bottom john lander/A; **157** top imagebroker/A, bottom MG; **158** BF; **159** left Navin Mistry/A, right Photodisc/A; **160** left INSADCO Photography/A, right MG; **161** top left Dinodia Images/A, top right Bon Appetit/A, bottom MG; **162** left WoodyStock/ A, right David Hosking/A; **163** top left Rob Crandall/A, top right BF, bottom Geraldine Buckley/A

Shrub and Flower Garden Fruits
Page 164 flowerphotos/A; **166** left All Canada Photos/A, right Martin Hughes-Jones/A; **167** top right MG, centre Martin Hughes-Jones/A, bottom LL; **168** top Javier Etcheverry/A, centre John Maud/A, right MG; **169** left Arco Images GmbH/ A, top right MG, bottom BF; **170** left Corbis RF/A, right MG; **171** left Holmes Garden Photos/A, top right blickwinkel/A, bottom MG; **172** left BRUCE COLEMAN INC./A, bottom left Steffen Hauser/botanikfoto/A, right MG; **173** left Dave Zubraski/A, right MG; **174** left WoodyStock/A, right Brian Hoffman/A; **175** left Reino Hanninen/A, right MG; **176** left Leander/A, right imagebroker/A; **177** left Danita Delimont/A, right MG; **178** left Nigel Cattlin/A, right flowerphotos/A; **179** top Gilles Delacroix/GWI, bottom right Bon Appetit/A; **180** left John Glover/A, right Niall McDiarmid/A; **181** left John Glover/ A, top right MG, bottom right Holmes Garden Photos/A; **182** left CuboImages srl/A, right Frank Blackburn/A; **183** left Frank Blackburn/A, centre Bob Gibbons/A, right MG; **184** left mike lane/A, right Bob Gibbons/A; **185** top Kris Butler/A, bottom left WILDLIFE GmbH/A, bottom right jack sparticus/A; **186** top left Simon Colmer and Abby Rex/A, top right WH, bottom Daniel Dempster Photography/A; **187** top right Don Smetzer/ A, centre blickwinkel/A, bottom left FLPA/A; **188** blickwinkel/ A; **189** top right Todd Bannor/A, bottom left GPL/A

Nuts
Page 190 PC; **192** left imagebroker/A, right Kirk Anderson/A; **193** top blickwinkel/A, bottom left flowerphotos/A, bottom right MG; **194** bottom Arni Katz/A, top Nigel Cattlin/A; **195** top left Organica/A, centre Grant Heilman Photography/ A, top right MG; **196** top Eyebyte/A, bottom Steffen Hauser/botanikfoto/A; **197** top left blickwinkel/A, top right John Glover/A, bottom MG; **198** left blickwinkel/A, right blickwinkel/A; **199** top David Lawrence/A, bottom left Andrea Jones/A, bottom right MG; **200** left Tony Watson/A, right Holmes Garden Photos/A; **201** top MG, bottom left Elizabeth Whiting & Associates/A, bottom right Jim Lane/A; **202** top blickwinkel/A, bottom Karl Hausammann/A; **203** top left Nigel Cattlin/A, top right MG, bottom Arco Images GmbH/A; **204** top imagebroker/A, bottom MG; **205** left blickwinkel/A, right MG; **206** top left Arco Images GmbH/A, top right Nigel Cattlin/A, bottom left imagebroker/A, bottom right MG; **207** bottom left Leonide Principe/A, centre blickwinkel/A, right MG; **208** left blickwinkel/A, right Arco Images GmbH/A

The Fruit Garden
Page 210 PC; **212** left PC, right Andrea Jones/A; **213** John Glover/GPL; **214** top PC, bottom FY; **215** top left and bottom PC, top right FY; **216** left FY, right PC; **217** Dave Bevan/A; **218** top left BF, top right and bottom PC; **219** top PC, bottom BF; **220** BF; **221** BF; **222** SM; **223** top FY, bottom Stephen Robson/GPL; **224** BF; **225** FY; **226** left PC, right BF; **227** FY; **228-9** FY; **230** left PC, right FY; **231** FY; **232** top and bottom left FY, bottom right PC; **233** top left PC, top right BF, bottom left FY; **234** PC; **235** left PC, right BF; **236** PC: **237** BF; **238** left Paul Debois/GAP, right PC; **239** BF; **240** FY; **241** left PC, right BF; **242** top BF, bottom PC; **243** PC; **244-245** BF; **246** MG; **247** left MG, right PC; **248** from *The Gardener's Assistant*, by Robert Thompson, revised edition edited by William Watson; Gresham Publishing Company, 1901.